AF653848

Concurrent Engineering in Product Design and Development

Concurrent Engineering in Product Design and Development

Editor

IMAD MOUSTAPHA

ARAB SCHOOL OF SCIENCE AND TECHNOLOGY (ASST)

PUBLISHING FOR ONE WORLD

NEW AGE INTERNATIONAL (P) LIMITED, PUBLISHERS

(formerly Wiley Eastern Limited)

New Delhi • Bangalore • Chennai • Guwahati • Hyderabad
Jalandhar • Kolkata • Lucknow • Mumbai • Ranchi

Visit us at **www.newagepublishers.com**

Copyright © 2001, Arab School of Science and Tenchnology
Published by New Age International (P) Ltd., Publishers
First Edition: 2001
Reprint: 2011

All rights reserved.
No part of this book may be reproduced in any form, by photostat, microfilm, xerography, or any other means, or incorporated into any information retrieval system, electronic or mechanical, without the written permission of the copyright owner.

Branches:

- No. 37/10, 8th Cross (Near Hanuman Temple), Azad Nagar, Chamrajpet, **Bangalore** - 560 018. Tel.: (080) 26756823, Telefax: 26756820, E-mail: bangalore@newagepublishers.com
- 26, Damodaran Street, T. Nagar, **Chennai** - 600 017. Tel.: (044) 24353401, Telefax: 24351463 E-mail: chennai@newagepublishers.com
- CC-39/1016, Carrier Station Road, Ernakulam South, **Cochin** - 682 016. Tel.: (0484) 2377004, Telefax: 4051303 E-mail: cochin@newagepublishers.com
- Hemsen Complex, Mohd. Shah Road, Paltan Bazar, Near Starline Hotel, **Guwahati** - 781 008.Tel.: (0361) 2513881 Telefax: 2543669, E-mail: guwahati@newagepublishers.com
- No. 105, 1st Floor, Madhiray Kaveri Tower, 3-2-19, Azam Jahi Road, Nimboliadda, **Hyderabad** - 500 027. Tel.: (040) 24652456, Telefax: 24652457, E-mail:hyderabad@newagepublishers.com
- RDB Chambers (Formerly Lotus Cinema)106A, 1st Floor, S.N. Banerjee Road, **Kolkata** - 700 014. Tel.: (033) 22273773, Telefax: 22275247, E-mail:kolkata@newagepublishers.com
- 16-A, Jopling Road, **Lucknow** - 226 001. Tel.: (0522) 2209578, 4045297, Telefax: 2204098 E-mail: lucknow@newagepublishers.com
- 142C, Victor House, Ground Floor, N.M. Joshi Marg, Lower Parel, **Mumbai** - 400 013.Tel.: (022) 24927869 Telefax: 24915415, E-mail: mumbai@newagepublishers.com
- 22, Golden House, Daryaganj, **New Delhi** - 110 002. Tel.: (011) 23262370, 23262368, Telefax: 43551305 E-mail: sales@newagepublishers.com

ISBN (10) : 81-224-1309-9
ISBN (13) : 978-81224-1309-0

₹ 495.00

C-11-07-5688

Printed in India at Glorious Printers, Delhi.

PUBLISHING FOR ONE WORLD
NEW AGE INTERNATIONAL (P) LIMITED, PUBLISHERS
4835/24, Ansari Road, Daryaganj, New Delhi-110002
Visit us at **www.newagepublishers.com**

Preface

This book is the result of a concentrated joint effort by a number of leading experts on concurrent engineering (CE). Drawing from various fields of engineering and industrial production, and emphasizing the role and impact of simultaneous product and process design and development, the authors of the book have managed to present a comprehensive presentation of the major issues involved. Recent development in Information Technology (IT) that have made an immediate impact on CE methods and practices have also been taken into account.

Organizational cross functional structures needed for concurrent engineering are highlighted as well as the essential ingredients for achieving business success through adopting concurrent engineering.

The book also covers the requirements for a successful implementation of concurrent engineering through the innovative use of enabling tools and technologies within the organization, and externally, through the extended enterprise concept.

Concurrent product planning and development using Quality Function Development (QFD) is presented through a case study with an example drawn from the automotive industry.

The role of Product Data Management (PDM) Systems and data requirements in concurrent engineering is discussed in conjunction with data exchange standards and STEP.

Imad Moustapha

Contents

SECTION ONE
Lecture Notes

SECTION TWO
Short Papers

Arab School of Science & Technology

The Arab School of Science & Technology (ASST), a pan-non-profit organisation, was founded in Damascus in 1978 by an initiative from the Kuwait Institute for Scientific Research (KISR), in Kuwait, and the Scientific Studies and Research Centre (SSRC) and the Supreme Council of Sciences, in Syria.

Through the organisation of high level Meetings and Seminars lectured by some of the best known international experts, ASST aims at providing high level educational programmes to Arab scientists in fields considered crucial to the progress of the Arab countries.

So far, ASST's meetings have dealt with subjects such as: Electronics, Energy, Environment, Mathematics, Informatics, Composite Materials, Planning, Product Development, Reliability and Sensors.

Nonetheless, plans to expand into other areas such as biotechnology and the transfer and development of technology are being studied.

ASST aspires to create for each subject a regular forum in certain parts of the Arab World, but until plans are finalised the meetings will continue to be held in Syria and Kuwait who has joined in recently represented by Kuwait Foundation for the Advancement of Science (KFAS), Kuwait Institute for Scientific Research (KISR) and Kuwait University.

Objectives of ASST

Through its programmes, the School aims at reaching the following objectives:

1. Bring Arab Scientists up-to-date on the latest scientific developments, and state-of-the-art technologies in the field under study.
2. Facilitate direct contact among Arab Scientists, and between Arab Scientists and their international counterparts, to create a favourable atmosphere for scientific and technological cooperation.

3. Make Arab scientists working abroad aware of their home countries resources, and encourage them to contribute to their scientific and technological development.
4. Provide the international scientific community with an overview of the scientific activities in the Arab countries through the publication of each School meeting proceedings which cover the scientific and technological developments in the Arab world.

Concurrent Engineering in Product and Design Development

Damascus, October 21-27, 1996

SPONSORS

- Regional Office for Science & Technology for the Arab States (Rostas)
- Kuwait Foundation for the Advancement of Science (KFAS)
- Kuwait Institute for Scientific Research (KISR)
- Kuwait University
- Atomic Energy Commission (AECS), Syria
- Higher Institute of Applied Sciences & Technology (HIAST), Syria
- Scientific Studies & Research Center (SSRC), Syria

SCIENTIFIC COMMITTEE

Amr Armanazi
Chairman,
Scientific Studies & Research Centre
Damascus, Syria

Imad Moustapha
Scientific Studies & Research Centre
Damascus, Syria

Mahmoud Anbar
Scientific Studies & Research Centre
Damascus, Syria

Ghassan Assi
Scientific Studies & Research Centre
Damascus, Syria

Khaled Sawan
Scientific Studies & Research Center
Aleppo, Syria

Jamal Said
Higher Institute of Applied
Sciences & Technology (HIAST)
Damascus, Syria

Mohamed Ali Haji
Kuwait Institute for Scientific Research (KISR)
Kuwait

SCIENTIFIC CONSULTANT

Prof. Adnan Aswad
Industrial & Manufacturing Systems Engineering
The University of Michigan-Dearborn
4901 Evergreen Road
Dearborn, Michigan 48128-1491, USA

ASST SECRETARY-GENERAL

Ahmad Haj Said

ASST ORGANIZING COMMITTEE

Alia Kouatly
General-Relations Administrator

Violet Kalemkerian
Secretary

Lecturers

Adnan Aswad
The University of Michigan-Dearborn
School of Engineering
Industrial & Manufacturing
Systems Engineering
4901 Evergreen Road, Dearborn
Michigan 48128-1491, USA

Hamid R. Parsaei
Department of Industrial Engineering
304 J.B. Speed Building
University of Louisville
Louisville, Kentucky 40292, USA

Sammy G. Shina
Mechanical Engineering Department
University of Massachussetts-Lowell
1 University Avenue, Lowell
Massachussetts 01854-2881, USA

Timothy Collins
Department of Electronics
Bournemouth University
Talbor Campus, Fern Barrow
Poole BH 12 5 BB
Dorset, UK

D.J. Gonzales
General Motors Corporation
Warren, USA

Peter J. Sackett
Director, The CIM Institute
Cranfield University
Cranfield, Bedford MK43 OAL, UK

Sa'ad Medhat
Head of the Office of Research
Bournemouth University
Poole BH 12 5BB
Dorset, UK

Imad Moustapha
Scientific Studies & Research Center
P. O. Box : 4470
Damascus, Syria

John Driscoll
Department of Mechanical Engineering
University of Surrey
Guildford, Surrey, UK

Short Papers Contributors

M. Ammar Al-Salka
Scientific Studies & Research Center, Division 2000
P. O. Box 4170, Damascus,
SYRIA

M. Esmat El Sarha
National Research Center
El-Tahrir Street
Dokki, Cairo 12622
Cairo,
EGYPT

Carlos Cziulik
Department of Mechanical Engineering
University of Surrey
Guildford-Surrey, GU 2 5XH
ENGLAND

Imad Sabouni
Scientific Studies & Research Center
P. O. Box : 4470
Damascus,
SYRIA

Aziz I. Said
Faculty of Engineering
Ain Shams University
1 El-Sarayat St. Abde Basha Square
Abbassia, Cairo, EGYPT

Nihad El Chazly
National Research Center
Mechanical Engineering Department
El-Tahrir Street, Dokki
Cairo, EGYPT

Tarek Mansour Turbakieh
Sun Office for Engineering Consultations
Benghazi, Jamal Abed Nasser Street
Tajouri Building Appt. No 309
P. O. Box : 21 Benghazi, LYBIA

Mohamed A. El Hamalaway
Professor of Computer Engineering
Department of Systems and Computers Engineering, Faculty of Engineering
Al Azhar University, Cairo
EGYPT

SECTION ONE
Lecture Notes

1

The Concurrent Engineering Organization

Adnan A. Aswad

Professor, Department of Industrial & Manufacturing Systems Engineering
The University of Michigan-Dearborn, USA

Abstract

The various definitions of Concurrent Engineering (CE) within the context of the product development cycle are introduced. The necessary requirements for implementing CE are outlined, and the need for building cross-functional structures is particularly stressed. Different models of such structures and their characteristics are described, and examples of such structures from the automotive industry are illustrated.

Keywords: *Concurrent Engineering, Simultaneous Engineering, Parallel Product Development, Organization for Design and Manufacturing, Team Organization.*

1. Introduction

The first concurrent engineer might well have been the blacksmith. He designed the horseshoe on demand, manufactured and installed it, and sold and maintained it, if necessary. However, as products became complex, and technologies more specialized, producer organizations became large. Consequently, communication channels among the various specialized units of these large organizations started to impede information flows, thus delaying design and manufacturing cycles, impairing quality, and increasing costs. During the past decade, intense global competitive pressures have forced many organizations to examine closely their product development processes as to quality, costs, and delivery schedules. Improving the effectiveness of, and the coordination between, the product and manufacturing engineering functions was identified as an obvious early target. Such coordination was sought through a parallel rather than a sequential product development process, which came to be known as simultaneous or concurrent engineering. Perhaps the most publicized case in the American automotive industry to date is Ford Motor Company's Taurus/Sable vehicle line (Peters [11]). This very successful program was done in a timely manner, at a reasonable cost, and with high quality.

As applications of concurrent engineering (CE) concepts matured, other functions in the product development cycle (PDC), such as marketing, product planning, material flow, and sales, began to be incorporated. With this expansion of CE beyond its initial boundaries, fundamental organizational and cultural changes were necessitated and began to take hold.

In general, the implementation of concurrent engineering requires:

1. An integrated information base and means for interactive communications for accessing information simultaneously and in a timely manner.
2. Methodologies for analysis and synthesis, in order to implement effective planning and communications, *e.g.* quality function deployment and design for manufacturing and assembly.
3. A cross-functional organizational structure, in order to facilitate the realization of development projects in a timely and cost effective manner.

In this paper the various definitions of CE are reviewed, and the characteristics of the concurrent development methodology that distinguish it from a serial development methodology are compared. Examples of various organizational structures for implementing CE are cited and discussed.

The reader is referred to Stark [16], Braithwaite [3], and Reddy (1993) [14] for a discussion of the information requirements in CE and to Aswad and Knight [2], Shina [15], and Parsaei [10] for the various analysis-and-synthesis and cost-effectiveness methodologies.

2. Definitions and Requirements for Concurrent Engineering

The term simultaneous engineering (SE) preceded that of concurrent engineering (CE), and at present both are used synonymously. During the mid-1980s SE was primarily concerned with a strong representation of manufacturing considerations in the initial product design stages. This orientation is reflected in a 1986 definition by the Society of Automotive Engineers:

> *"SE is defined as the integration of the roles of the design engineer and the manufacturing engineer."*

The Society of Manufacturing Engineers (SME) used, in 1987, the following expanded definition:

> *"SE is design, manufacturing, and quality engineers working together to improve manufacturing processes and techniques to respond to customer demands of faster delivery times, increased product variety and higher quality products.'*

In a study for the US Department of Defense, the Institute for Defense Analysis (IDA), which came to be Known later as DARPA, defined CE in 1988 as:

> *"...a systematic approach to the integrated, concurrent design of products and their related processes, including manufacture and support. This approach is intended to cause the developers, from the outset, to consider all elements of the product life cycle from conception through disposal including quality, cost, schedule, and user requirements.'*

This last definition is encompassing and covers the activities of the total life cycle of the product, and advocates the objective of the early coordination of decision making among the various organizational units of an enterprise. Similar definitions could be found in Prasad [12], Shina [15], Parsaei [10], and others. A comprehensive discussion of these is given by Prasad [12]. We will use the recent 1992 definition by Cleetus [5], which explicitly includes the added organizational aspects of *team values, trust,* and *sharing*:

> *"Concurrent Engineering is a systematic approach to the integrated development of a product and its related processes — from conception to disposal — that emphasizes response to customer expectations and embodies team values of cooperation, trust, and sharing in such a manner that decision making proceeds with large intervals of parallel working by all life-cycle perspectives, synchronized by comparatively brief exchanges to produce consensus."*

3. Concurrent and Serial Product Development Phases

Various organizations follow a plethora of product and process development cycles (PDC). Characterizing the phases of the product development cycle (PDC) helps to put in perspective some of the organizational issues involved. We will define a generic process that is similar to that advocated by Ulrich and Eppinger [18], but containing seven phases that we will describe briefly:

3.1. Mission statement

The *mission statement,* which is also known as the *design brief* or *charter,* should contain a general description of the product, the target market segments, and customer categories and specify the primary and secondary business goals as to market share, profit margins, and the product's projected life cycle.

3.2. Market and concept definition

Customer demands are identified through various market survey techniques; competitive benchmarking studies are conducted, the functional technical design requirements are identified, design and manufacturing feasibility is determined, and cost estimates are projected.

3.3. System-level concept generation and selection

In this phase, various design concepts that satisfy the functional design requirements are generated. The design that best satisfies these requirements in terms of quality, cost, and delivery is selected, and the product architecture is determined.

3.4. Detail product design

Detailed specifications of product dimensions, materials, and tolerances are made. Special and standard components are identified, and make or buy decisions are made.

3.5. Prototype testing and refinement

Prototypes of the selected design are tested for functionality, manufacturing and assembly feasibility, reliability, and cost. The *alpha* prototypes are refined, and thereafter the next generation *beta* prototypes are built with "production-like" processes.

3.6. Process planning, production planning and control

Actual production processes of the final design are planned. Production control and quality assurance plans are drawn up.

3.7. Production ramp-up and refinement

In this final phase, a pilot production run is carried out with the purpose of familiarizing and training the work force, discovering and correcting production problems before full production levels are reached. Subsequently, the product is *launched.*

The above seven phases are interdependent, and the degree of their dependencies is a function of the product architecture, the available production capabilities, and the organizational structure of the producer. In Fig. 1.1, the phases are depicted with substantial overlaps between each pair, thus conceptually representing the concurrent engineering approach. This is in contrast to a purely sequential or serial approach, where each phase starts after the completion of the previous one, which eventually results in a longer development cycle. Krishnan [8] characterizes the degree of the overlaps between phases as indicative of their dependency and partial information sharing. On the other hand, the ordering of the phases represents their precedence relationships. The product development cycle time in this case will be greatly influenced by the phase having the longest duration.

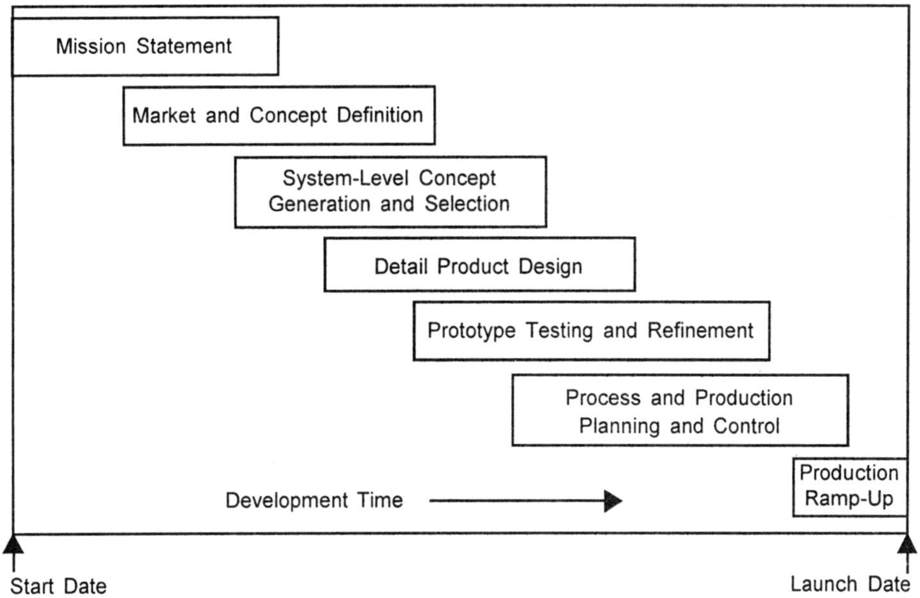

Fig. 1.1: Concurrent Product Development Cycle

Prasad [12] states that "optimum concurrency" occurs when the start points of each phase begins to the farthest left of the diagram as much as possible, while satisfying the following conditions:

1. Maintain the precedence of the phases.
2. Minimize the horizontal overlap between consecutive phases.
3. Maximize the independence of the tasks.

He adds that "In general, there is greater affinity and dependence between pairs of activities which are adjacent to each other. The farther away the activities are positioned from each other, the lesser would be the degree of affinity or the need for information transfer among them." Thus, in phase five, prototype testing and refinement requires more information sharing with detailed design, in the immediately preceding phase, than with market and concept definition in the earlier, second phase. Clark *et al.* [4] maintain that from the information processing point of view, the sequential approach is more characteristic of a batch communications environment, while the concurrent engineering approach is more consistent with a dialogue communications mode between upstream and downstream design groups.

4. Organizational Structures: Concepts and Examples

An organization is composed of *groups* of people involved in communicating *decisions* in order to achieve a set of common *objectives* through *division of labour.* In the functional type of organization (*e.g.*, department) the information flow occurs vertically. However, the need for a common base of information in complex product concurrent development necessitates that organizational structures adapt to the information processing requirements of the tasks to be achieved. Cross-functional structures promote, *via* lateral communication, the needed integrated decision making. Following the seminal work of Galbraith [6], we cite seven types of lateral (cross-functional) structures listed in increasing order of complexity and administrative cost:

4.1. Informal liaison

A structure between two managers who engage in solving a problem that might affect them jointly. This relieves the vertical hierarchy from an information and decision "overload condition." However, it may result in suboptimal decisions that might not be in the best interests of the global organization.

4.2. Formal liaison

A means to formalize the interdepartmental communications as the intensity of information processing between two functional departments increases (*e.g.*, an engineering liaison person who is formally assigned and located in the manufacturing plant and acts as a conduit for expediting information between the two functional units).

4.3. Task force

When the number of functional departments that must reach a joint decision increases (usually more than two), then a task force is constituted with representatives of the departments affected by the problem. Such a task force is temporary and is dissolved after recommending a set of solutions to the affected functional managers.

4.4. Teams

A structure of "permanent" task forces formed to provide solutions for frequently recurring problems. Teams may be formed at various levels of the organizational hierarchy and possess decision making power. For example, a specific product team might consist of department managers from marketing, engineering, and manufacturing who solve problems within their jurisdiction but refer bigger problems upward to a higher authority.

4.5. Champion integrator

Typically a high-level manager serves as the champion integrator by facilitating information processing between functional managers both vertically and horizontally. The champion's role is thus to assure that the best decisions that are consistent with the overall organizational objectives are made and not to make the best decision personally. The champion typically reports directly to the general manager and exercises influence from having access to information and by providing it in an unbiased manner to various functional managers and task force and team leaders. It is a delicate role that requires a person with a high sense of achievement and a high degree of loyalty to the overall organization. This is the model followed by Cadillac Motor Car Division, in addition to a hierarchical matrix organization described by Walklet [19].

4.6. Cross-functional manager

This individual performs the same functions of the champion above but with the added formal authority to make and approve decisions. A functional manager does not report directly to the cross-functional manager. However, he or she derives power from the general manager, who is the position's immediate supervisor, and possibly through the budget control process. Fig. 1.2 illustrates such a case at Komatsu Ltd., whereby the "plant control manager" serves in this role of cross-functional manager and reports dually to the plant manager and the corporate office.

4.7. Cross-functional matrix

This mode is appropriate whenever a greater integration of specialized skills is needed on a larger scale than around distinguishable programs or products. Such integration requires a group of managers with cross-functional expertise and the authority to make decisions. Such group or committee members are usually members of both the functional departments and the program office and thus are subject to dual reporting relationships in a matrix structure. The committee is usually headed by the functional member who has the relevant expertise and has the largest portion of responsibility in a particular program. Often, goal conflicts arise between functional managers and the cross-functional committee heads. To resolve these conflicts, effective policy deployment is essential in order to achieve consistent decisions that serve the overall goals of the organization. Fig. 1.3 illustrates such a matrix structure, which is used by Toyota Autobody Company, a division of Toyota Motor Company.

The seven types of cross-functional organizational structures are not mutually exclusive, and it is conceivable that one or more types might coexist at different levels in a single organization. For example, the Komatsu Ltd Type VI structure, illustrated in Fig. 1.2, has the "plant control manager" serving as the cross-functional manager for the distinct engine manufacturing activity. Yet this is only one of the many cross-functional organizational structures at Komatsu Ltd.

Toyota Autobody uses the Type VII cross-functional matrix management structure, as illustrated in Fig. 1.3. The structure incorporates the plan-do-check-action (PDCA) philosophy, often referred to as the Shewhart/Deeming cycle of total quality control, where the plan and do phases are implemented in a matrix within the larger matrix of the check and action phases. The cross-functional

CROSS-FUNCTIONAL MANAGEMENT

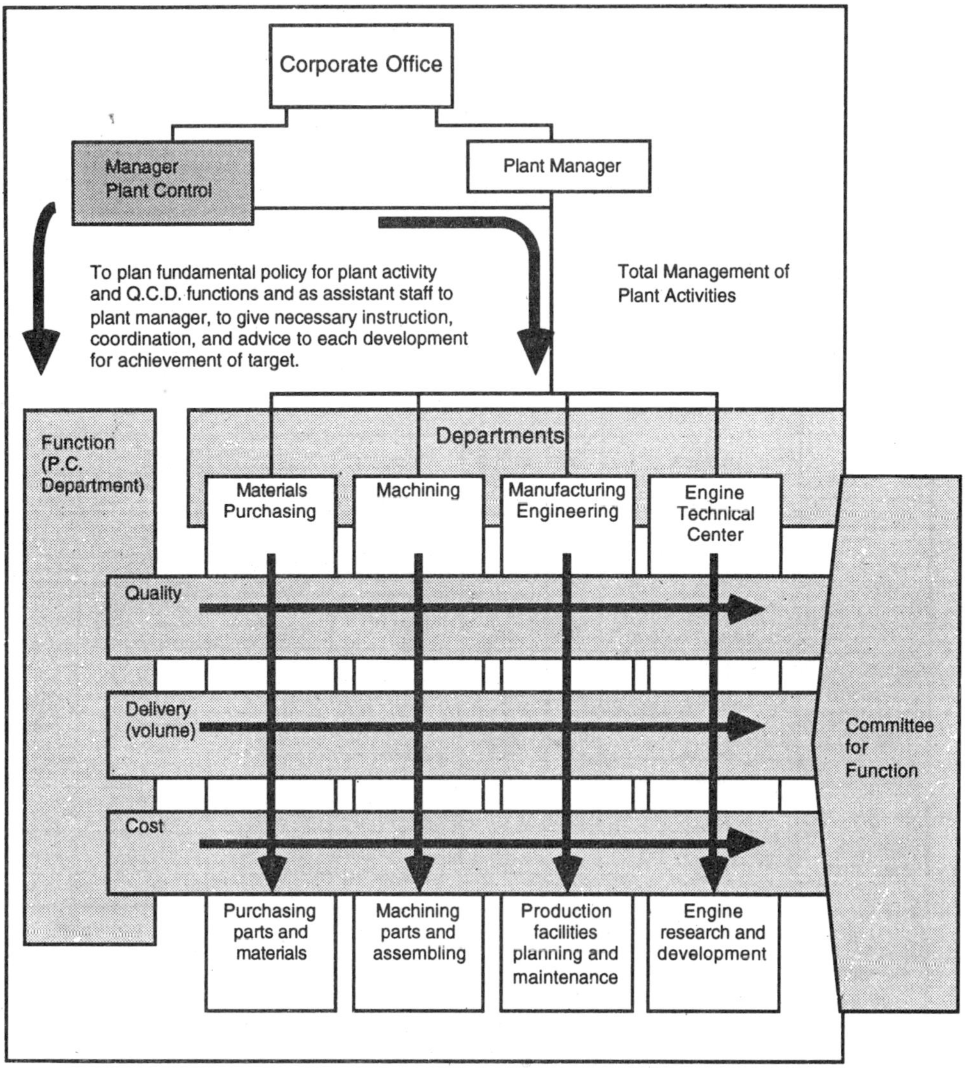

Fig. 1.2: Cross-Functional Management (Courtesy: Komatsu Ltd.)

committees for specific programs are denoted by dotted boundary lines and have members from each relevant functional group and program. They ensure the consistency of decision making in program planning and control (check). The line functions, which are in charge of the resources, perform the actual work (do) and provide the necessary skills for assuring the integrity of the product. The cross-

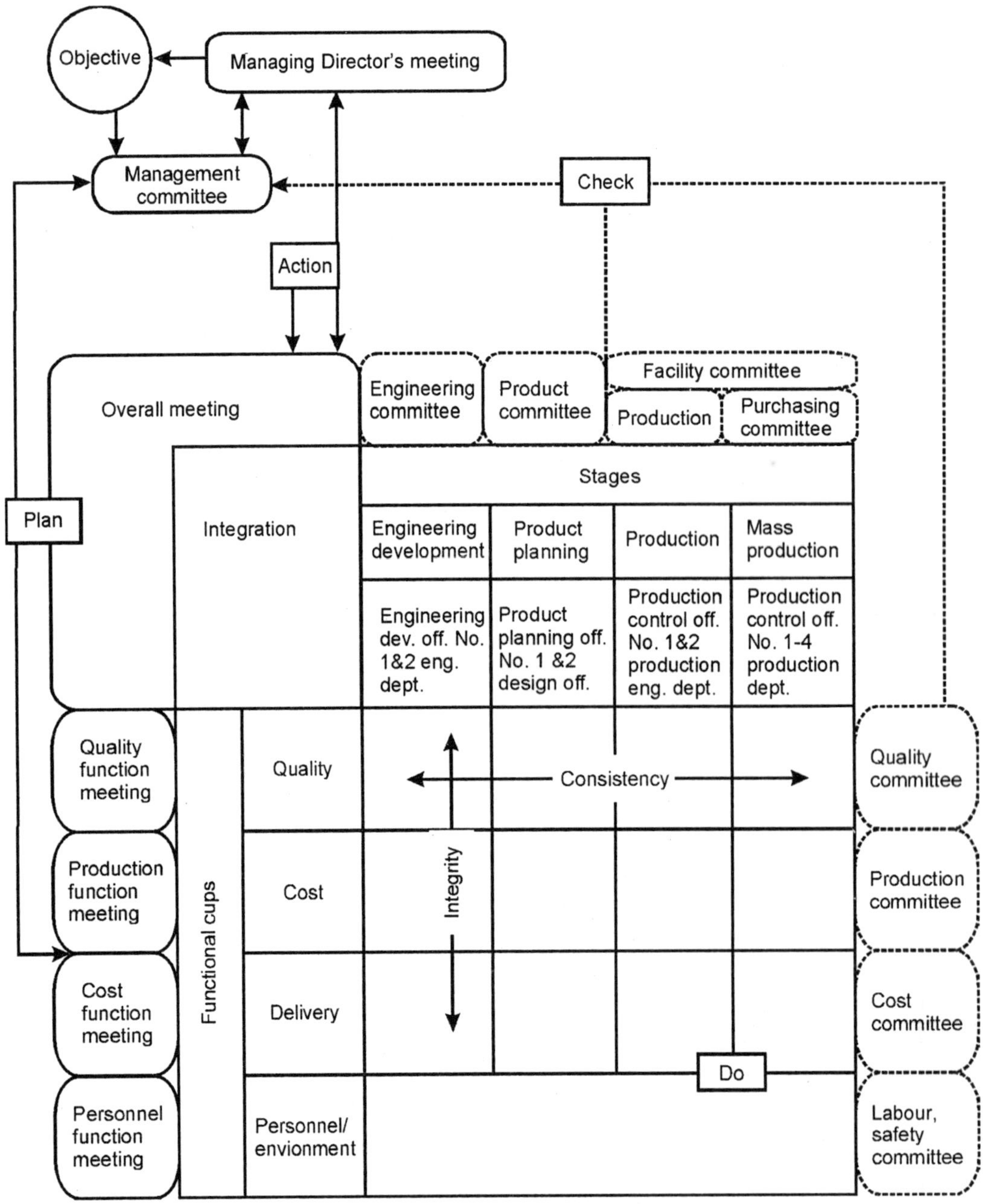

Fig. 1.3: Cross-Functional Matrix Management (Courtesy: Toyota Autobody Company)

functional matrix management structure is a complex system that requires a large number of meetings to process information effectively in order to ensure consistency of decisions.

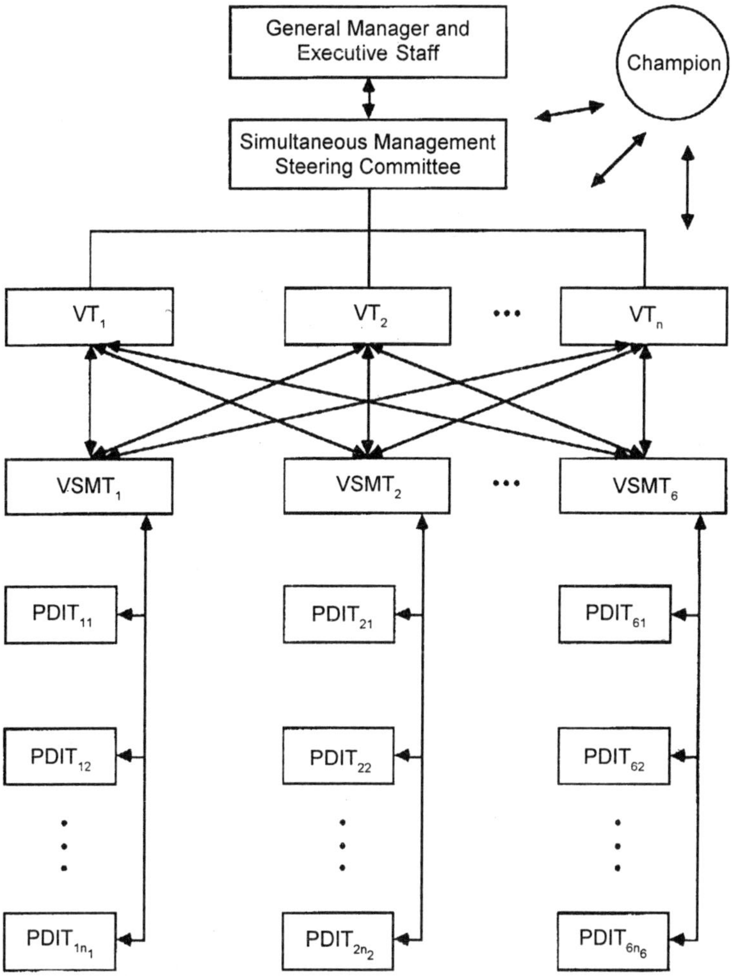

VTi — ith Vehicle Team, i=1, ..., n
VSMTi — ith Vehicle System Management Team, i = 1, ..., 6
PDITij — jth Product Development and Improvement Team for ith VSMT, i = 1, ..., 6; j = 1, ...ni

Fig. 1.4: Cadillac Motor Car Division Hierarchical Matrix Organization

The hierarchical matrix organization of Cadillac Motor Car Division is depicted in Fig. 1.4. Here the members of each product development and improvement team (PDIT) are involved in the detailed simultaneous engineering design of a product and its associated manufacturing methods. PDIT membership includes not only product and manufacturing engineering representatives, but also, for example, finance and customer satisfaction and supplier representatives. These members report dually to their functional line departments as well as to a vehicle system management team (VSMT), whose leader is responsible for a somewhat independent vehicle system (*e.g.*, chassis/power train, seats and interior trim, electrical/electronic). In turn, each vehicle development program is conducted by a vehicle team (VT), which draws on the resources of the various VSMTs. Vehicle team membership consists partly of members of the VSMTs. A simultaneous management steering committee coordinates the VTs and reports to the executive staff led by the general manager. The champion (Type V) also reports to the general manager and facilitates information processing in this hierarchical matrix structure.

The common factor in the above three matrix-structure examples is the multiple reporting relationships. A cross-functional team might consist of individual members who contribute their efforts as needed, ranging from part time to full time. Galbraith [6], based on studies performed at DoD and NASA, suggests that a mixture of part- and full-time personnel contributes the most to project performance indicators of cost and schedule and provides organizational flexibility. He further recommends the use of a higher proportion of part-time people in a project in order to take advantage of the matrix organizational structure.

The question arises as to how to ensure that the most qualified rather than the most dispensable individuals are released from their departments to join the cross-functional team. Nemoto [9] recommends that a company-wide system of rotation be used. Such a system provides training and widens the professional and interpersonal skills of the participants. Thus, every employee becomes an indispensable member of the organization.

5. Modes of Organizational Leadership

Hayes *et al.* [7] address the issues of organizational leadership in relation to development project management. They propose four project leadership modes, which are illustrated in Fig. 1.5:

1. Functional
2. Project Team
3. Lightweight Project Matrix
4. Heavyweight Project Matrix.

The functional mode corresponds to the individual departmental structure which was prevalent in American and European auto and other industries for most

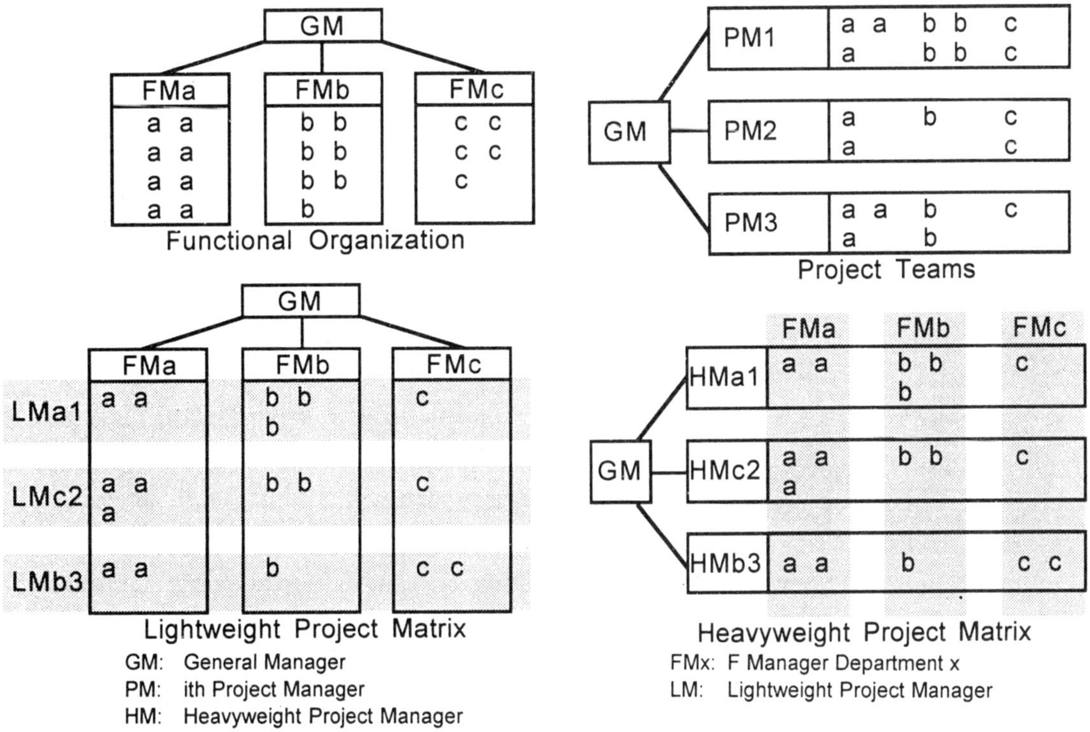

Fig. 1.5: Organizational Leadership Modes (adapted from Hayes *et al.* [7])

of the century. No individual has responsibility for the entire product or project. Coordination is achieved *via* meetings, liaison, and rules of procedure. This mode is not conducive to effective product development, and definitely is the antithesis of practicing concurrent engineering principles. Many firms have moved from this type of structure to one or a combination of the next three modes for implementing their product development activities, although this mode is still prevalent in research activities where in-depth specialization and competence are prerequisites.

The second mode of the project team is a special case of the matrix structure in that a team of specialists are dedicated to the execution of a single project; thus, it might be called a "Vector Structure." Team members report to a single manager, who is both the functional and project manager. This is suited for specialized "technology-push" product management modes, *e.g.* a venture capital firm beginning with a technology and then trying to find a market for it.

The last two structures are the matrix organizations that are suited for implementing concurrent engineering in the development of "market-pull" - type products, but with differing leadership modes.

The lightweight project manager (LM) is typically responsible for the coordination of the development activities using liaison representatives. LMs have less power and status than functional managers, and little influence outside the particular product development project. They have no direct marketing contact and are not responsible for product concept generation. As such, this structure and mode of leadership might be suited for established rather than new product development, since only minor changes in product and process design might be necessitated.

On the other hand, the heavyweight project manager (HM) has more responsibility and authority for product development. The project team members still work for their functional areas; however, the HMs have direct access to their services. The HMs are responsible for product planning and concept generation for new products. They are typically involved in meeting customers, actively working with the engineers, monitoring prototype, testing, and production activities. Generally they become involved in and responsible for the whole development cycle.

Clark and Fujimoto [4] found from a study of twelve Japanese, eleven European, and six U.S. organizations that the Japanese project managers exercised more authority than their U.S. counterparts, while the European organizations relied more heavily on the functional form of organization. Japanese companies tended to place potential heavyweight project managers as apprentices with existing HMs, in order to train and groom them for the future. The apprenticeship period might last for more than one product cycle, until that person is deemed capable of assuming the responsibilities of the HM. Another important aspect in the apprenticeship process is the matching of the person to the product. For example, a risk-taking and aggressive person would probably not be the best choice for the development of a sedate family car.

The writer has no knowledge of any apprenticeship training programs in American automotive firms. They generally tend to promote to the position of project manager those personnel who have been rotated working in many different areas of the company, and who have considerable seniority. They typically originate from the ranks of product planning, as opposed to engineering. However, there is a recent trend to intensify the formal training of engineers in managerial disciplines, including concurrent engineering, and to restructure into matrix organizations.

6. Conclusion

There is a demonstrable need of coordinating the activities of the product development cycle in order to improve the effectiveness of the process. Concurrent engineering (CE) principles must be applied in order to fulfill this need, to achieve the goals of developing products that possess high quality, at a competitive cost, and marketed in a short cycle time. The implementation of CE requires the design of an integrated information base, the utilization of analysis and synthesis methodologies, and the building of an effective cross-functional organizational structure.

The goals of meeting quality, cost, and timeliness or delivery (QCD) are generally shared by all the elements in an organization. Indeed, these are superordinate goals and should serve as the common conduits of communications between functional lines and as catalysts for cooperation between vertical functional lines, making cross-functional management a reality. Thus, instituting cross-functional structures in an organization should be the first step toward implementing concurrent engineering principles.

We have discussed in detail various types of cross-functional structures and the main modes of leadership in a matrix organization. Although current matrix organizational structures utilize lightweight project managers, there are sustained efforts to migrate toward the heavyweight manager leadership mode.

References

1. A. Aswad, "Policy Management: A Perspective on Japanese Practice," *Proceedings of the 1988, Institute of Industrial Engineers Integrated Systems Conference,* October 1988, pp. 73-76.
2. A. Aswad and J. Knight, "Comparative Aspects of QFD and Simultaneous Engineering," *Proceedings of the 21st International Conference on Automotive Technology and Automation,* Wiesbaden, Germany, November 1989, pp. 141-155.
3. K.S. Braithwaite, *Object Oriented Database Design: Concepts and Application,* Academic Press, 1993.
4. K.B. Clark and T. Fujimoto, *Product Development Performance: Strategy, Organization, and Management in the World Auto Industry,* Harvard Business School Press, 1991.
5. K.J. Cleetus, "Definition of Concurrent Engineering," CERC Technical Report Series, Research Notes, CERC-TR-RN-92-003, West Virginia University, Morgantown, WV, 1992.
6. J.R. Galbraith, *Organization Design,* Addison Wesley, 1977.

7. R.H. Hayes, S.C. Wheelwright, and K.B. Clark, *Dynamic Manufacturing: Creating the Learning Organization,* The Free Press, 1988.
8. V. Krishnan, *Design Process Improvement: Sequencing and Overlapping Activities in Product Development,* Doctoral Dissertation, Massachusetts Institute of Technology, Boston, MA, 1993.
9. N. Nemoto, *Total Quality Control for Management: Strategies and Techniques from Toyota and Toyota Gosei,* Prentice Hall, 1987.
10. H. Parsaei and W.G. Sullivan (eds.), *Concurrent Engineering,* Chapman & Hall, 1993.
11. T. Peters, *Thriving on Chaos,* Knopf-Random House, 1987.
12. B. Prasad, *Concurrent Engineering Fundamentals* — Volume 1, Prentice Hall PTR, 1996.
13. R. Reddy, "The DARPA Initiative: Encouraging New Industrial Practices," *IEEE Spectrum,* July 1991, pp. 26-32.
14. R. Reddy, K. Srinivas, and V. Jagannathan, "Computer Support for Concurrent Engineering," CERC Technical Report Series, West Virginia University, Morgantown, WV, 1993.
15. S.G. Shina, *Concurrent Engineering and Design for Manufacture of Electronic Products,* Van Nostrand Reinhold, 1991.
16. J. Stark, *Engineering Information Management Systems: Beyond CAD/CAM to Concurrent Engineering Support,* Van Nostrand Reinhold, 1992.
17. J. Turino, *Managing Concurrent Engineering, Buying Time to Market,* Van Nostrand Reinhold, 1992.
18. K.T. Ulrich and S.D. Eppinger, *Product Design and Development,* McGraw-Hill, 1995.
19. R.H. Walklet, "Continuous Improvement and Simultaneous Engineering," Society of Automotive Engineers, paper no. 890162, 1989.
20. R.I. Winner, J.P. Pennell, and M.G. Slusarczuk, "The Role of Concurrent Engineering in Weapons System Acquisition," Institute of Defense Analysis (DARPA) report R-338, Washington DC, December 1988.

2

Concurrent Engineering: The Essential Ingredients for Achieving Business Success

Professor Sa'ad Medhat
Ph.D, M.Phil, C.Eng, MIEE, MIEEE, MACM
IBM Professor of Concurrent Engineering and Intergraph
Bournemouth University, Fern Barrow, Poole BH 12 5BB UK

Abstract

Concurrent Engineering describes an approach management in response to competitive needs to reduce time-to-market with shortened development cycle at lower cost, through multi-disciplinary teamworking, communication, shared tools and data, and simultaneity of functional operation. This paper reviews these issues in the context of engineering management and discusses the changing role of organisation, information technology and the means by which success can be measured. The paper emphasises the importance of embracing requirements engineering with a whole product life cycle perspective and extending these considerations to the marketplace.

The full and effective implementation of Concurrent Engineering requires significant and innovative use of enabling tools and technologies across the boundaries within the organisation and externally throughout the supply chain and with the customer.

1. Introduction

The electronics industry was amongst the first to embrace Concurrent Engineering. There has been a significant widening of interest beyond the original electronics industrial sector to now include many other industries such as aerospace, chemicals, mechanical, IT, communications and consumer goods. Many new subjects and issues are now allying themselves to Concurrent Engineering, with participation at conferences on the subject over the last five years seeing a transition from being Academia-led to now being Industry-led. For example, industry made up 60 per cent of the CEEDA '96 Conference (Concurrent Engineering & Electronic Design Automation) delegates this year, outnumbering the academics for the first time and following a year on year trend. A clear indication of the growing awareness, importance and acceptance of Concurrent Engineering to future industrial progress and success.

Our own undergraduate and postgraduate Concurrent Engineering degrees, which we pioneered in the UK at Bournemouth University, are flourishing. Blue chip companies are already accepting our students with skills that are equipping them to play an effective role in the management of advanced technology. The National Council of Systems Engineering is now well established and is playing an important role in the development and dissemination of Concurrent Engineering, as is the Institution of Electrical Engineers.

This is all testimony to the wide realisation that Concurrent Engineering is developing rapidly with direct relevance to the industrial and commercial challenges that face us today, and even more vigorously in the future.

Concurrent Engineering has expanded and developed to reach out beyond its beginnings of simply looking at smarter ways for the design and manufacturing communities to work more effectively together. Today, the customer and requirements engineering are now being addressed with a cradle to grave perspective, for improved innovation and product development management, new technology introduction, all the way through the product life cycle to include the eventual withdrawal of the product from the marketplace — to then be replaced by an even better product that has benefitted by having followed the same route.

Other disciplines are converging with Concurrent Engineering in response to the need for organisations to meet their ever increasing competitive challenges. Reducing time-to-market and product introduction costs are now being joined by the need to examine the dynamics of change within the organisation, managing technology and processes, and business process re-engineering.

Multi-media, virtual prototyping and client/server computing are now being adopted and introduced into the Concurrent Engineering communication tool kit for improved co-operative working and co-location.

2. Time-to-Market

The microelectronics industry sector has seen its time-to-market plummet over the last decade from typically four years to four months, driven by improving technologies and increasing competitive activity.

Another example of this dramatic trend is in the personal computer industry. As this business got underway in the early 1980's, a typical PC had a production life of two and a half years. Today, computing power is doubling every year, and the growth of information is doubling every two years. Manufacturers now introduce replacement PC products every six months, and new options every month. Their products now spend more time in development than they do in production. Other industries are paralleling this trend.

This time-to-market contraction has introduced huge pressures on the design and manufacturing process, inventories, ROI, marketing and after sales support. The need for industry standards and re-useability is now even more important.

All organisations are facing change in response to these pressures and those imposed by competition, customers and their ever changing needs, suppliers and the new and more innovative ways in which everyone in the total supply chain needs to work. Information technology developments continue to accelerate dramatically and are raising challenging questions as to how such technology should profitably be exploited in support of Concurrent Engineering.

We are all experiencing widening horizons in terms of those who now need to be involved in our systems, sometimes on a global basis. Already, we are seeing the emergence of teleworkers. The concept of the portable, mobile and remote office is now a reality needing to be integrated into the workplace. Electronic data interchange (EDI) between companies and their suppliers is well established.

3. Organisation & Information Technology

Information Technology (IT) will need to be tightly coupled with Concurrent Engineering as part of what needs to be done to effect the changes that will enable companies to improve their business performance. It is therefore critical to look closely at the question; "Which data do we communicate, and to whom?" To answer this, it will be necessary to examine how business goals and the organisation are realigned to deliver these improvements. Companies will need to continue to reposition themselves to best respond to these pressures. Performance within the company has to improve, and likewise, performance working with other companies, be they customers or partners, must also improve.

The last three decades have seen a progression away from a simple and occasional use of a mainframe computer hidden in the darker recesses of the company. In recent years there has been a rapid move towards IT becoming distributed and used in a highly interactive way.

The number of workers in all branches of industry, commerce and government using these systems has introduced a need for ease-of-use by people who do not see computing as their primary role.

There is an essential need for systems integrity and affordable performance that will meet both the end-users' needs and those of the clients and suppliers of the company.

Today, we are seeing continued refinement of the client/server or distributed system computing concept. What can be expected to emerge in the next few years is an "anyhow to anyone" networking approach. Organisations, large and small, will be running their businesses using distributed systems which will extend to communicate directly with their suppliers' and customers' systems, through broadcast systems, superhighways like Internet, and other value-added services. Web browsers, personal digital assistants like the Apple Newton, and other mobile devices able to recognise voice and hand writing, respond to touch input and other multi-media concepts will gain ground.

This change is all very well, but it is not just a question of changing our approach, or our system, or even what we do. We must be sure that al those involved understand, and as partners, agree the changes, recognise their new or modified role, and be able to see and capitalise on the advantages in these changes if this is to succeed. These partners of change include the customers and the supply chain, as well as the people within the organisation. From this follows what I call the "3-D" partner. The three **D**'s refer to the fact they will each be **D**irected by their respective job objectives, with **D**ifferent skills and geographically **D**ispersed within and without the enterprise.

4. Performance Metrics

Customer and marketplace perspectives have a profound effect on Concurrent Engineering and the upstream design, production and supply-chain management. Somehow, companies must involve their customers in defining product specifications and service, to ensure that customer expectations will be surpassed. In an ever more vigorous competitive environment, maintaining customer interaction and loyalty is a critical paradigm for the nineties and beyond.

One of the first issues that needs to be addressed at the commencement of a new product life cycle is to identify and quantify performance metrics. That is not new of course. We have always needed to persuade our Finance Director or Venture Capitalist that enthusiasm for starting a new product is tempered by a sound business plan. It is imperative to show that the required level of working capital will attract appropriate levels of revenue, market share, cost savings, return on investment and assets. The business plan will need to demonstrate a desirable break-even schedule, and indeed a schedule that reduces cycle time when compared to earlier product development experiences, and those that can be expected from competition. These plans will need to ensure that customer requirements will be met, and risks identified and contained.

But in today's environment, heavily influenced by competition and price sensitivity in the marketplace, the critical question is "but how do I know that my new product development proposals will exceed our customers' expectations?" This is a loaded question and raises its own implicit challenges. For example, "What are these expectations? How can they be determined? Are they stable? Are they realistic or credible?".

This is where Concurrent Engineering can act as a catalyst to draw together all the disciplines that have already been mentioned, such as business process re-engineering — and invoking tools such as client/server computing.

5. Conflicting Perceptions of Requirements

Consider the question of how a customer's perception of their own requirements for a new product be compared to the supplier's perception of the same customer's requirements. Experience shows startling and concerning results in many cases — conflict! [Fig. 2.1].

For complex projects, perhaps involving internationally dispersed customers, product development, production sites, distribution, marketing channels and after-sales service operations, a familiar adage surfaces - "if only we didn't have to worry about customers or competition we wouldn't have nearly so many problems." Technology-led product developers start with what they perceive to be an application that can use a new technology. All too often what is witnessed is a solution looking for a problem. As time goes on, ideas, designs and processes become increasingly fixed and even

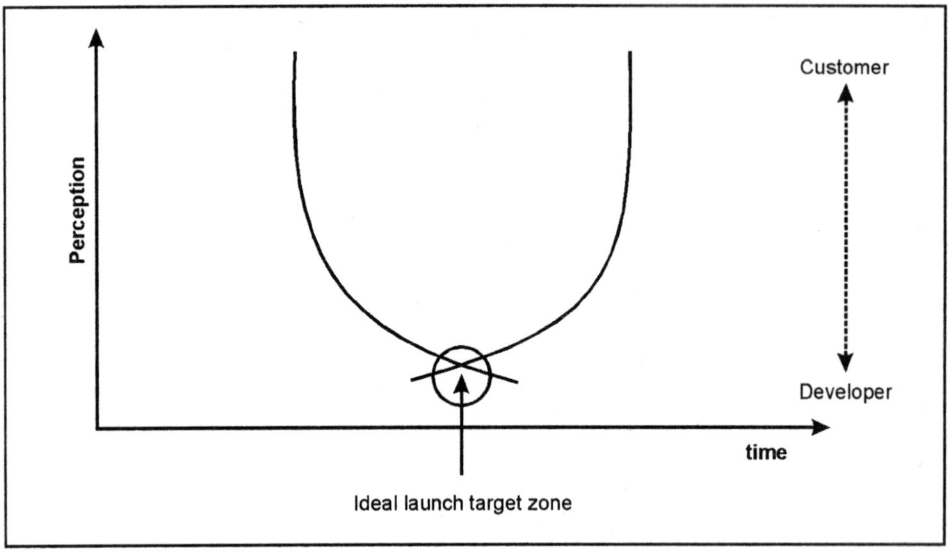

Fig. 2.1: Requirements conflict between supplier & customer

entrenched. The "we can't change it now" syndrome becomes the received wisdom from the development and production teams, in what I call the "unattended case".

We have all seen references to celebrated and prestigious large companies running into trouble with products that turn out to be totally unacceptable in the marketplace, and then see these unfortunate products hurriedly withdrawn at significant cost to both reputation and the balance sheet. So often the blame lies at the door of poor basic communication, a lack of appreciation of the wider picture and lack of shared vision with the customer.

Conversely, if we return to our comparison and look at the customer's view of requirements comprehension, initially, the customer often has to real appreciation of what technology might offer or how it can be commercially exploited. Nor does a customer really have the time or motivation to think ahead in this way. But as time progresses, new needs do get articulated and requirements begin to crystalise in the customer's mind.

Then, of course, other ideas follow to provide the other half of the equation that contributes to the eventual divergence between the supplier and the customer.

Only by getting close to the customer, seeing requirements through their eyes and using this knowledge to feed forward into the early design process will the catastrophe be avoided — and indeed give the supplier a chance of converging with the target in the marketplace.

6. Concurrent Engineering and the Customer

Consider a stream of products successively moving through a development process (Fig. 2.2). The process is the combination of all those corporate functions typical of a design, manufacturing and marketing based company. Concurrent Engineering encourages all the players to make the earliest start - in parallel to the extent feasible. Hopefully, the company will have learnt from the experiences of earlier products in their marketplace - their own and those of their competition. Some of these experiences can be incorporated and earlier elements of design can be re-used in the new product, following a process of continuous improvement. Other marketplace and product insights should also be taken into account. Thus the aggregate of these experiences and observations from product history are also then appropriately fed forward to influence and enhance the new product.

We are living in highly volatile business environment with new technologies emerging and mature technologies becoming obsolete, often at the most inconvenient times. Customers will change their views as a result of their own competitive pressures. There will continue to be fluctuations in national and international economies — be it the cost of money, exchange rates or preferential trade agreements.

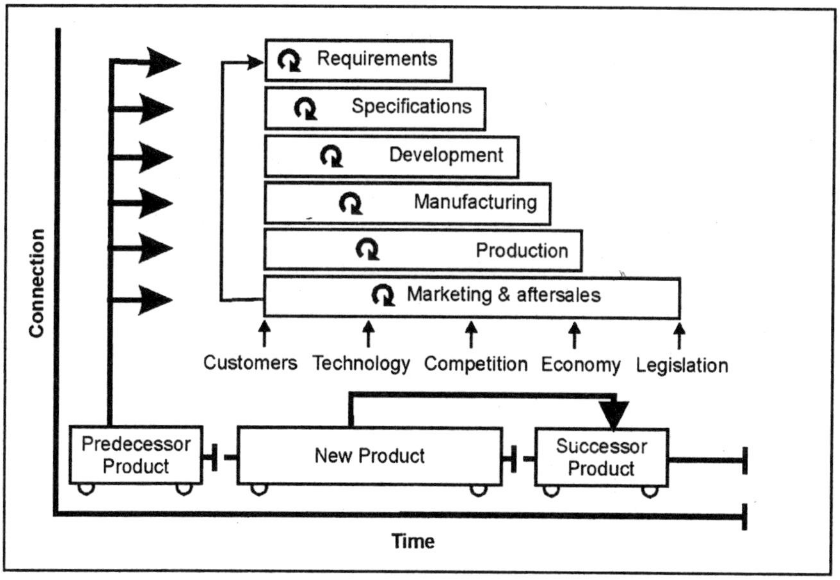

Fig. 2.2: Meeting customer requirements through concurrent engineering

Legislation, to address safety, the environment and changing industry standards all serve to keep us on our toes. Viewpoints and processes are evolving. The "conflict" model between the supplier and customer belongs to those earlier days when suppliers assumed they knew best, and competition had only a relatively modest effect for the most part.

Today, there is increasingly intense competition, best demonstrated by the successes of the Pacific Rim economies, and evidence of significant development from China and others. But it won't stop with national economies. Customers are now far better informed, far more discerning and far more demanding. By contrast with the "conflict" model, the "customer connection" model of world class companies today, exhibits strong links between supplier company and customer, a full appreciation of the intended marketplace, the process of requirements engineering and how the sum of all these nurtures and drives the new product development process throughout its life cycle.

7. Summary

This paper has briefly reviewed the evolution and drivers behind Concurrent Engineering, and highlighted the competitive marketplace considerations that will influence Concurrent Engineering. The critical success factors that will help to establish the environment for Concurrent Engineering are:

- Understand the customer, without which it will be very difficult to remain competitive and avoid the attendant costs of not getting it right first time.
- Elevate the customer to that of an essential partner. They represent the opportunity that companies address and define the environment within which Concurrent Engineering approaches are directed.
- Create a product development team that includes all the key functional players from the organisation — design, production, finance, marketing and after sales support.
- Involve suppliers and subcontractors early. Ensure that they understand the customers' requirements appropriately, know what is wanted and why, and that they recognise their role in the Concurrent Engineering environment that they have been invited to join.
- Simulate product performance and the manufacturing process early and

communicate this to every partner in the team, including the customer and supply chain.

- Establish strong links of communication between all the partners — throughout the company, amongst the supply chain and the marketplace.

References

1. *Journal of the Society for Computer Simulation International on Simulation in Concurrent Engineering*, Edited by S. Medhat, ISBN: 1-56555-054-4, May 1993.
2. *Proceedings of the International Conference on Concurrent Engineering and Electronic Design Automation* (CEEDA 94), Edited by S. Medhat, SCS/IEE. ISBN: 1-56555-074-9, Bournemouth April 1994.
3. *Proceedings of the International Conference on Concurrent Engineering and Electronic Design Automation* (CEEDA 96), Edited by S. Medhat, IEE/EPIC/DTI. ISBN: 1 900345 05 6, Bournemouth January 1996.

3

The Enabling Tools & Techniques for Successful Concurrent Engineering Implementation

Professor Sa'ad Medhat

Ph.D, M.Phil, C.Eng, MIEE, MIEEE, MACM

IBM Professor of Concurrent Engineering and Intergraph Design Automation, Head of the Office of Research, Bournemouth University, UK

Abstract

As the pressure to achieve and maintain competitiveness continues in order to retain or regaining market share, companies often react to such challenges by changing their management, engineering, production and customer support processes.

Commonly, the first steps in implementing change is seen to be centred around the formation of product development teams. These teams included representatives with different expertise, such as design, manufacturing, quality assurance, purchasing, marketing, field service and computer-aided design support. Change has also included relaxing policies that inhibited design changes and providing greater authority and responsibility to members of design teams. Managing change in a manufacturing environment requires a more systematic method of concurrently designing both the product and the downstream processes for production and support. This systematic approach is fundamentally known as 'Concurrent Engineering' (CE).

This paper will also discuss the need to achieve a multi-disciplinary team working environment as a prerequisite for facilitating a CE strategy. In doing so, it will highlight some of the organisational barriers and will suggest management initiatives to overcome these difficulties.

The paper will also examine the role of enabling technologies such as shared digital product data, engineering data management, CAE/CAD, computer aided manufacturing, technical and industrial networking to achieve reduced product development cycles, whilst improving the quality of products. Programme deployment plans and implementation pitfalls will be highlighted. The challenges the organisation faces in implementing a CE strategy will be examined. In conclusion, this paper will highlight recommendations from experience gained by companies who have implemented CE.

1. Definitions of Concurrent Engineering

In the UK, the Computer Integrated Manufacturing Institute Definition of Concurrent Engineering is: "the delivery of better, cheaper, faster products to market by a lean way of working using multi-discipline teams, right first time methods and parallel processing activities to continuously consider all constraints".

In the US, the term is similarly defined by the Institute of Defense Analyses as: "a systematic approach to the integrated, concurrent design of products and their related processes, including manufacture and support. This approach is intended to cause the developers, from the outset, to consider all elements of the product life cycle from conception through disposal, including quality, cost, schedule, and user requirement".

2. Introduction

In the modern market place product life-spans are decreasing whilst product complexity is increasing. The rallying cries heard in the corridors throughout the manufacturing industry have become 'reduce time scales!' and 'right first time design!' as they strive to hit the rapidly closing 'window of opportunity' for their vital new product. Therefore, companies are increasingly looking to the promise of Concurrent Engineering to help deliver the goods.

Concurrent Engineering represents a sea-change in the approach to steering projects from concept to customer. By providing a wide range of new methods and software tools to an inter-departmental project team, an environment is created where the mix of disciplines allow all aspects of product development to be tackled in parallel with enhanced efficiency. Cutting free from the shackles of 'Departmentalism', product styling, electronic and mechanical product detail design, manufacturing engineering, process planning and sales preparation are carried out largely simultaneously. Successful practitioners of this methodology have realized dramatic reductions in their new product 'time to market' and as a result have enjoyed substantial commercial advantage.

Ranking the order of Competitive Priorities through the 1990s include the following:

- Introducing new products quickly.
- Offering fast, dependable deliveries;
- Offering consistently low costs;
- Providing high performance products and service;
- Providing reliable/durable products;
- Customising products and services to customer needs;
- Ensuring profit in price competitive markets.

Competitive dominance can be achieved by:

- Advanced manufacturing and information technology (CAD/CAM, MRPII, JIT...);
- Time compression from conceptual design through detailed design and production engineering to manufacture;
- Total quality management (TQM);
- Concurrent engineering.

Some of the benefits claimed by many companies such as Boeing, IBM, AT & T and Hot point have included:

- Reduced design to manufacture lead times by running activities in parallel;
- Reduced information loops;
- Improved inter-departmental information transfer;
- Brought design and preparation for manufacture closer together;
- Having common objectives, reporting structure, tools, data, controls and monitors;
- Having an increased flexibility;
- Having a team focus on project.

These claims have been substantiated by the following example:

- Development time 30-70 per cent less

- Engineering changes 65-90 per cent fewer
- Time to market 20-90 per cent less
- Overall quality 200-600 per cent higher
- Productivity 20-115 per cent higher
- Sales 5-50 per cent higher
- Return on assets 20-120 per cent higher

The benefits that a supplier gets as a result of implementing concurrent engineering include:

- Shorter time to market;
- Lower product development costs;
- Higher product quality;
- Improved manufacturing costs;
- Lower re-work costs;
- Lower testing costs;
- Reduced services costs;
- Increased profit margins.

As a result, the supplier of course, gets lower life cycle costs, longer mean times between failures, shorter mean times for repair, reduced expenditures for automatic test equipment or other specialised support equipment, the ability to utilise lower skill level personnel for maintenance activities, reduced spares inventories and more operational availability.

The integration of new product development and processes is the key to concurrent engineering. In the traditional sequential method of product development, information flows are in one direction and processes follow each other sequentially without significant feedback. However, with the concurrent approach, information flows are bi-directional and decisions are based on consideration of downstream as well as upstream inputs. The processes are conducted in parallel and unison to the maximum that is feasible for total teamwork involvement at all times. Achieving this sharing of information normally requires both organisational and technological change (see Fig. 3.1).

The philosophy of concurrent engineering is not new. The terms 'system engineering', 'simultaneous engineering' and 'producibility engineering' have been used to describe similar approaches.

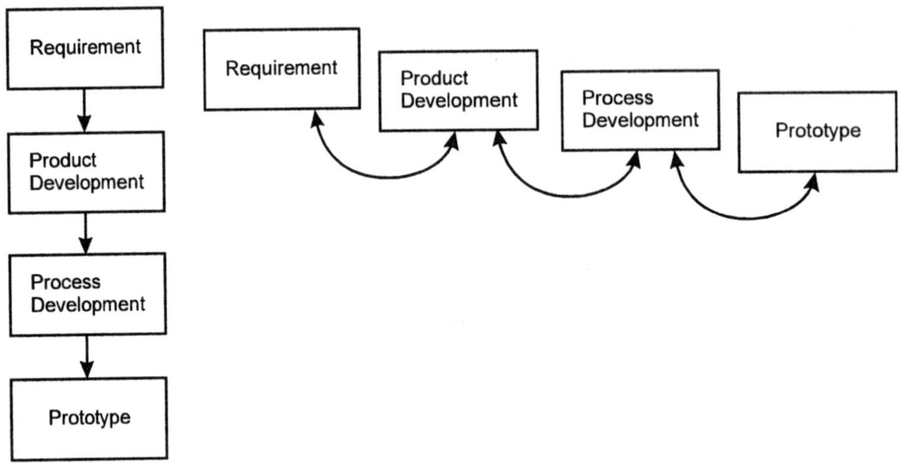

Fig. 3.1: Sequential *vs.* Concurrent Engineering Development Cycle

3. Multi-Disciplinary Teams

In Concurrent Engineering, the key ingredient is team work driven by customers' requests and a clear understanding of the market place. People from many departments collaborate during the life of the product — from ideas through product launch to eventual product withdrawal from the market place — to ensure that it reflects customers' needs and desires.

Marketing, engineering, and manufacturing, for example, work together from the outset to anticipate problems and bottlenecks and to eliminate them early on. In so doing, they avoid delays in bringing the product to market and costly failures in service. Accounting and purchasing have their input too, and help to ensure low product cost and reliable supplies of parts and materials.

With CE, no longer does marketing give product specifications as a '*fait accompli*' to engineering. No longer does engineering design get passed 'over the wall' to manufacturing. Instead, all work together.

Concurrent Engineering requires fundamental changes in the way individuals and functional organisations go about their work. Most of the organisational barriers to concurrent engineering stem from traditional line structures, many levels and fragmented departments. They include:

- Problems divide into unconnected pieces;
- Resistance to change due to functional bureaucracy;
- Poor lateral communications and sharing of responsibility;

- High specialism and fragmented technical departments;
- Analyse problems to fit organisation; and
- Parochialism.

Involvement of representatives of manufacturing early in the design process is a minimal step in this direction.

Most discussions with industry indicate that companies form teams which include marketing, production, engineering, support, purchasing and in some cases the ability to contribute to the design effort by early identification of potential problems and by timely initiation of actions to avoid bottlenecks.

The ability to work effectively as a member of a team is critical. Using multidisciplinary teams is not equivalent to forming committees where members often delay decision making; instead these teams get faster action through early identification and solutions to problems.

4. The Management Role

Thus, the critical success factors for effectively employing Concurrent Engineering in recognition of need for highly effective communication, new management approaches, teamwork, and wide perspective of a market driven environment. Thus, leadership at the highest corporate levels driving continuous quality and productivity improvement is a prerequisite for the success of the changes associated with implementing CE.

Management led initiatives that need to be employed include the following:

- Emphasizing attention to customer needs and quality improvement;
- Improving horizontal integration of the organisation;
- Promoting employee involvement in generating new ideas for improvement;
- Requiring engineering comparisons of proposed products and competitive offerings; and
- Establishing closer relationships with suppliers to include supplier involvement during conceptual design phase.

Implementing CE will be different for each company and customization is best left to the owner of the problem, the company. There are, however, some clear guidelines which apply to all CE teams and which if followed will increase the team performance.

- Provide a clear goal: both in terms of team performance (*e.g.*, completion date) and expected product performance;
- Select quality members from all functions with full time commitments;
- Limit core team size not more than 8;
- De-emphasize function: members should be identified with team task not function;
- Measure team performance: no individual measures;
- Give individual feedback: based on agreed project plan with clear responsibilities;
- Provide principled leadership: recognizing the value of achieving concurrence and adhering to the CE principles; and
- Give top-level management support: only top-level support can guarantee success under new conditions.

It is important to recognize that the above is a typical list and no team needs all of these to succeed.

In implementing these guidelines, top management must ensure the followi

- Encourage motivation of new multi-disciplinary teams;
- Ensure group members have a secure sense of membership and are perceived as valuable members;
- Empower members so that skills and talents are developed;
- Allow participation in decision making process; and
- Encourage freedom of thought, initiative and creativity.

5. Communication Challenges

In a dynamic and changing environment, an appropriate communication infrastructure is paramount. In the Automotive, Aerospace, Electronics and Computer industries, where products are becoming more complex through the introduction of multi-functional teams and technologies, paths of communication are thus becoming more diverse and complicated.

For example, a 15 person team will have 105 paths of communication, a 30 person team will have 435 paths and extremely complex projects including 1,000 personnel in the project would have 499,500* paths of communication! This example

---

* Formula: $\frac{N(N-1)}{2}$ (where N is the number of persons involved).

illustrates the need to integrate the product data and to keep **all** personnel involved, informed about every activity in the product development stage.

Open architecture environments containing Design Automation tools, project management tools and integrative databases assist in the monitoring and communication processes. They enhance the communication of innovations, requirements and definition for the product development cycle as a whole. The failure to integrate and disseminate will lead to confusion and a subsequent breakdown in both communication and direction.

An obvious area of conflict is in the nature of communication itself. The teamwork method requires effective communication, however when different disciplines combine, respective personnel each have their own language or jargon indigenous to their area of expertise. Use of these words in team discussions can inhibit or even alienate other group members from participating. A common vocabulary must therefore be defined and agreed upon by the group.

In a group situation, purposes are often varied. The need to reach a consensus is vital to productive output. In reaching a consensus, the group should use collaborative communication rather than informative or procedural communication. Collaborative communication will ensure that a creative environment of interactive ideas and shared goals exist. This interactive perspective will channel group "conflict" in a positive way, to produce originality of thought.

6. Implementing Concurrent Engineering

Implementing concurrent engineering within an organisation requires the following:

- Management commitment and leadership;
- Understanding of the current situation;
- Developing a concurrent engineering organisation; and
- Continuous improvement to key processes.

The minimum elements that make up concurrent engineering are listed below:

- Design for Performance;
- Design for Manufacture;
- Design for Test;

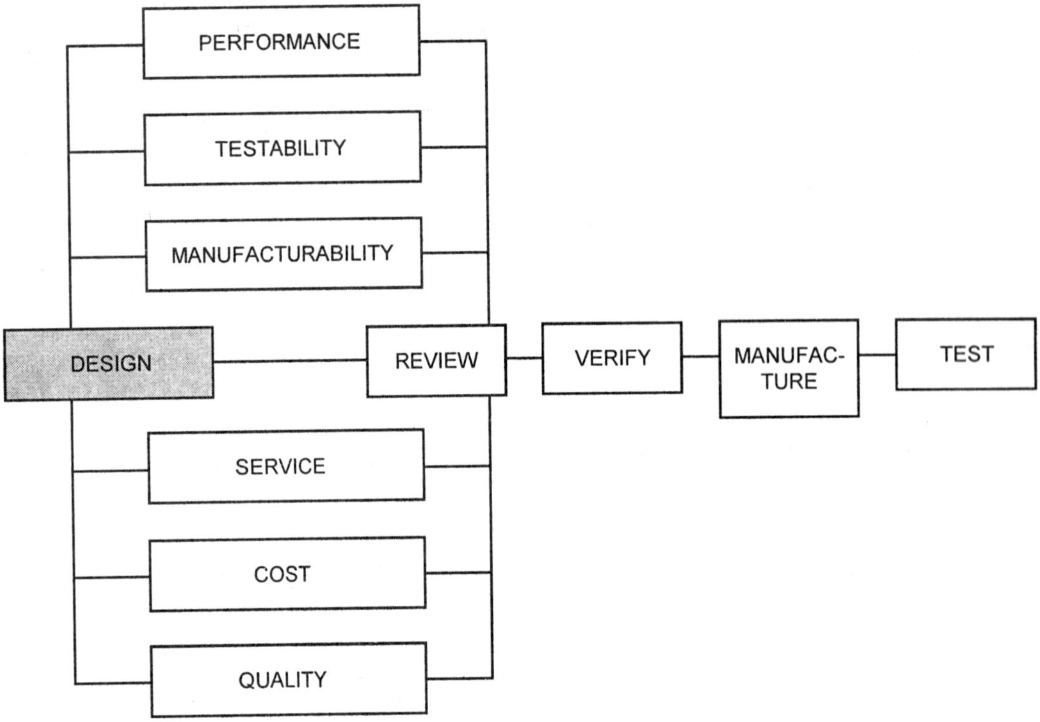

Fig. 3.2: Concurrent Engineering Process

- Design for Quality;
- Design for Service; and
- Design for Product Cost Goals.

Design for performance means making sure that all customer performance requirements are met, that the product operates at the required speed, that human factors such as operation, assembly and disassembly and safety have been considered and that the product meets or exceeds the reliability requirements.

Design for manufacture means using the minimum number of parts (consistent with the other trade-offs such as testability or maintainability), using standard components wherever possible (thereby minimizing the number of different part types), facilitating error free assembly and integrating the product with the production process.

Design for test means that for example, all aspects of testing to meet manufactory safety and other legislation and conference to agreed specifications are achieved at cost, schedule and complexity circuits are partitioned into manageable blocks, that circuit control has been provided, that circuit nodes are visible, that automated test has been facilitated and that built-in test has been included as applicable.

Design for quality means selecting high quality components, using the proper derating calculations, fitting the product into its end-use environment, making sure that the mean time between failures is appropriate and that the 'look and feel' of the product conveys quality. In other words, making sure that the product meets (or exceeds) the customer's expectations.

Design for service includes such simple, but often overlooked, ideas like making sure that all items are accessible, replacing fuses with circuit breakers, physically partitioning the system into modular functions, including built-in test as appropriate and considering or implementing a remote diagnostic or integrated diagnostics strategy.

The successful implementation of all of these elements may require the help of specialists in packaging, production, testing, safety, ergonomics, etc. The key is to make the design team (and therefore the designers themselves) responsible for the successful and balanced implementation of all the characteristics required of the final product. Therefore, concurrent engineering ensures effective, quantitative trade-offs regarding all of the requirements listed above.

7. Concurrent Engineering Techniques

Important techniques that can be used when implementing concurrent engineering are:

Computer-based design and support tools, and formal methods.

7.1. Use of computer-based design and support tools

CE is much more than just team work. Computer Aided Design, (CAD), Engineering (CAE), and Manufacturing tools play a big role. Systems for sharing and managing design information are vital in large projects.

In the CAE field, the technology is evolving rapidly, and new tools, methods, operating systems, data base managers, computers etc., are being continually introduced. It is therefore important to maintain the integrity of transported engineering data in the Computer Aided Engineering (CAE) environment.

In the concurrent engineering approach, many different processes and tools from different engineering disciplines are used. Each tool has a unique data requirement, 'experience' and 'knowledge' and can be used in a different or unique context or domain of knowledge/expertise. From this arise some of the problems that sequential CAE systems face.

Efficient data manipulation is fundamental to the success of CE whether the process is automated or not. The data base in a DA system should support multiple access for use in different applications at the same time, while the necessary protection systems to ensure data integrity is maintained throughout such actions.

Ordering, and cross-referencing data frequently when handling large structured data particularly engineering design is essential. Object orientated databases (OODB) offer an efficient solution to design tool and vendor suppliers. OODB are arranged in a hierarchy. Designs will reference components, for example. Data associated with the design (such as the name) can be changed without affecting component data. This is not possible with Relational Databases.

The advancement and continuous evolution of DA (Design Automation) will be necessary to handle the explosion in system complexity which is projected to double every three years during the 1990s. DA will therefore become an essential requirement for system designers. The future design environment could look like that in Fig. 3.3.

To support complete specifications, design automation will begin to focus on the definition of an electronic system. This re-focusing gives a more complete integration of the *How* so that the cognitive process can shift to *What*. The *How* concept is moving beyond speeding up each design step to incorporating the entire processes. Once a new product has been defined, the requirements can be further defined and analyzed using system modeling and analysis tools. Today, once the requirements have been written, the design implementation can begin immediately by dividing the specification among designers.

Design automation is bringing to this process an executable model through which the company and the customer interact with the requirements validation, and would combine simulation with animation, to become visually informative and exciting — in effect, a "virtual prototype". Automated requirements validation will be more thorough as well as less error prone than manual review. It is cheaper and easier and often faster to experiment with a *Soft Prototype* (a design on the computer) than with physical prototypes. This validation would require two parts: a method to describe the requirements in a coherent and complete manner, and a tool environment that can exercise the descriptions. This method will express the virtual prototype by taking advantage of graphical capture of those requirements. The key

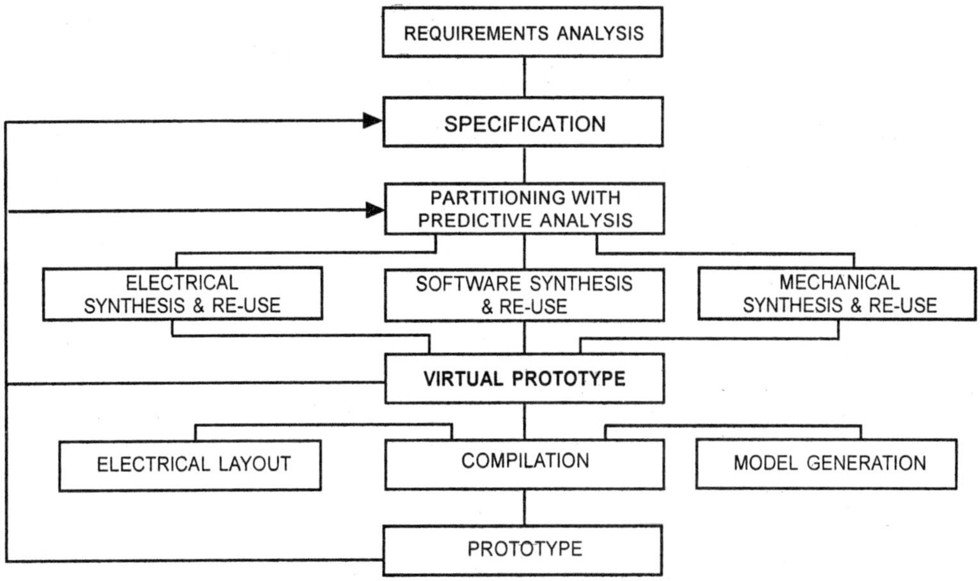

Fig. 3.3: Virtual prototyping, the new design environment

to verification at this stage is being able to define the system without assigning specific functions to electrical, software or mechanical implementations. System engineers require complete freedom in describing and exercising functional flows and system components. Partitioning and predictive analysis will give System Designers the ability to quantitatively compare the results of different partitioning decisions. Using a format like today's business spread sheets, designers can calculate the effects of placing system functions into specific disciplines (clectrical, software and mechanical) and specific components. The data within the calculations will be generated by the design automation using existing design databases and implementation tools. This concept, however, is still at its infancy and perhaps it will initially be more suitable for defense and aerospace products.

Concurrent Engineering cannot be bought in a box. It is a philosophy, a way of doing things. However, the process can be automated to benefit complex product design.

Frameworks have now been introduced by many CAD vendors to automate the design process and to manage databases. Often entirely separate frameworks are needed to carry out the management functions on one hand, and to integrate the various engineering tools on the other. Therefore, this introduces the idea of a hierarchy of frameworks. An integrated tool suite without the design management facilities, may be itself integrated into an 'enterprise' wise framework that provides engineering management tools.

Clearly, in this tangled web of design automation there is a need for standardization. Currently, there is no standard way of providing inter-tool communications. There is no database consistency, data library formats or even data representation standards. New standards are essential if frameworks and the automation of concurrent engineering are to be widely accepted. The CFI (CAD Framework Initiative) was formed in 1988 to address precisely these three issues. CFI provides a Forum for users and vendors to agree framework standards. The minimum requirements for the tools needed for the successful implementation of CE are listed below:

- CAE *frameworks* which support *all* engineering tasks;
- Library elements that can be re-used at various levels of integration;
- Common languages and formats for design information;
- Common data bases and file servers at all integration levels;
- Synthesis tools that include CE; and
- Expert system rule checking.

It is important to have common languages and data bases that can be accessed concurrently by each of the functional disciplines that make up the product team. It is also *essential* to have user friendly systems that don't need a life time to learn!

The concept of 'Open Architecture' in the context of Design Automation implies data which are created by one tool and subsequently used and augmented by others. Data must accurately reflect these multiple discourses rather than just harmonizing the transport of data between two tools. This ensures that automation of tasks will be more efficient, integrated and flexible in the context of the design cycle.

CAD tools cannot only assist in the validation of a proposed design, but can also be used in synthesizing the design itself.

Rule-based systems are sometimes used in synthesis. In attempting to provide rule-based design methods several companies are developing practical applications of expert systems. CALS and AECMA are two of the recently developed standards that could facilitate the implementation of a concurrent engineering environment.

CALS is an acronym for Computer Aided Acquisition and Logistic Support. This is a strategy generated by the United States Department of Defense. The

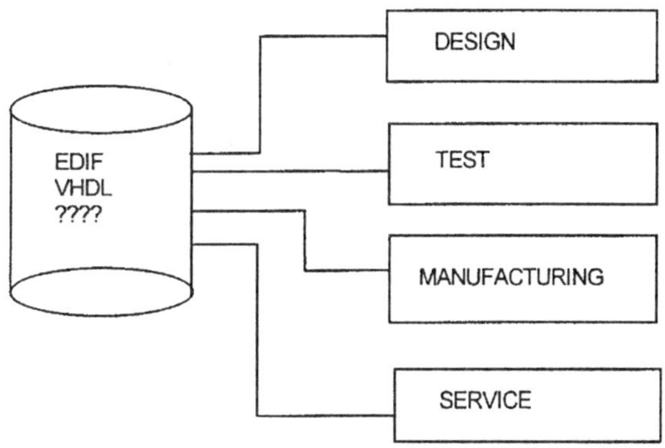

Fig. 3.4: A common language and common data base, which provides the ability to transcend levels of integration and CAE workstation platforms and operating systems, allowing the full automation of CE.

CALS strategy uses digital data processing techniques to integrate technical information and enhance the processes for acquisition, design, manufacturing and support of weapon systems. The interest shown towards CALS within the European Union is further emphasized by the compilation of new standards by AECMA — the Association Europeenne des Constructeurs de Material Aerospatial, concerning standard data formats and interchange of technical information. The AECMA range of specifications can be used as standards for the communication of technical information within the CALS strategy. The objectives of CALS are:

- To accelerate the integration of reliability and maintainability design tools into contractor computer aided design and engineering systems;
- To encourage and accelerate the automation and integration of contractor processes for generating weapon systems technical data in digital form;
- To rapidly increase DoD's capability to receive, share, distribute and use logistic technical data in digital form to improve weapon system maintenance, training and spare parts procurement.

The main direction of CALS is the automation of weapon system technical information throughout the system's life cycle. AECMA plays a part as standards for electronic interchange of technical data. Enhancing the design process by incorporating quality features is a multi-disciplinary effort. It can be seen that Concurrent Engineering plays a key role in the CALS strategy.

7.2. Use of formal techniques

Formal approaches include techniques such as Statistical Process Control. Design of Experiments, Design-for-Assembly, Value Engineering and Quality Function Deployment, some of which date back to the 1930s. Although formal methods are used for many purposes, they are all designed to improve the understanding or control the behavior of processes, products, mechanisms, and other entities. If used effectively, these new methods and tools can open up a new era in the design, production and engineering, yielding sharply reduced life cycle costs, shorter design cycles and improved quality. There are three key techniques that can be used:

- Quality Function Deployment (QFD);
- Taguchi Methods; and
- Design for Manufacturing and Assembly (DFMA).

7.2.1. Quality function deployment (QFD): QFD is a powerful tool for understanding the 'voice of the customer' to specify requirements and focus the activity of cross functional teams. QFD consists of two things: well developed formats and style of organizational behavior that facilitates a holistic response to customer needs. The formats — matrices and charts that have been developed on the basis of experience over the past 16 years — guide the work and provide for easy, standardized documentation during product development and production.

The series of weighted cross-comparison matrices and charts create a flowchart that supports decision making for the important product-development activities that lead to production: product planning, design, process planning, and production planning. The formats also help ensure that work is properly documented in a form that is easily recognizable and understandable by everyone in the organisation. For example, machine operators can trace any specific production operation back through the series of charts (Fig. 3.5) and see exactly how the operation helps achieve the needed part characteristics, which help meet the design requirements, which, in turn, are responsive to customer requirements.

It's convenient to think of QFD as consisting of four activities. In the product planning activity, customer requirements are deployed into product-expectation characteristics and specifications that then become design requirements. In the design activity (parts deployment), the design requirements established during product planning are deployed through the concept and design.

Cross-functional teams using QFD as a set of planning and communication routines are currently the most effective way known to cut through barriers to good design. QFD focuses and co-ordinates skills within an organisation, first to design and then to manufacture and market goods that customers want to buy.

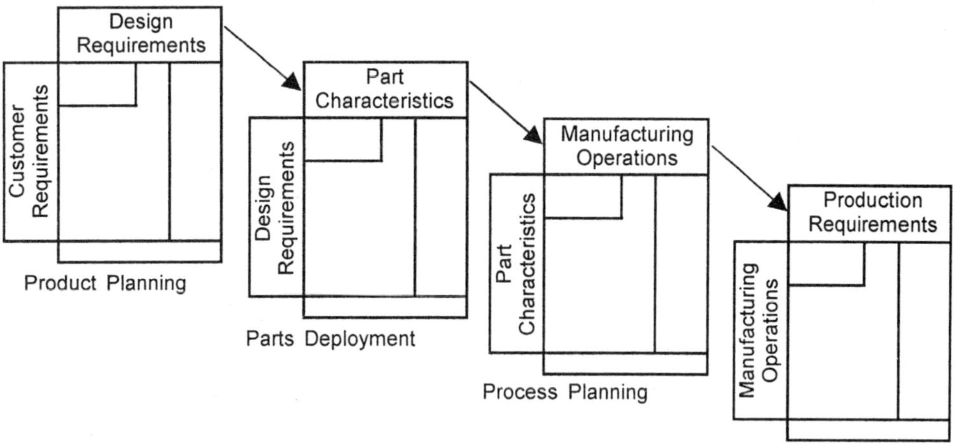

Fig. 3.5: Quality Function Deployment Charts & Matrices – deploy customer requirements and related technical requirements all the way down to factory floor.

7.2.2. Taguchi methods: Taguchi methods support a philosophy of design that leads to robust products by tuning critical parameters of systems before conventional tolerancing processes. The basic idea is the provision of a set of techniques for studying the effect of variables which affect the product or process with the aid of the smallest possible number of experimental trials. Experimenting with design variables, becomes very quickly an onerous task. For example, a problem with 15 variables each with two values, would require 32,768 different experiments to investigate all the possible permutations. However, using Taguchi's efficient experimental design technique only 16 experiments would be required to give the same effect. This experimental efficiency is achieved through the application of balanced array tables used to design the 16 experiments. In simple terms this technique has the same effect as football teams changing ends at half-time to eliminate any field advantage.

'Parameter Design' involves selecting system parameters and target values for design variables that make the product and processes robust. Robust is defined as being insensitive to the effects of variability such as environment, manufacturing processes and deterioration in use. It is perhaps understandable that without a knowledge of Taguchi's experimental techniques the average designer would be put off by the monumental task of trial and simulation facing him in order to optimize his design.

*7.2.3. **Design for manufacture & assembly (DFMA):*** DFMA is the powerful structuring of common-sense design from which the original use of the phrase 'simultaneous engineering' was coined. Designing for manufacture and assembly early in the design process is a technique that goes way beyond the articulation of best practice axioms for engineers. However, the number of parts and assembly operations in a design does drive cost and simplification does lead to improved reliability.

A number of companies have developed quantitative methods for enhancing the DFMA capability of designers. These methods attempt to predict both assembly costs and component manufacturing costs at the earliest stages of product design yield, with varying degrees of sophistication, 'productability coefficients'.

There have been some spectacular applications of DFMA techniques to product design. For example, since 1984, Philips has reduced the number of parts in its compact disc player by 75 per cent. It has simplified VCR's by parts reduction of 55 per cent, tuners by 45 per cent, and amplifiers by 40 per cent; Swatch, the Swiss watch maker, has reduced the number of components in its watches from 150 to 51 etc.

8. Concurrent Engineering Implementation Issues

Many organisations lack perspective on Concurrent Engineering. They view it as implementing improved design automation systems, focusing on producibility or establishing teams. CE is a combination of strategy, organisation, the development process, techniques and tools. The implementation of CE concepts must be effectively planned and managed. The implementation of product development teams is a starting point. Explicit guidance must be provided for these teams to be successful. The early involvement through teams and the application of CE techniques necessitates changes in the product development process to achieve real benefits.

Programme Actions

- Early functional involvement
- Customer & subcontractor involvement
- Co-location
- Training
- Quality Function Deployment
- Bench-marking.

Enterprise Actions

- CAD-3D/Solids and EDA
- CAE/Analysis Tools
- EDM System
- Product Development Team
- Guidelines
- Standard parts libraries
- Lessons learned System
- Cost Models & DFM/A Tools
- Supplier involvement.

The programme deployment plan should take into account the following considerations:

- Staffing — sufficient early involvement;
- Program organisation — Product Development Teams;
- Co-location;
- Training;
- Facilitators;
- Selection of tools & techniques;
- CAD/CAE deployment;
- Development Methodology;
- Policies (*e.g.* standardization); and
- Strategy (*e.g.* teaming, sourcing, technology, process investment).

Some of the pitfalls when implementing CE include:

- Limited CE perspective — management believes that they have achieved it;

- Not a high priority; treated as a fad or novelty strategy;
- Lack of understanding of how to manage change, involve employees or to change the culture;
- Teams formed but no guidance given;
- No leadership or follow-up; imperative lost;
- Lack of time or investment in training process improvement; systems or guidance;
- No plan, accepted responsibilities or co-ordination; and
- Policies & rewards system not aligned to support CE.

9. Conclusions and Recommendations

The pressure to be excellent at engineering will continue to increase with the pervasive nature of intense global of competition. Being a Concurrent Engineering company is now a fundamental part of maintaining a competitive advantage. The following list of recommendations has been identified from the lessons learned by companies who have implemented CE:

- Apply a structured and formalized programme of work;
- apply top-down leadership and bottom up implementation;
- Breakdown departmental barriers and address the culture;
- Teams and co-location are key to success;
- Training is necessary;
- Address the business process; and
- Ensure continuous improvement.

Concurrent Engineering can work for small companies as well as larger organisations by focusing on the main core strengths. Sometimes it is necessary to re-engineer part of the organisation to be able to be responsive, lean, effective, and therefore competitive. Thus it is important for companies to consider pro-actively and continually the setting of challenging goals for their next new products uncompromising the quality or customer satisfaction.

References

1. *Proceedings of the International Conference on Concurrent Engineering and Electronic Design Automation* (CEEDA 91), Edited by S Medhat, Woodhead Publishing Ltd. ISBN: 185573 054 5, Bournemouth March 1991.

2. *Journal of the Society for Computer Simulation International on Simulation in Concurrent Engineering*, Edited by S Medhat, ISBN: 1-56555-054-4, May 1993.
3. *CADD Journal*, March 1994.
4. *Proceedings of the International Conference on Concurrent Engineering and Electronic Design Automation* (CEEDA 94), Edited by S Medhat, SCS/IEE. ISBN: 1-56555-074-9, Bournemouth April 1994.
5. IEE Computing & Control Division Colloquium, 8 June 1995, London, UK. Paper Title: *Concurrent Engineering — Getting it Right First Time.* ISSN 0963-3308.
6. IEEE Engineering Management Conference, 28-30 June 1995, Singapore. Paper Title: *Engineering Data Management and it's Role in Implementing a Concurrent Engineering Environment.*
7. CE 95, Concurrent Engineering Research and Applications. Paper Title: *Defect Analysis and Predictive Modeling for Efficient Electronic Product Development in a Concurrent Engineering Environment.* Washington, DC. August 23-25, 1995.
8. CIM'95- Computers in Manufacturing, September 1995. NEC. Session 15. Paper Title: *Introduction to Concurrent Engineering.*
9. Chapter Title: *Concurrent Engineering at IBM Storage Subsystems Development*, Marshall SE, Medhat SS, Pratt GR, Rook J. Editors: Backhouse CJ, and Brookes NJ. Publisher: Design Council/Gower. 1996
10. Advanced Technology Management through Concurrent Engineering. Special feature Editor IEE, *Computing and Control Engineering Journal*, April 1996.

4

Quality Engineering: The Tools and Techniques Available to the Engineer

Timothy Collins

Lecturer in Concurrent Engineering Methods

Department of Electronics, Bournemouth University, UK

Abstract

A new economic age is upon us. The advance of new technology, the ever decreasing lead times, the 'quality conscious' customer and the increased overseas competitive pressures have meant that companies have had to take steps to survive within the global village. Among them has been the adoption of the Concurrent Engineering (CE) framework which stresses customer driven planning, multi-disciplined team working, continuous improvement and employee empowerment.

A key component of Concurrent Engineering is the adoption of tools that assist in creative thinking and problem solving. This paper presents a brief overview of the tools available to engineers in the quest for quality attainment. It will attempt to demonstrate the effectiveness of these tools as an aid for the decision making process.

1. Introduction

The global village is now a highly competitive and ruthless arena where one soon realises that Darwin's law of survival of the fittest applies without exception. A new economic age has developed, mainly created by the advances of Japan.

Japanese products are now considered to be of the highest standard and competitively priced, so much so that companies have adopted Japanese sounding brand names to assist sales.

However, the Japanese experience took a long time to flourish. In the immediate post war period most Japanese products had a reputation for poor quality at low prices. Considering many of the quality pioneers were developing the strategies in Japan in the 1950's, it is clear that the elapsed time required to establish a reputation for quality can be substantial.

For short term visionaries the future looks bleak. A company that does not change will succumb to market forces and perish. The fittest will survive. Those who are willing to change, to learn, to adapt, to constantly improve will win. The others will not.

Many issues have to be addressed in the search for higher quality products. Education at all levels is vital to the success of industry. Employees should be trained in the various techniques. They should be given control of their own destiny and have a vital part in the future of the company.

Managers should be given the necessary skills to guide teams and to motivate staff.

The education process should also filter through to Universities.

At Bournemouth University, engineering students are being given the opportunity to learn about quality and how it will affect them. This will give them a competitive edge for their own career development and will instill the quality process within the companies they will soon be working for.

High quality products at competitive prices are no longer the sole domain of Japan.

2. Quality, Cost and Value

According to most dictionaries, the word quality is defined as 'the degree of excellence' [OXF82] and usually refers to a product or service. This can have various meanings - it may possess desirable attributes that may distinguish it from other products, or, when goods are in short supply the concern may centre on availability.

But in essence it is more than this. It is "the totality of features and characteristics of a product or service that bear on its ability to satisfy a given need" [ISO92]. The word *totality* is the key to the modern approach. It encompasses all stages of the product life cycle, and all members of the process, from customer through to distributor.

W.E. Deming [DEM86], an American industrialist, also pioneered a new radical wave of quality understanding in Japan in the 1950s. He believed that quality also consisted of a mathematical phenomena — variation. His belief was that variation should be monitored using techniques developed by the English statistician, Walter Shewhart — the control chart. This would allow trends in the process being discovered far earlier than had been possible previously. More importantly it was a simple tool that could be understood by the shop floor. The quality flood gates had opened to the masses.

3. The Samurai's 7 Swords

It is a well known fact that the ancient samurai carried 7 swords into battle. It was inevitable that the Japanese would then seek seven tools for which they would start their rejuvenation after World War II. According to Ishikawa [ISH82], the seven tools that were chosen were:

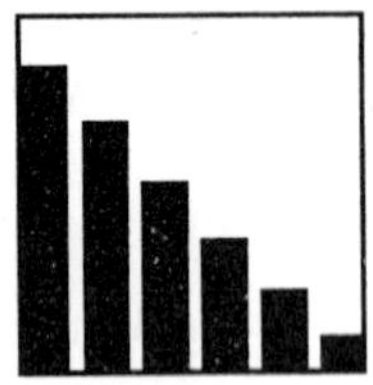

1. The Pareto Chart is a simple method of descriptive statistical analysis, wherein data is categorized by cause, and vertical bars are constructed with the height of each bar. It was devised by the Italian economist, Pareto, who studied the distribution of wealth in the population and concluded that about 20 per cent of the people held approximately 80 per cent of the wealth. This is known as the Pareto rule.

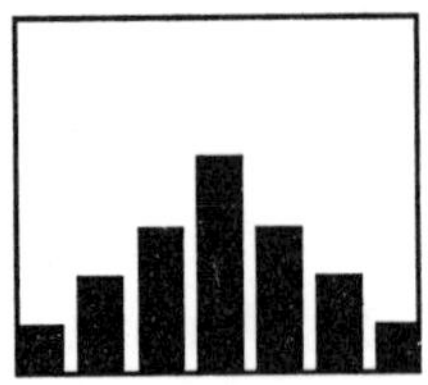

2. The Histogram is a bar chart with the vertical bars ordered horizontally by value of a random variable. It will then give a visual representation of the probability distribution for the variable being studied. It will also give an indication of the central tendency, dispersion and symmetry.
3. The Check Sheet is a data collection tool from which a histogram or Pareto chart may be constructed. Ideally the check sheet should have areas assigned to categories. For example, employees working in the production process should tally events occurring by the appropriate category during the process.
4. The Ishikawa diagram (or fish bone diagram), is used to associate multiple possible causes with a single effect. Thus, given a particular effect, the

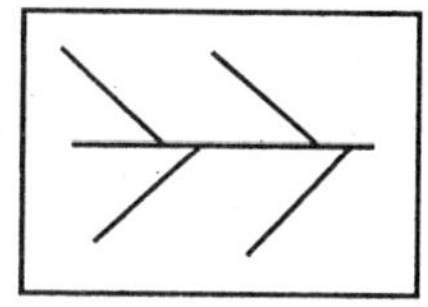

diagram is constructed to identify and organize possible causes for it. The primary branch represents the effect (the quality characteristic that is intended to be improved and controlled) and is typically labeled on the right side of the diagram. Each major branch of the diagram corresponds to a major cause (or class of causes) that directly relates to the effect. Minor branches correspond to more detailed causal factors. This type of diagram is useful in any analysis, as it illustrates the relationship between cause and effect in a rational manner.

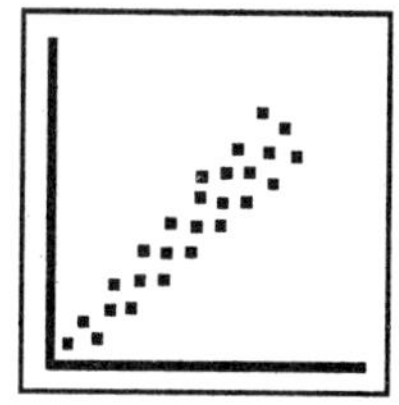

5. A Scatter Plot is a presentation of data on an *x–y* coordinate system. From this, a visual representation can be ascertained of the relationship between two variables. If there is an indication of some relationship between the variables, the statistical techniques of regression and correlation are used to build a parametric model.
6. Flowcharts are pictorial representations of a process. By breaking the process down into its constituent steps, flowcharts can be useful in identifying where errors are likely to be found in the system.
7. Statistical process control charts are used to monitor data from a process. It was designed by Walter Shewhart in the 1920's, but was updated by W.E. Deming in the 1950's where common/special causes were investigated. The chart consists of a centre line (at the nominal value of a controlled variable), bounded by control limits beyond which variability is considered to be unacceptable. Data is then plotted on the chart to visually represent the variation within the process. Trends can then be seen and corrective actions taken.

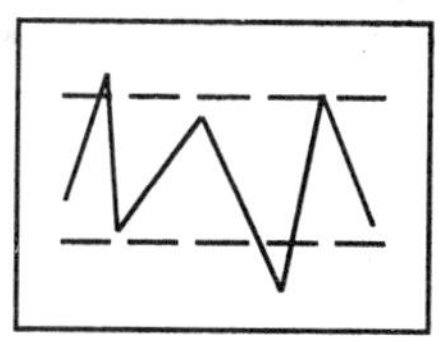

4. Quality Function Deployment

The main goal of any company professing to be 'quality conscious' must include focusing on the customer and customer satisfaction. However, such a declaration must be backed up with a solid framework to work with. Such a framework is provided for with Quality Function Deployment (QFD).

QFD has been defined as 'a systematic way of ensuring that the development of product features, characteristics, and specifications, as well as the selection and

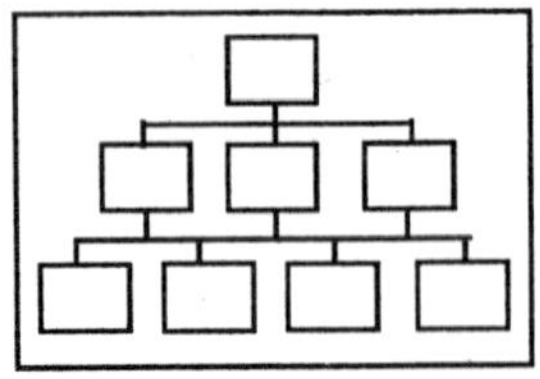

development of process equipment, methods and controls, are driven by the demands of the customer or marketplace.' It is a tool for translating the voice of the customer (customer requirements) into appropriate company requirements at each stage of the product life cycle.

There are basically four stages in the process [SUL86]:

1. *Customer requirements planning* Translates customer expectations, 'the voice of the customer', in the form of market research, competitor analysis and technological forecasts into the desired and specific product characteristics
2. *Product specifications* convert the customer requirements plan for the finished product into its components and the characteristics demanded.
3. *Process and quality control plans* identify design and process parameters critical to the achievement of the requirement.
4. *Process sheets* derived from 3, are the instructions to the operator.

The thread of customer requirements initiating and running through this procedure provides the basis for commonality of purpose [MAN88]. An outline of the steps to be taken is as follows:

> The customer requirements derived from market research or competitor analysis are simply stated on a simple matrix. It involves the expansion of basic wants into secondary and tertiary elements. From this is developed a matrix of product control characteristics that will enable the customer requirements to be met. The relationship between product characteristics and customer requirements are ranked in order of importance and thus an evaluation of customer wants not being addressed can be ascertained. Various adaptations of this matrix can then be used such as competitor evaluation that enables direct assessment of the proposed specification and determines the potential positioning of the product design against the competition.

There are a number of publicised successes that have realised the full potential of Quality Function Deployment. [MAN88] cites a Japanese automotive manufacturer that have reduced costs by 61 per cent and cut lead times for product development by a third. This has also been accompanied by a reduction in the number of product design changes.

5. Taguchi Methods

Through a continuing record of success, Genichi Taguchi convinced both management and engineers that quality improvement could be achieved with a low cost, simple, recipe-like methodology [PIG91].

Taguchi asserts that [NOO95] the quality of a product is a function of key product/performance characteristics. A high quality product performs near the ideal value of this characteristic (target value) consistently throughout its life span and under all operating conditions.

He estimates that there is an actual "Loss to Society" from the failure of that product to attain its ideal value. This loss is incurred by the consumer (through short product life times, increased maintenance and repair costs), the company (increased scrap and rework, warranty costs, damage to the company's reputation, eventual loss of market share) and to society in general (pollution and safety).

Taguchi has developed a three method approach for reducing variability around the target value:

1. System Design
2. Parameter Design
3. Tolerance Design

Parameter design is the most widely used technique and demonstrates the fundamental thinking in Taguchi's techniques. An example of this can be seen with the INA Tile Company (TAG86] in the 1950's who were faced with high variability in the dimensions of its tiles it produced. The company had purchased an expensive new tunnel kiln in order to increase productivity, but the high variability remained. After further investigation it was found that the temperature of the tiles at the centre of the pile experienced lower temperatures than those at the edge. Since redesigning the kiln was too expensive it was decided to investigate the tile mixture. Parameter design was used to overcome the effects of the uneven temperature by selecting, through a series of experiments, the controlling factors that have the most influence on the tile mix. It is not intended to fully present an account of these techniques as they are fully explained elsewhere [TAG86]. Summarising, experiments are performed to test the effects of changing selected factors. The optimisation is then arrived at through the evaluation of the Signal to Noise ratio.

6. Conclusion

This paper has given the reader the briefest glimpse of the tools available to the engineer. It was not intended to be an exhaustive list but a demonstration that extremely powerful tools exist and that they have a proven track record.

However, Snee [SNE86] has highlighted that total quality be divided into three elements:

1. Philosophy
2. Policies and Procedures
3. Tools

It is vitally important to create an environment where quality can flourish. This can only be achieved by having leaders who are dedicated to continuous improvement. The implications for the organisation are huge. Barriers must be broken, multi disciplined cooperation put into place and a laser beam of common purpose established. This will allow a framework for a planned approach to quality improvement through prevention rather than inspection.

References

1. [DEM86] W.E. Deming, *Out of Crisis*, Cambridge, MA, 1986.
2. [ISH82] K Ishikawa, *Guide to Quality Control*, Tokyo: Asian Productivity Organisation, 1982.
3. [ISO92] "ISO 9000", Geneva, Switzerland: International Organisation for Standardisation, 1992.
4. [JUR89] J.M. Juran, *Juran on Leadership for Quality*, New York: Free Press, 1989.
5. [MAN88] S.M. Manton, "Engineering for Quality", James Clayton Lecture, *Proc. Instn. Mech. Engrs.* Vol.202, 1988.
6. [NOO95] H. Noori, *Production and Operations Management*, McGraw Hill, 1995.
7. [OXF82] *The Concise Oxford Dictionary*, New York, Oxford University Press, 1982.
8. [PIG91] J.J. Pignatiello, "The Ten Triumphs and Tragedies of Genichi Taguchi", *Quality Engineering* 4(2), p.p. 211-255 (1991-92).
9. [SNE86] R.D. Snee, "In Pursuit of Total Quality", *Quality Progress*, August 1986
10. [SUL86] L.P. Sullivan, "Quality Function Deployment", *Quality Progress*, pp. 39-50, June 1986.
11. [TAG86]G. Taguchi, "Introduction to Quality Engineering", Asian Productivity Organisation, 1986.

5

Manufacturing Strategy Decision Support Tools: Linking Corporate Vision to Measures of Manufacturing Performance in Concurrent Engineering

Peter J. Sackett

Cranfield University, Cranfield, Bedford, UK

Abstract

There is little reported work on the interface between high level business strategy and operations manufacturing strategy. New business philosophies and new manufacturing technologies are increasing the importance and the dynamic nature of this interface. This paper draws upon the convergence in enterprise and manufacturing strategies apparent in the established theories and models and relates these to the practical application of Concurrent Engineering.

Through case studies this text examines manufacturing strategy for different business types. Corporate strategies emanating from a range of leading companies are related to the Company's manufacturing goals. A generic platform for describing this integration is clearly presented. The author develops this form through enterprise-wide Competitive Dimensions into a customisable, Business Environment and Manufacturing Technology/ Programme Specific, support framework. This generic framework links the Competitive Dimensions, the Manufacturing Enterprise Business Process Chains, and the Manufacturing Typology; each is selectable and customisable for a specific manufacturing business operation. The result is a method of decomposing business goals into aggregate business specific Manufacturing Performance Indicators. These are linked to Measures of Manufacturing Performance and directly related to a Manufacturing Technology or a Manufacturing Programme Component of Concurrent Engineering.

Keywords: *Concurrent Engineering, Decision Support, Manufacturing Performance, Manufacturing Strategy, Tools,.*

1. Introduction

The competitive pressures facing manufacturing business are formidable. These pressures lead to requirements for greater cooperation across the total business value chain in a way that is quite unlike classical business practice. Manufacturing systems seeking outstanding success must see themselves as part of multiple value chain systems directly delivering to the enterprise vision. In the past the challenge of manufacturing business was to realise performance within the factory or confines of the service system provider. The challenge to manufacturing in the late 1990s is to realise inter enterprise performance across the value chain [1]. This organisational form — The Extended Enterprise, demands that the adoption and implementation of new manufacturing ideas is not just compatible with business objectives but proactively supportive [2]. A senior manager comtemplating the local adoption of a technology needs to be able to determine its potential contribution to realising the total enterprise vision. This vision may have been set in a remote corporate headquarters and is probably couched in a terminology which is distant from the concerns of the manager. The impact of the investment on the value chain, the Extended Enterprise, may be ill defined [3].

This problem is significant with the selection and implementation of Advanced Manufacturing Technologies (AMT) but it exacerbated in the case of the plethora of what we define here as Advanced Manufacturing Programmes now emerging. Concurrent Engineering, Just-In-Time, Manufacturing Process Re-Engineering, Lean Manufacturing, Agile Manufacturing are examples of Advanced Manufacturing Programmes (AMP).

Manufacturing business is becoming more volatile. A decade ago Puttick [4], reported that a common question posed by chief executives is 'what technology or technologies should I buy to achieve my business objectives?'. In 1996 executives might also ask 'how can I use Concurrent Engineering', and 'what parts of my business should I re-engineer first?'. These questions are being posed in the context of achieving increasingly demanding business objectives. The new business philosophies and the new manufacturing philosophies of the late 1990s are increasing both the importance and the dynamic nature of the interface between high level business strategy and operations manufacturing strategy. Developments, particularly the rate-of-change in the competitive environment, are generating new requirements for manufacturing decision support tools [5, 6]. In these circumstances doing the right thing is perhaps even more important than doing things right which has been the focus of the 1990's style Business Process Re-engineering [7].

These changes create the requirements for a coherent, up-gradable and locally customisable decision architecture to provide a creative support system at the business strategy/manufacturing strategy interface. At the user level, existing decision support tools, whilst based in sound manufacturing business theory, typically serve a corporate management objective of prediction, optimisation and control. Usually they have been developed for highly specific market/technology/time point application; often they are appropriate to large organisations and staff-intensive support mechanisms. They have been associated with top down financial accounting and control systems [8].

The application domain for an appropriate tool is not restricted to large organisations. The European manufacturing base, including Small and Medium Sized companies, is being encouraged by member state governments to adopt both Advanced Manufacturing Technologies and Programmes. Manufacturing technologies do not give a manufacturing advantage; they provide a market based means of survival through product excellence and operations resilience. These new application requirements must be reflected in the decision support tool architecture.

A range of manufacturing decision support tools for use by managers on their own personal computers, applicable across industry sectors and customisable to local and individual need are required.

Good decision support tools will augment creativity and innovation inherent in the manufacturing manager's environment. This paper describes the framework for a personal decision support system addressing the selection and application of alternative manufacturing philosophies such as Concurrent Engineering.

2. Manufacturing Context

Senior managers face a plethora of new Advanced Manufacturing Technologies alongside a growing number of Advanced Manufacturing Programmes, for example: Concurrent Engineering, Agile Manufacturing. These technologies and programmes have far reaching consequences that are not easily evaluated in their contribution to enterprise strategy. The stimulus for the development of the decision support tool framework described here is the authors' belief that the use of appropriate Advanced Manufacturing Technologies and Advanced Manufacturing Programmes is directly related to the ability of the company to quantify the likely impact of the Technology/Programme on the business. Generic decision support tools to facilitate this quantification of impact are not readily available. The functionality and the architecture of such a tool have not been well defined. It is dangerous to adopt Concurrent Engineering just because it is fashionable.

3. Process Map

The decision process adopted constructs and deploys a common framework endorsed by the literature and through in-depth access to industrial data determines and develops a common interface to support the decision making activity described. Using the data collected a top-down cascade was followed from the Corporate Vision, together with a bottom-up cascade from Manufacturing Programmes and Technologies. A detailed study created a common format hierarchical decomposition map of the business to manufacturing strategy link via six process steps to identify cross sector applicable Competitive Dimensions (Fig. 5.1).

The top-down cascade starts with the Corporate Vision. This may normally be directly extracted from the company annual report. It should comprises a succinct challenge to all company employees. Chrysler recently used: 'Not the biggest, just the best', as its vision statement. Our next level is the enterprise mission. This defines the framework in which the business operates and usually includes a sense of direction for the future. For example: Ford Motor Company is a worldwide leader in automotive products and services.... to continually improve our products and services to meet customer needs, allowing us to prosper as a business....' The Enterprise Mission specifies the basis of competition for the particular business unit under consideration; it is the reason customers will buy the products/services offered by the enterprise. This often requires workshop/interview activities with senior management to build a coherent high level common view. The Critical Enterprise Success Factors are what the enterprise has to be good at to succeed. Usually there are three to eight critical success factors for an organisation. An example for a manufacturing company might be 'pre-eminent manufacturing', or 'low cost producer'. This is the extent of the business strategy. The interface with the manufacturing Strategy is the Competitive Dimension set.

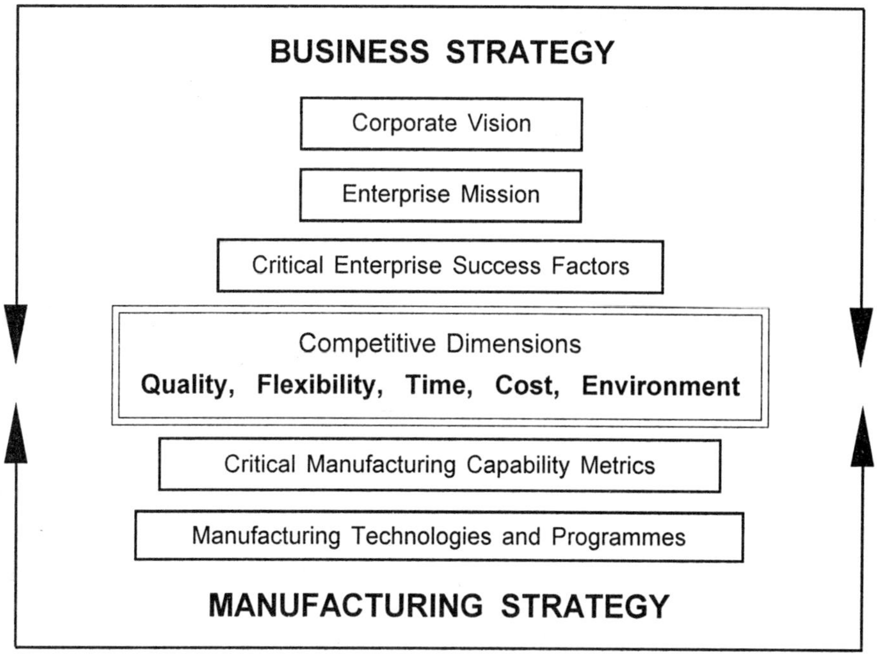

Fig. 5.1: Common Format Strategy Decomposition Map

The bottom-up cascade starts with the Manufacturing Programmes and Technologies. A Technology might be robotic assembly, a Programme might be Concurrent Engineering. These examples pose totally different successful implementation issues. 'What gets measured gets done'; so the Manufacturing Capability Metrics adopted are the key to success in these or any other manufacturing investment. They must be determined against appropriate criteria before implementation. These can then also be used as a basis for ongoing performance assessment should the Programme for Technology be adopted. The Manufacturing Capability Metrics arise from, and are directly associated with the each specific Programme or Technology: they are not determined by the Critical Enterprise Success Factors. Critical Manufacturing Capability Metrics interface with the success factors through the Competitive Dimensions.

The means for developing this process was through access to senior personnel and sensitive documentation on high level corporate strategy and operations objectives. For the purposes of this paper data is presented drawn from non-current strategy. This provides for model validity. Any similarity with current similar enterprise operations does not have commercial significance; interpretation of the data sourced is entirely the authors responsibility. Case studies illustrate the process and support validation of the outcome.

4. Case Studies

4.1. Automotive

The Ford Motor Company's ambition is to be seen as best in class in all operations. The Board believed that the Company has to improve its competitive stance in each of the industry's core technologies and operating systems. In this context, core technologies are defined as the functions required for the manufacture and assembly of a motor vehicle including: Forging (of engine blocks, camshafts), Welding, Component Assembly. Operating systems are defined as the underlying methodology or philosophy that governs the method of working including: Just-In-Time, Concurrent Engineering. In 1993 Ford Motor Company increased its emphasis on customer satisfaction as a goal. In pursuit of this the competitive strategy was to provide a low cost and differentiated product. The Company identified product differentiation combined with quality at a competitive price as being the main driver in the market place.

As indicated in the Company's Annual Report, special emphasis was being placed on; developing new products, improving quality, reducing time to market, improving efficiency of processes and becoming more productive.

The tactical position adopted by the Company was to develop new quality products at a lower cost while reducing product development, manufacturing and assembly lead times. Prior to Global reorganisation in January 1995, Ford European Manufacturing and Engineering Operations were divided in to two business groups; Vehicle Operations and Powertrain Operations. Each has its documents strategy ("Technology Cycle Plan"). The strategies concentrate on the implementation of a manufacturing plan in Ford's European operations. They identify core technologies, project plans, short and long term goals, time scales and proposed budgets. The Company corporate goal was translated into the Corporate Vision and Enterprise Mission statements.

The Corporate Vision is interpreted as, to be a Low cost producer of highest quality products that provide best customer value.

The Vision statement incorporates a degree of industrial comparison, intimating that the Company aims to be the industry leader.

The Enterprise Mission can be seen as providing processes, skills, tooling facilities and procuring materials to efficiently produce the highest quality automotive components and vehicles at world class timing... be a world wide leader in automotive and automotive related products and services.

The Vision and Mission are consistent with each other, identifying customer value as the objective. The manufacturing strategy and the corporate strategy both seek overall cost leadership. There is also a degree of correlation in the tactical position adopted. They both seek to position the enterprise among the industry leaders and place special emphasis on the competitive dimensions of quality, timing, and cost.

The Company's use of the term 'Timing' was examined in detail. It was found on close evaluation, to embrace the Flexibility and Time elements normally described in the literature. After the determination of these Competitive Dimensions the Company's documentation identified the long term goals. The strategy documents do not show how the Environment fits into their overall vision and mission although legislative aspects impinge on this area.

The Company sub-divide these long term goals into both short term and medium term goals to form objectives. Examples of the short and medium term goals on environmental issues are respectively: coolant systems without need to recycle filters, swarf and coolant in special purpose tunnels.

The next stage of the manufacturing strategy is to identify which core technologies would be most closely associated with the achievement of these manufacturing goals. The Company document that the achievement of the Timing and Low Total Cost goals would best be achieved through the implementation of Simultaneous (Concurrent) Engineering, Total Productive Maintenance and Integrated Manufacturing Teams.

The Company's process is that Manufacturing Technologies are then investigated with the specific aim of achieving these goals. They are assigned start dates, due dates and a budget. The Company identifies the implementation of the plan necessary for the achievement of these goals, vision and mission statements:

Reaching "among the leaders." in most areas becoming the 'leader' in selected areas.

These "areas' and "selected areas" are defined as the industry's core technologies and operating systems.

The Vision to Mission cascade uses the Vision statement which at the top level is Best Customer Value. The Critical Enterprise Success Factors from the basis of assessment and are; Customer Satisfaction, Low Cost Producer, Pre-eminent Manufacturing. The Enterprise Mission Statement is directly linked to four Competitive Dimensions: Quality, Flexibility, Time, Cost. The successful achievement of the Corporate Vision must be measurable against specified goals directly driven by manufacturing plan objectives.

Upward cascading from the manufacturing plan is via the competitive dimensions of most significance to the Company. The Company's manufacturing plans can be formatted so that their measures of success can be related to the Quality, Flexibility, Time, Cost, Environment dimensions. The operating systems encompass the specific core technologies. The decomposition map is shown in Fig. 5.2. The Company has defined clear objectives for each of the operations within the Engineering & Manufacturing and the Powertrain groups.

4.2. Aerospace

The ten largest commercial aircraft manufacturers achieved sales of US$ 41,323 million during 1993. Aerospace companies typically operate world-wide and exports may account for the majority of sales. In the UK, British Aerospace has refocused its strategic direction back to its roots in aerospace and defence. As one of the world's few fully integrated aerospace and defence contractors, core engineering and technological strengths provide the basis of competition. British Aerospace is primarily an Assemble-to-Order and an Engineer-to-Order (customisation of products to specific customer requirements) business. In this respect it is similar to US aerospace companies examined by the authors. The annual report of companies in this sector typically state that the Corporate Vision is best customer value on whole product life cycle cost which specifically includes product life time support. The Enterprise Mission is usually to remain a competitive world-class, high technology, manufacturing company. A recent world wide survey by Ingersoll Engineers found a mature global industry with competition based on cost, quality, and rapid response times, and little differences from nation to nation.

The company used in this example is operated as a set of Strategic Business Units. These may be operationally integrated or not depending on the relationship to the business division. They achieve their individual Enterprise Mission through contract specific self determination in the realisation of the Critical Enterprise Success Factors. Despite the diversity of the strategic business units, Critical Enterprise Success Factors are common to the total enterprise, here they are: Low cost producer, High quality in products and processes, High product capabilities (performance, product attributes).

Fig. 5.2: An Automotive Strategy Decomposition Map

One particular Business Unit is examined, and for clarity on the decomposition map only the Advanced Manufacturing Programmes are presented in Fig. 5.3. Ongoing improvement in Quality is sought but is less of an issue currently following substantial efforts and achievements over many years. The driver for Flexibility improvement is associated with realising better product introduction processes which are seen as high priority. These are to be realised through, amongst other measures; late customisation, common platform engineering, modular design. Reductions in Time and Cost are identified as important in the face of intense international competition.

The widespread roll out off Advanced Manufacturing Programmes piloted in certain sites has great potential. The implementation of world class manufacturing techniques at one site reduced lead times on a defence system by over 50 per cent. In-house inventory has been reduced by more than half. At another site project

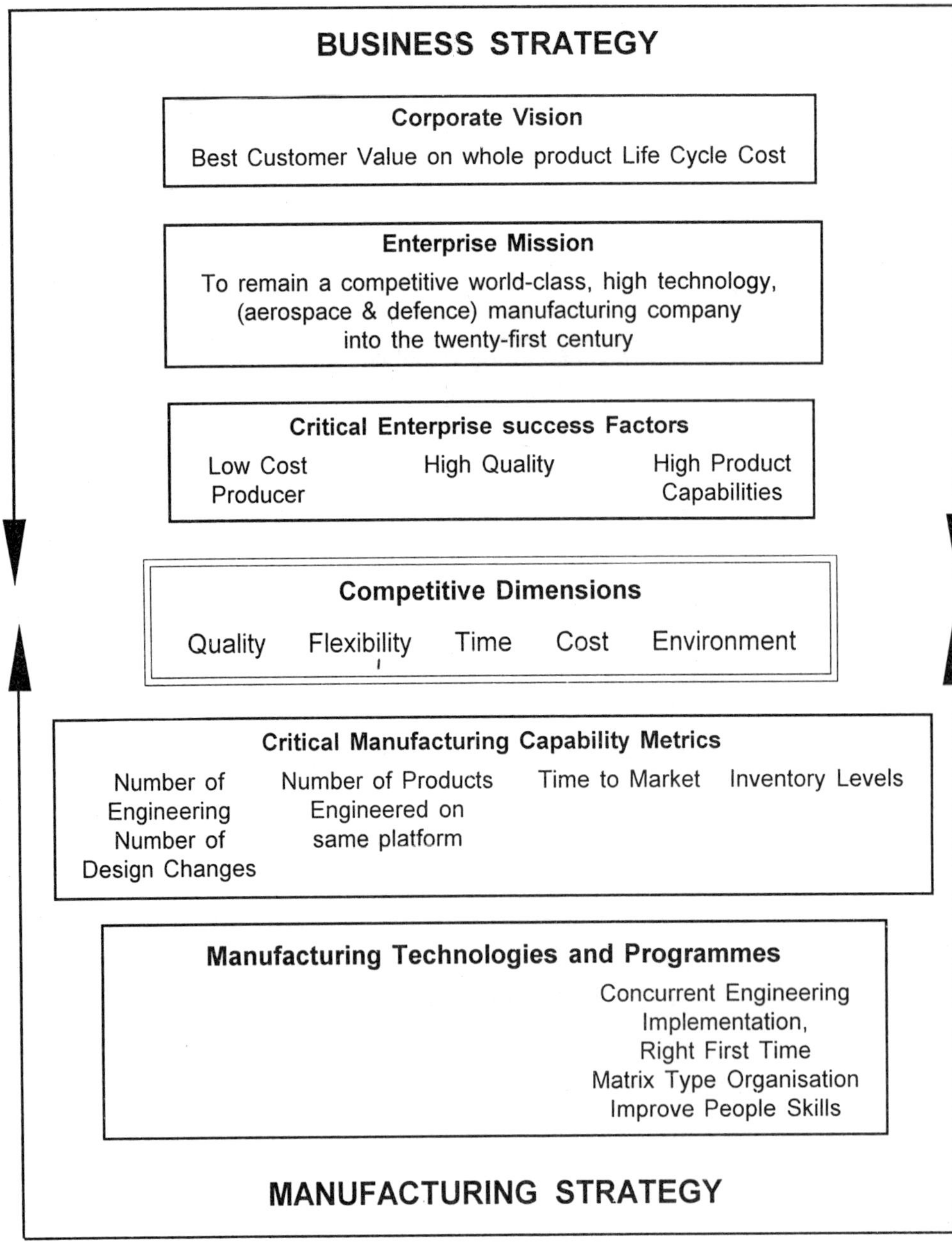

Fig. 5.3: An Aerospace Strategy Decomposition Map

completion of orders for one aircraft type was achieved in 35 per cent of planned time through the implementation of a Concurrent Engineering Programme.

The Company has in-depth experience in Advanced Manufacturing Programmes. A meeting with executives at Company Headquarters provided discussion points with respect to Concurrent Engineering implementation. This Programme is seen as addressing in particular the Competitive Dimension of Time. The Critical Manufacturing Capability Metric is identified as Time to Market. The cross relationship to other manufacturing metrics is shown through the expectation that the Concurrent Engineering programme will be measured via metrics more directly associated with Competitive Dimensions other than time. These include: number of engineering drawings, number of design changes, ratio of spend in each of the Concurrent Engineering phases, single geometry platform. Benefits are also seen to arise at a detail beyond that presented in Fig. 5.3. Other Programmes impinge on this achievement such as matrix structures, co-location of teams, and Just-in-Time. Dramatic achievements have been reported in these programme areas by for example Boeing, Fokker and Short Brothers'.

4.3. Steel

The steel industry represents an apparently different industry type to the automotive and aerospace sectors so far considered and offers further insight into the model presented. Amongst possible future scenarios are those where steel will no longer perceived as a commodity, but a highly sophisticated product which is made-to-order to customer's specification. Some steel companies will then have a reputation for designing and manufacturing special steels. These steels will not be mass-produced and manufacturing systems will have to change to reflect this trend including a re-examination of decisions based on achieving economies of scale. Under this scenario the steel industry would closely resemble the automotive and even aerospace types addressed earlier.

From the 1992-93 Annual Report to Shareholders: 'British Steel is a low-cost and internationally respected steel producer, one of the most important companies in one of the world's key industries. Strength and adaptability stem from constant attention to cost reduction, product quality and customer service at all times and through all market conditions. British Steel is the UK's Sixth largest manufacturing exporter with overseas sales accounting for around half its total business.' During the tax year 1993-94 British Steel reported a substantial pre-tax profit. It is one of the few profitable steel manufacturers in the world. The strategy decomposition map in Fig. 5.4, presents a different viewpoint from the automotive and aerospace examples. It reflects the visible scale of the industry and the basis of competition

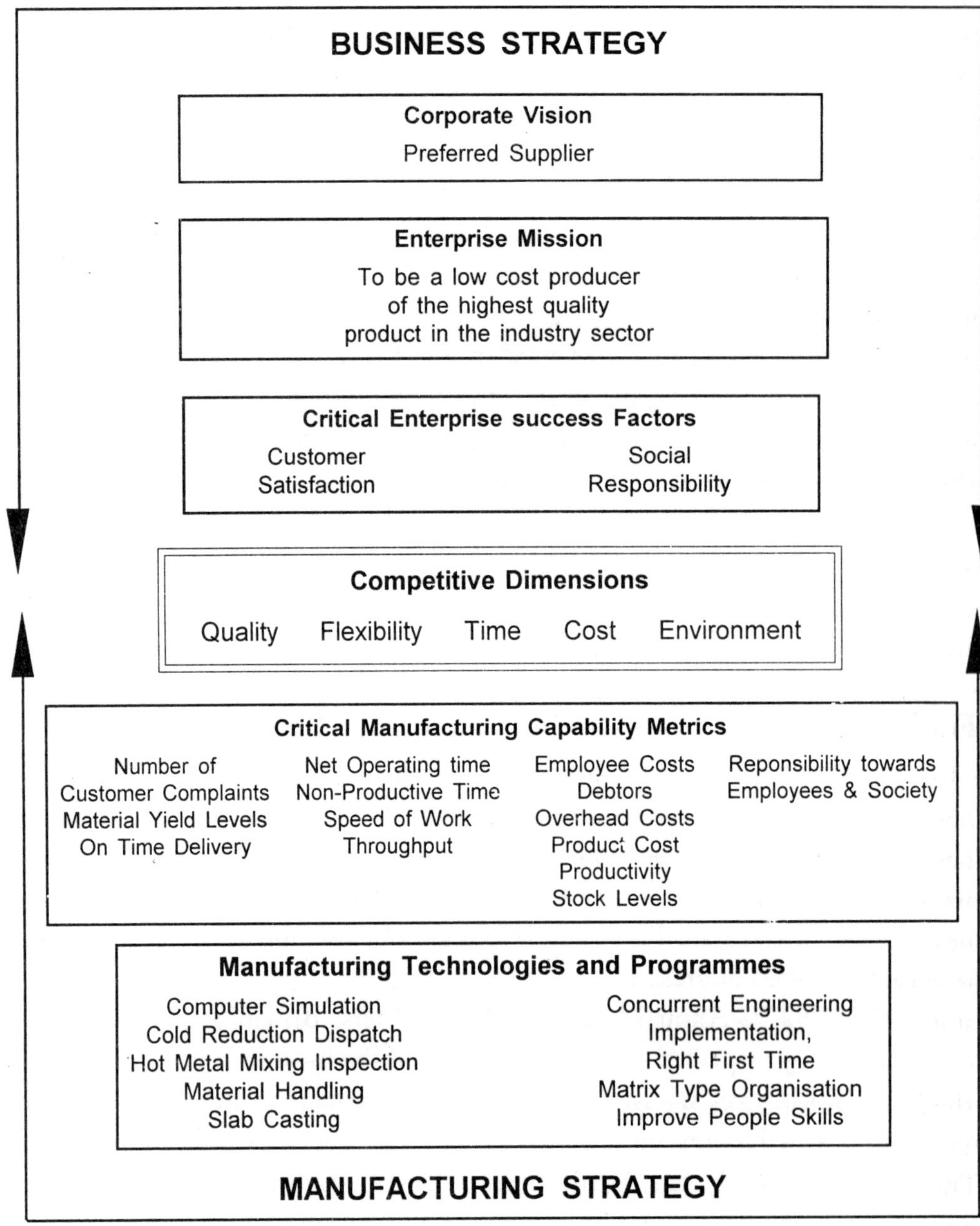

Fig. 5.4: A Process Industry Strategy Decomposition Map

very distinctly in the two Critical Enterprise Success Factors of Customer Satisfaction and Social Responsibility.

The manufacturing strategy for the steel company reflects the highly capital intensive nature of the industry. This huge overhead can dictate the strategic thinking. Minor changes to productivity/plant efficiency determine difference between profit and loss. The steel industry has striven for economies of scale by building larger facilities. The use of larger, specialised facilities has often been at the expense of flexibility. In the medium size strip products plant considered here over £150 million has been invested over the last decade in a plant which covers almost 1000 hectares. The strip product range produced includes coated and uncoated steels for use in general engineering, the automotive industry and household appliances such as washing machines.

The scope of the Advanced Manufacturing Technologies and Programmes implemented and planned in the steel industry does not reflect the traditional image of the industry. Very high conformance to customer on-time delivery is sought coupled with aggressive objectives in the plant order throughout time. On-time delivery is interpreted as a critical Manufacturing Capability Metric under the Quality Competitive Dimension. Flexibility does not currently have a clear metric specifically associated with it. Time and Cost metrics are process orientated. Environment is a specific Competitive Dimension with well defined metrics.

5. Framework

The European Commission BRITE EURAM Fundamental Research Project, Number 7094, [9] has demonstrated that to formalise and apply the link between business strategy and manufacturing strategy requires the measurement of 3 macro factors. These factors are: the product and market drivers, the specific manufacturing business processes, and the choice of manufacturing philosophy. The decision tool framework is expanded to reflect this and in application constitutes a 3 dimensional decision space. The axes of the decision space are: the determinate Competitive Dimensions of the business, the Manufacturing Enterprise Business Process Chains, and the Manufacturing Typology adopted. The generic framework is a Hexahedral in Fig. 5.5.

This format provides a robust and customisable method of decomposing business goals and relating them to manufacturing issues. Corporate Vision can be mapped by visible and meaningful business metrics to the selection and successful

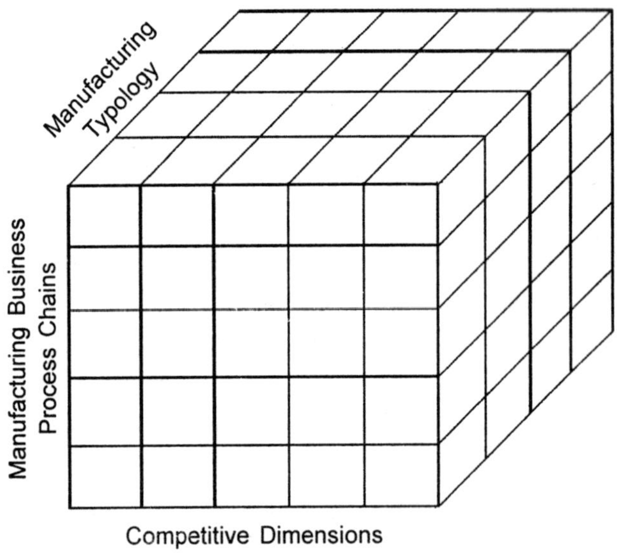

Fig. 5.5: The Hexahedral

implementation of manufacturing technologies and manufacturing programmes. The 3 axis of the hexahedral are now examined in turn.

5.1. Competitive dimensions

The Competitive Dimensions, there can be up to 5 in a manufacturing business, are at the heart of a common format, 6 process step, hierarchical decomposition map. The Corporate Vision can be cascaded down; the Manufacturing Technologies and Programmes can be cascaded up; to the Competitive Dimensions of the business.

The Manufacturing Metrics arise from, and are directly associated with each specific Programme or Technology: they are not determined by the Critical Enterprise Success Factors. Critical Manufacturing Capability Metrics interface with the success factors through the 5 Competitive Dimensions: Quality, Flexibility, Time, Cost, Environment.

5.2. Manufacturing business process chains

A consideration of a single Competitive Dimension is still too coarse a division for manufacturing decision making. A focus on a business process in conjunction with a single Competitive Dimension allows the specific impact of a manufacturing change to be both analysed and controlled. Business Process examination has become a catch-all for management of change activity across all enterprise functions.

Here we are only concerned with those processes that directly impact manufacturing. Too often the full opportunity for performance enhancement arising from technology investment has been lost because the manufacturing business process impacts are blurred. The measured, and therefore the achievable, benefits have been limited to the local environment of the technology or programme. The Critical Enterprise Success factors need to be tightly related to a Manufacturing Business Process to achieve meaningful impact. The full range of manufacturing activity is grouped here under the 5 Manufacturing Enterprise Process Chains: the Manufacturing Process Chain, the Co-Development Chain, the Product Configuration Chain, the Customer

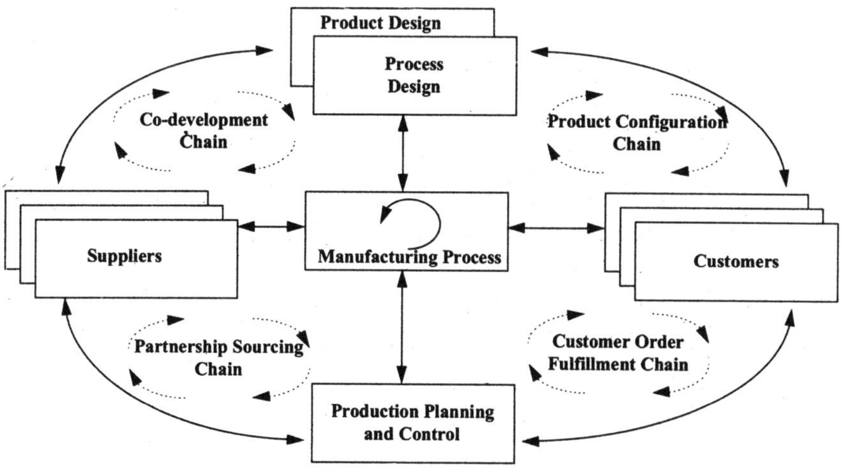

Fig. 5.6: Process Chains

Order Fulfilment Chain, the Partnership Sourcing Chain. The enterprise positioning of these chains is shown in Fig. 5.6 and each described below.

The Manufacturing Process Chain embraces all the activities directly involved in the physical production of the enterprise product or delivery of the enterprise service. It maybe located within a single plant or include geographically remote manufacturing sites. In the Extended Enterprise all the Manufacturing Chains are likely to interact with remote sites.

The Co-Development Chain contains all the activities directly involved with the supplier knowledge and capability contribution to the product design and process design activities. In the limit the co-development may occur wholly in the remote members of the chain. This has been described as black box engineering. Normally the objective is to reach levels of excellence through an appropriate contribution of expertise by all the process chain members.

The Product Configuration Chain is the product/service design and delivery process specification. It is normally achieved in conjunction with a market needs analysis. It will include volume, quality, conformance and delivery performance alongside the legislative issues.

The Customer Order Fulfilment Chain contains all the activities involved in the planning, data transmission, control, measurement and shipment of product to customer order requirements.

The Partnership Sourcing Chain is the activity directly involved in the co-ordination of vendor supplies to the manufacturing process. It includes planning requirements, selecting suppliers and achieving performance criteria.

5.3. Manufacturing typology

The customer order decoupling point forms a basis of describing manufacturing enterprise typology [10]. It provides a sharper graduation than the classic 'mass' or 'batch' or 'continuous' manufacturing process based terminology. As a part of the structured framework we require a business driven categorisation; customer order point decoupling point provides a neat and appropriate solution. This enterprise typology defines the following 4 modes:

- Make-To-Stock (MTS)
- Make-To-Order (MTO)
- Assemble-To-Order (ATO)
- Engineer-To-Order (ETO)

This typology provides an excellent means of differentiating manufacturing organisations. There is a well founded belief that competitive pressures are moving leading organisation operation across this spectrum from left to right, Fig. 5.7. It is accepted that we are moving from an era of mass production of stock items to mass customisation of unique product; engineer-to-order is gaining in importance. Many companies are finding that the engineering effort involved in the Engineer-To-Order typology is overwhelming their traditional systems; this is one reason for the increase in interest in Concurrent Engineering and many other Programmes which facilitate the effective use and reuse of scarce engineering resource.

Put simplistically, Make-To-Stock is physical resource intensive, Engineer-To-Order is information resource intensive and this provides a basis of categorisation of manufacturing business.

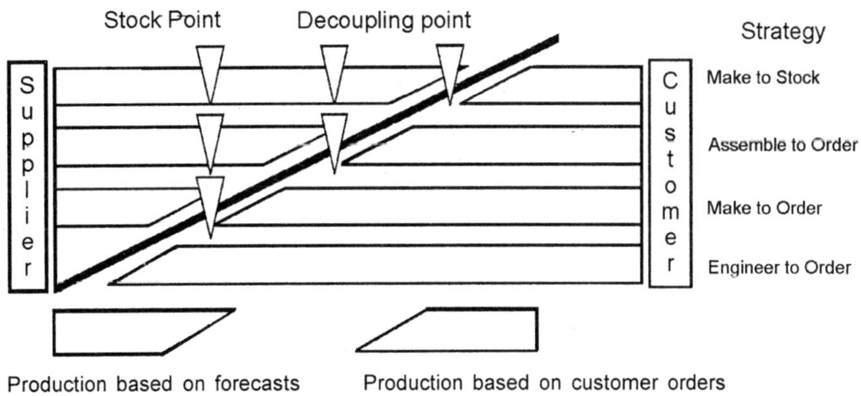

Fig. 5.7: Customer Order Decoupling

This typology has a good theoretical basis and works well in larger companies where the scale of business and individual business units provides clear boundaries to typology operation. Practical application by the author in the SME base, particularly for advanced business forms, has proved more difficult. Here even the smaller business sub units often display instances of two or more typologies on the same product line/product cell. The typology may therefore be difficult to apply.

An alternative classification is the use of Puttick Grids [11]. These can be represented as a quadrant with dimensions of Complexity and Uncertainty. Complexity is a means of measuring the large number of both physical product items and product/process knowledge entities that must be managed in even the smallest manufacturing business. These are greatly influenced by the type of product being delivered. Uncertainty arises from the unpredictable behaviour of the market place. Again this has as a prime driver, the nature of the product. At one time uncertainty was considered to apply to the production environment as well as the market; now we recognise that production environment uncertainty can be managed to a level where it does not impact the business typology.

The resulting typology provides four basic Complexity/Uncertainty manufacturing business types. For example a company manufacturing incandescent light bulbs would be classified as low Complexity (product)/low Uncertainty (market). In the same way that the trend in European business needs to be from Make-To-Stock to Engineer-To-Order, in the European arena successful, sustainable business needs to move towards the high Complexity/high Uncertainty quadrant. Companies in this quadrant might, for example, manufacture special capital equipment, high

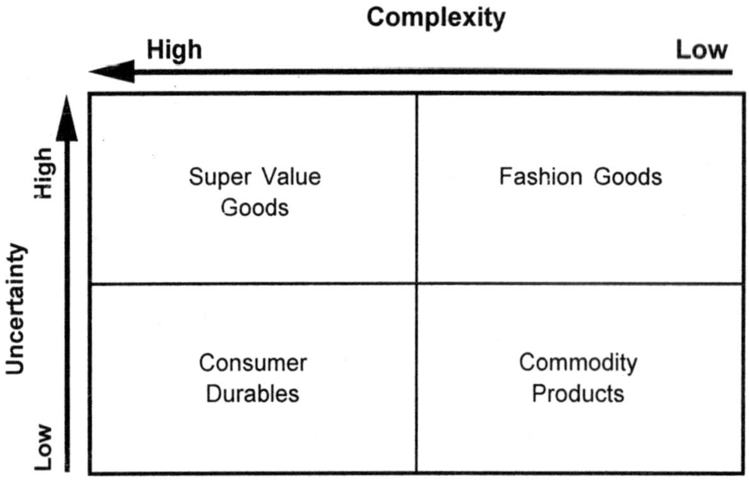

Fig. 5.8: Product Complexity Uncertainty Matrix

service level or individual to customer, items. The recent EUREKA Factory for the future study classified this quadrant as Super Value Goods, see this EUREKA study has directly addressed the needs and characteristics of future manufacturing systems for Small and Medium Sized Enterprises. This four grid typology is particularly suited to categorisation of smaller and advanced operation manufacturing businesses. It is simple to apply.

6. Architecture

The Competitive Dimensions, the Manufacturing Business Process Chains, and the Manufacturing Typologies may now be combined so that the Hexahedral referred to earlier can be elaborated. Fig. 5.9 represents the framework for a manufacturing environment where the order decoupling point is clear.

Other manufacturing environments use a similar scheme but adopt the Uncertainty/Complexity grid typology in Fig. 5.10. In both environments the Manufacturing Typology has four classes.

The high level Corporate Vision statement is decomposed via the five Competitive Dimensions, and deepened by the five Manufacturing Business Process Chains and the four Manufacturing Typologies. The resultant hexahedral has a potential 100 unique manufacturing Performance Indicators. These Performance Indicators contain structures collections of measures suitable for bench marking against company and industry standards. Examples of these will be developed during a following session at this meeting. In practice a small subset applies to a

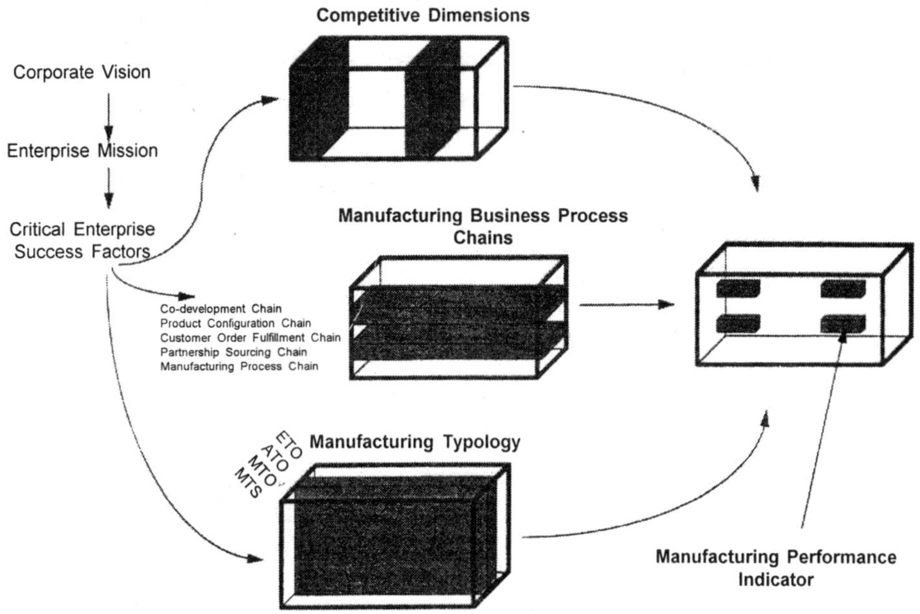

Fig. 5.9: Manufacturing Environment, Order Point Decoupling

particular decision environment. For example a manager contemplating an investment in an Advanced manufacturing Programme may be primarily concerned with three Competitive Dimensions of Cost, Flexibility and Time; be operating in the single, high Complexity/high Uncertainly Manufacturing Typology; be concerned only with the Design Configuration Chain. This situation presents just three Performance

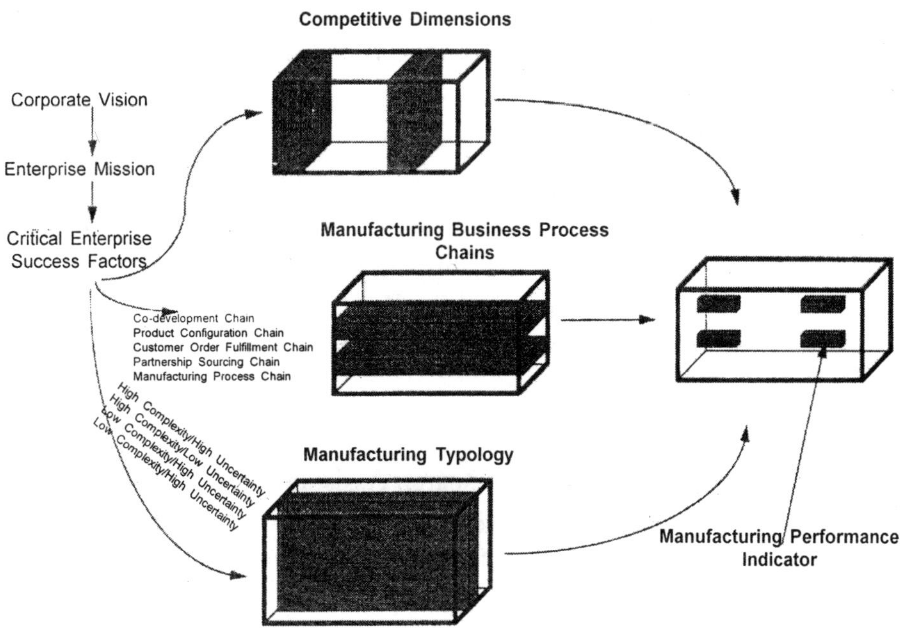

Fig. 5.10: Manufacturing Environment, Puttick Grid

indicators from the 100 Indicator envelope. These Manufacturing Performance Indicators can be cascaded into a series of Measures of Manufacturing Performance. For example; the Competitive Dimension: Cost, the Manufacturing Business Process Chain: Product Configuration and the Manufacturing Typology: Make-To-Order.

These define a particular sub set Manufacturing Performance Indicator envelope. The Measures of Manufacturing Performance addressing this space might include: number of design queries, time taken to answer queries, designer hours used, number of prototypes built. Experience to date has shown that there maybe 20-30 measures of manufacturing Performance for each Strategic Performance Indicator. An examination of these measures and the analysis tools adopted to relate manufacturing technology and programme features to the manufacturing measures is shown in Fig. 5.11.

7. Conclusions

A manufacturing business decision support architecture relating business goals with manufacturing strategy has been established. The framework is in the form of a hexahedral; it has widespread manufacturing business application. Alternative manufacturing typologies are accommodated.

The large generic decision support framework is readily customised to a particular business decision application. This greatly reduces the potentially overwhelming decision space. The result is a manageable decision support tool in terms of practical personal level application and the ability to handle complexity in the manufacturing environment. The framework forms the basis for a detail analysis tool relating specific manufacturing technology models to business driven measures of manufacturing performance. This facility is currently being Beta tested in a range of European industrial companies. It has particular application for Concurrent Engineering which has far reaching business impacts. The combination of an appropriate design model with a strategy support framework provides a means of managing the business processes impacted by Concurrent Engineering to realise high business performance.

Acknowledgements

Paul Lowenthal and Douglas Maxwell, Research Assistants at Cranfield University for their contributions to the framework presented.

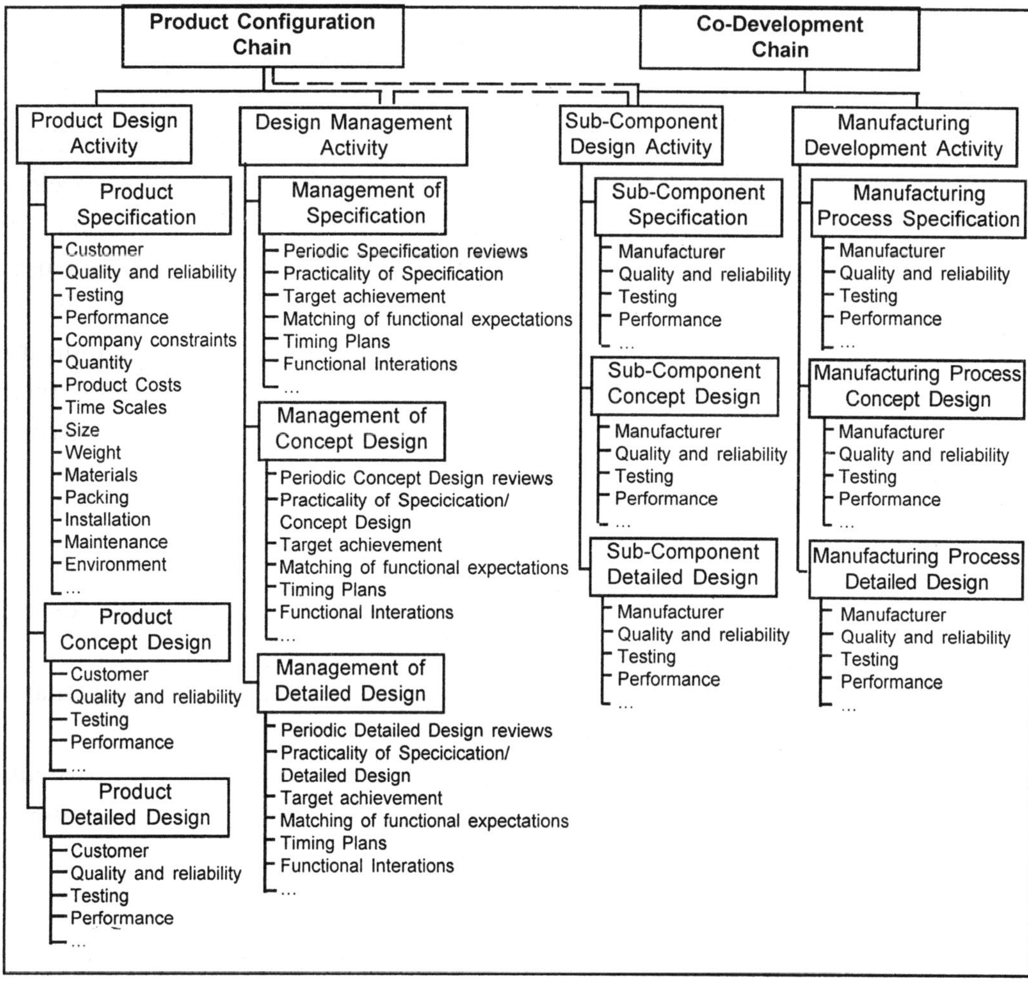

Fig. 5.11: Manufacturing Measures

This work has been partly funded under the European Commission, BRITE EURAM, Fundamental Research Programme, Project No. 7094. The Programme participants include: Ford Automotive Operations, British Steel, Daimler Benz, Kewill, Digital equipment, University of Karlsruhe, University College Galway, Cranfield University.

References

1. P.J. Sackett, "Using Your Resources Effectively", *Proc Computers in Mfg.*, Birmingham, U.K. Oct. 1990.

2. H. O'Neill, P.J. Sackett, "The Extended Manufacturing Enterprise Paradigm", *Management Decision*, Vol.32, No.8, Oct., pp42-49. 1994. ISSN 0025-1747.
3. H. O'Neill, P.J. Sackett, "The Extended Enterprise Reference Framework", *Proc. — BAYS '96*, Lisbon, Portugal, June 1996, Chapman & Hall, ISBN 041278890X.
4. J. Puttick, "Manufacturing Pull - Manufacturing Push, Springboard for Competitive Advantage", PA Consulting Group, London. 1986.
5. P.J. Sackett, J.C. Wortmann, J. Browne, "The Systems of Manufacturing — Manufacturing Business Challenges", Keynote Paper, *Proc. ASI 1994, ESPRIT ICIMS Network of Excellence*, Patras, Greece, June 1994.
6. P.J. Sackett, "World Class Manufacturing - Linking Future Scenarios, Strategies and Technologies", *Proc. Pro E User Conference*, Johannesburg, SA. 24 August, 1996
7. A. Trisoglio, "Manufacturing Complexity", The Strategy and Complexity Seminar, London School of Economics, London, July 1995.
8. P.J. Sackett, P.A. Lowenthal, D.J. Maxwell, H.O'Neill, 1996, "Business Strategy and Manufacturing Strategy — Mapping the Link", IJCIM, UK, awaiting publication.
9. S. Jackson, P.J. Sackett, "Advanced Manufacturing Business Integration Tool for Europe", *Proc. Logistics, Management and Production Organisation, EU Targeted Research Action No. 53*, Vouliagmeni, Greece, October 1995.
10. H.P. Wiendahl, P. Scholtissek, "Management and Control of Complexity in Manufacturing", *Anals of CIRP*, Vol.43, No.2, pp533-540, 1994.
11. Factory for the Future, EUREKA Project No. 1005; Department of Trade and INdustry, 151 Buckingham Palace Rd., London, or Forschungszentrum Karlesruhe Gmph, Postffach 3640, D-76021, Karlsruhe, 1995.

6

Developing Measures of Manufacturing Performance for Concurrent Engineering Implementation

Peter J. Sackett
Cranfield University, Cranfield, Bedford, UK

Abstract

A Framework to guide Concurrent Engineering practice and implementation is described. Through practical examples the role of Measures of Manufacturing Performance in realising and maintaining successful Concurrent Engineering by linking Corporate Vision with implementation issues is emphasised. A process to elicit participant by Concurrent Engineering team members in setting Measures of Manufacturing Performance is presented. These techniques provide direct guidance for developing company specific Measures of Manufacturing Performance to drive successful Concurrent Engineering implementation programmes.

Keywords: *Manufacturing Performance, Concurrent Engineering, Implementation.*

1. Introduction

The need to link Manufacturing Strategy via the Corporate Vision to Measures of Manufacturing Performance was described earlier [1]. This is particularly important when an issue such as the implementation of a Manufacturing Programme like Concurrent Engineering is being addressed. The goal of the particular implementation needs to be aligned with business issues. Without this linkage to the Corporate Vision the implementation will probably fail or deliver much less than has been promised. In this session we will develop Measures of Manufacturing Performance and customise these for specific business requirements of a Concurrent Engineering Programme.

Simplistically stated, the principle guiding the operational implementation of Concurrent Engineering is to improve communication throughout the product development process. This can be achieved through techniques such as process planning in the Manufacturing Enterprise Chains impacting the design activities, together with the use of Information technology and adoption of multi-discipline product development teams. This implementation guideline is not the goal of the Concurrent Engineering Programme. A definition of Concurrent Engineering, developed by Dr Evans at Cranfield University, reflects the significance of the technique and the importance of the implementation process in achieving business benefit;

> *"Concurrent Engineering is the delivery of better, cheaper, faster products to market, by a lean way of working, using multidiscipline teams, right first time methods and parallel processing activities to continuously consider all constraints".*

The challenge presented by this implementation process can easily overshadow the underlying reason behind the management decision to deploy the Concurrent Engineering technique. The effect can too often be a focus on the process and a loss of clarity on the end objective of the Concurrent Engineering Programme.

It can be readily and logically argued that extra time and effort spent in the front end design phases where most of the product cost is fixed, reduces the need for costly and time-consuming design changes later. This suggests that Concurrent Engineering is just common sense or god business practice. In which case many companies will naturally be applying the principles probably without using the label Concurrent Engineering. This type of implementation, Level 1 Concurrent Engineering, is indeed common. More important is the role of Concurrent Engineering in meeting business goals. This might mean making a better product. A product that is better for customers and manufacturers. A product that requires the implementation goes well beyond the mere avoidance of errors and oversights in our development process (Level 1 Concurrent Engineering).

In practice the adoption of high performance, Level 2, Concurrent Engineering is a resource hungry, potentially disruptive and costly operation. The potential benefits are great but the resource implications mean they need to be directly driven by the participating Company's own business goals.

The company's wide adoption of the language of Concurrent Engineering which has evolved over the last 5 years, is a cheaper and easier option even than Level 1 implementation. It should not be considered as an alternative to the real implementation of Concurrent Engineering. Examples of this vocabulary illustrate the potential impact if Level 2 Concurrent Engineering is to be realised:

> *'time/risk assessment profiles', 'parallel processing of design ideas', 'flat operation of multi-disciplinary teams', 'right first time processes', 'integrated product data management', 'beyond market needs conformance', 'zero defect build'.*

Minor changes to measuring, and therefore managing, the product development business process chains will not bring about the realisation of Level 2 Concurrent Engineering. However, the tools and techniques that come under the Concurrent Engineering header, especially multi-discipline product development teams, applied in a structured and planned way have been shown to give companies a significant boost in performance and productivity [2].

2. Practice and Implementation

Concurrent Engineering is a business process initiative potentially impacting the whole organisation. It alters what we do and the way that we do it and needs to be directly linked to the overall business strategy [3].

2.1. Business process

Concurrent Engineering implementation with the Manufacturing Enterprise Chains can be related to the re-engineering of a business process. Hammer and Champy [4], define a process as, "A collection of activities that takes one or more kinds of input and creates an output that is of value to the customer". This is a good high level description of the activities of a Concurrent Engineering team. Faced with this role objective, the team members have potentially unlimited scope and are likely to be daunted and frustrated. The Company's business strategy with respect to Concurrent Engineering needs to define the boundaries of scope. Again we can draw on Business Process Re-engineering to provide a guideline. MacDonald [5] defines three distinct management approaches to the scope of change. He describes process improvement, process design and process re-engineering. The Concurrent

Engineering team will find it useful to recognise the scope of their activities. This will be determined by the business requirements. Process improvement is incremental,

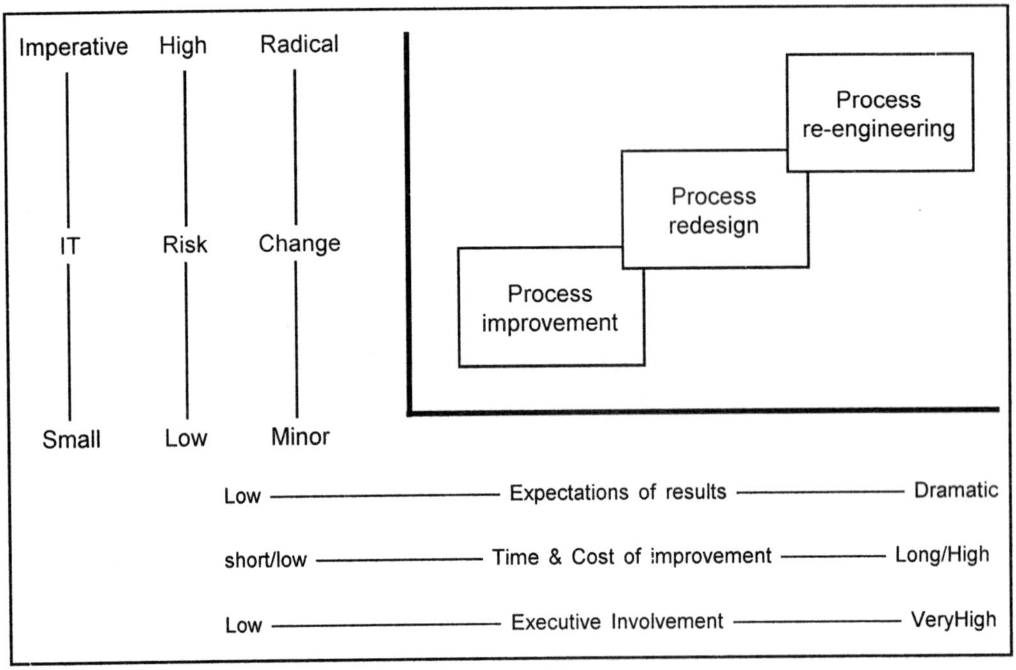

Fig. 6.1: Scope of Concurrent Engineering

implemented by the team over a period of time. Process redesign is more radical; cross functional boundaries are likely to be breached, tasks which do not add value will be phased out. Process Re-engineering delivers dramatic changes over a compressed time scale. Fig. 6.1 illustrates the impacts of these three categories.

2.2. Decision framework

The Concurrent Engineering implementation process can draw directly on the framework presented earlier in this meeting [1] in Fig. 6.2.

The five Competitive Dimensions; Quality, Flexibility, Time, Cost, Environment, may potentially all be influenced by a Concurrent Engineering Programme. For a particular business operation, 1 or 2, perhaps 3, of these dimensions will have special significance and priority. The others can be ignored, at least initially.

For example, the Competitive Dimension 'Time' may be particularly significant. Time-based Competition is now widespread. The opportunities for improvement have been identified by reference to the shortfalls in performance apparent in many

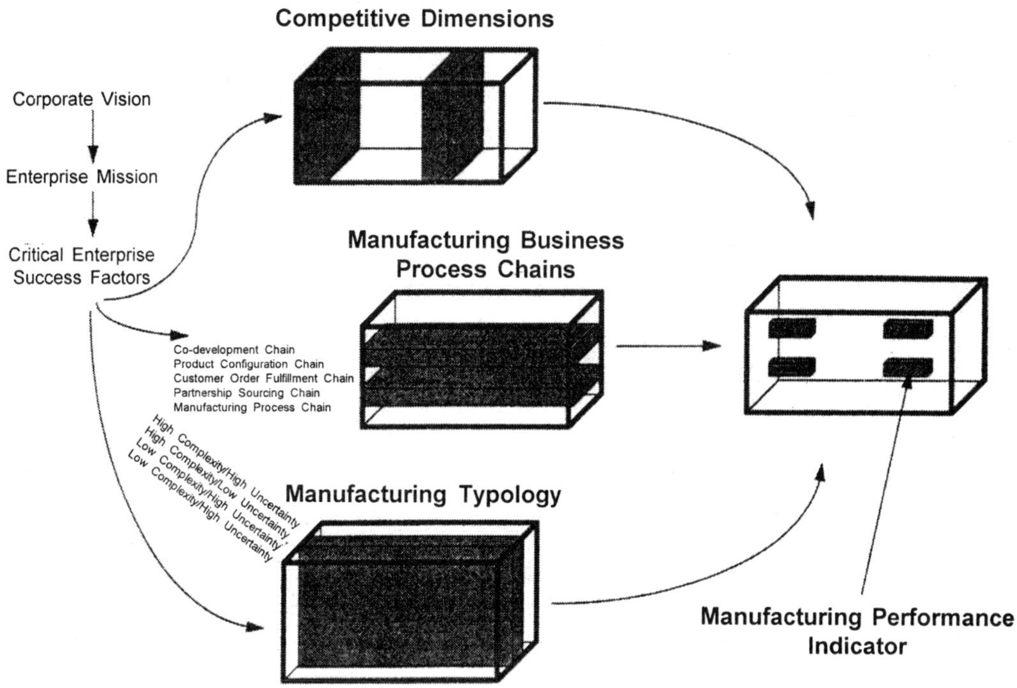

Fig. 6.2: Manufacturing Environment, Puttick Grid

industrial organisations. Brooks and Schofield, [6], summarise the results of a recent survey:

- most projects over run on time and cost
- value adding time often less than 15 per cent
- 50 per cent of resources dedicated to product innovation go to unsuccessful projects
- over 60 per cent of executives are disappointed with their new product development.

Returning to the Framework, the Manufacturing Typology will be selectable on the basis of either the customer order decoupling point or the product complexity/ market uncertainty matrix. It will be defined by the characteristics of the business unit under consideration. It is not determined by the use of Concurrent Engineering as a technique.

The third consideration, the Manufacturing Business Process Chains, are key to setting Measures of Manufacturing Performance for Concurrent Engineering.

The Manufacturing Business Process Chains most impacted by a Concurrent Engineering Programme are the Product Configuration Chain and the Co-development Chain. The other 3 Chains can often be ignored in this context, at least in the initial stages of Concurrent Engineering in Fig. 6.3.

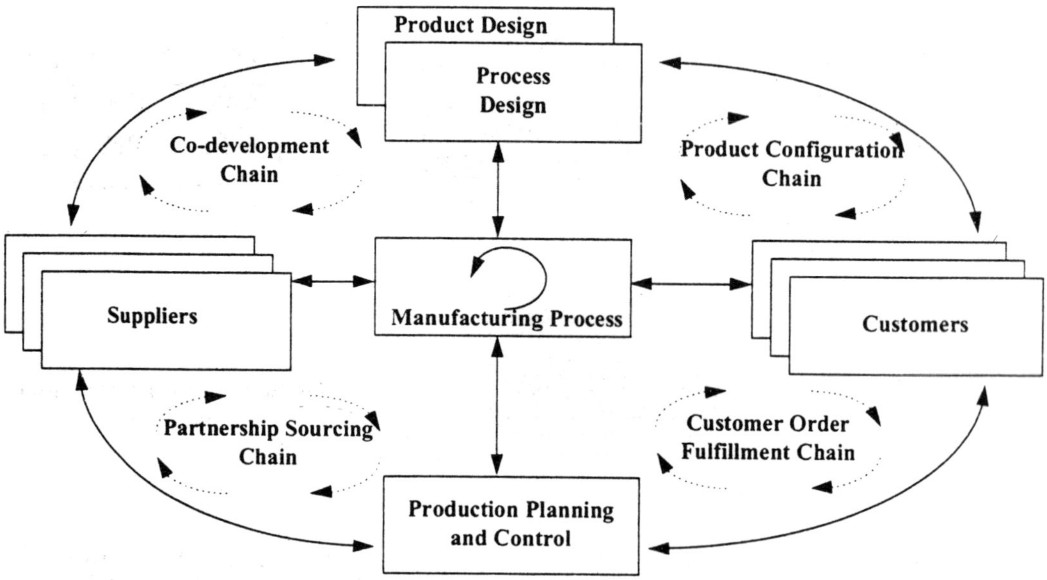

Fig. 6.3: Process Chains

The Co-development Chain is becoming increasingly important as companies focus on core business and use supplier capability to collaboratively develop components or even major sub systems of their final product. It embraces all the activities directly involved with the supplier contribution to the product design and process design activities. It needs to manage external knowledge and capability. In some cases the co-development may occur wholly in remote and separate members of the Chain. This can be described as black box engineering. Normally the objective will be to reach levels of product and process excellence through an appropriate contribution of expertise by all the members of the Co-development Chain.

The Product Configuration Chain is the product and/or service design and delivery process specification. It will normally be achieved in conjunction with a market needs analysis. It will include the proservice volume, conformance, and delivery performance and will often embrace legislative issues for alternative markets.

In practice the application of these Enterprise Chains requires a good understanding of the company's design process. Modelling of this process may be required.

2.3. Opportunities

The Competitive Dimension goals envisaged will not be achieved easily. There will normally be resistance to change, as traditional behaviours, values and ways of working are challenged. The most likely sources of resistance must be identified and eliminated [7, 8]. This applies even if just Level 1 Concurrent Engineering is being developed.

Level 2 Concurrent Engineering needs to be an empowered team based 'learning by doing' process. If the team is to be empowered to make their decisions, collectively and individually, they require specific, clear, workable and accepted, Measures of Manufacturing Performance linked coherently through to the Company's Corporate Vision. This can most readily be achieved by allowing the team to develop the Measures of Manufacturing Performance they will work to. A process to achieve this is now simulated in a Workshop session.

3. Developing Measures of Manufacturing Performance

The delegates participating in the Workshop session were reminded of the strategy decision support framework. The definitions of the Manufacturing Enterprise Chains were elaborated and displayed. The delegates were divided into two groups. One Group was allocated the Product Configuration Chain; the other Group was allocated the Co-development Chain. The common question was posed:

What Measures of Manufacturing Performance are needed to implement a Concurrent Engineering Programme in your Enterprise Chain?

It is necessary for each team to determine the Competitive Dimensions it will be particularly concerned with. Teams selected a company type against the typologies described. This provides substance and a reference point for debate and exchange of ideas. The Facilitator interacted on these issues taking into account the delegates areas of experience and expertise.

The participants were asked to think of successful development projects, or pockets of success within a project, that they had either been directly involved in or had observed in the past, or read about. They were asked to consider the Measures of Manufacturing Performance being used in these instances, even if they had not been specifically defined at the time.

The participants were provided with Post-it type pads and "Creative Silence" [9] was used to start a process of brainstorming. This involved the participants individually generating ideas and solutions in response to the question posed. One idea was written per post-it. Each participant then contributed their ideas singly and without comment from the group until all the ideas were represented. This approach prevents the first contribution presented overwhelming other potential contributors. It allows a diversity of ideas to be generated and group knowledge presented. Participants were encouraged to listen to one another, and only speak if a contribution needed clarifying. The groups were then asked to move their ideas into families on the wall. At the end of the exercise, the groups presented their outputs to one another. A discussion followed, comparing the output from each of the two groups. The text below shows a sample output structure for a large industrial firm. The discussion included the comments that Measures of Manufacturing Performance are likely to be numerous, they may fall into a general structure with local special impacts, clarity of the measure is essential, visibility and acceptance of measures is very helpful to team operation. Participants valued the opportunity to share the development of these measures and anticipated doing this in future applications.

4. Measures Proposed

The data presented below relates to a specific set of Competitive Dimensions and Manufacturing Typology. Sample Measures of Manufacturing Performance, grouped under generic headings and appropriate to the Chains include:

4.1. Product configuration chain

Product Design

Product Specification:
Customer
Quality
Performance
Company constraints
Reliability
Product Costs
Time Scales

Size
Weight
Materials
Packing
Installation
Maintenance
Environment

Product Concept Design:

Customer
Quality
Reliability
Testing
Performance

Product Detail Design:

Customer
Quality'
Testing
Performance

Design Management Activity:

Management of Specification
Periodic Specification Reviews
Practicality of Specification
Target Achievement
Matching Functional Expectations
Timing Plans

Management of Concept Design:

Periodic design reviews
.....
Management of Detail Design;
.....

4.2. Co-development Chain

Manufacturing Development Activity

Manufacturing Process Specification;
Manufacturer
Quality
Testing
Performance
Manufacturing Process Concept Design;
Manufacturer
Quality
Testing
Performance

Manufacturing Process Detail Design;
.....

Sub Component Design activity:

Sub Component Specification;
.....
Sub Component Concept Design;
.....
Sub Component Detail Design;
.....

5. Conclusion

Measures of Manufacturing Performance linked to a company's business goals can be developed by Concurrent Engineering Team Members. A process to develop these Measures has been presented. In application these Measures should then be used by the team to assess their own operational conformance to the company's business objectives.

The scope which Concurrent Engineering teams have needs to be related directly to the Company's business strategy. This can be defined by a simple model.

If the team based, 'learning by doing', Measures driven approach fails it is difficult to restart. For companies new to Concurrent Engineering it is advisable to launch the process on a very simple part of the product development process and a single Enterprise Chain for a modest complexity product. This process needs to be recycled and refined through regular use if it is to become institutionalised in accepted working practice.

The process outlined here can determine the key implementation issues specific to a particular Concurrent Engineering team. This can focus management effort and so quickly realise Concurrent Engineering benefits within the scope determined by the Company's business strategy.

Acknowledgements

Paul Lowenthal and Douglas Maxwell at Cranfield University for their substantial contributions to the content presented.

The European Commission support for the BRITE EURAM, 'AMBITE' Project.

Palie Smart, Dr Fiona Lettice and Dr Steve Evans at Cranfield University for their contribution to the research supporting the process used.

Computervision UK Ltd and the EPSRC, UK, joint sponsors, the FAST CE Project.

References

1. P.J. Sackett, "Manufacturing Strategy Decision Support Tools — Linking Corporate Vision to Measures of Manufacturing Performance in Concurrent Engineering", *Proc. Concurrent Product and Process Design and Development*, Damascus, Oct 1996.
2. S. Evans, F.E. Lettice, P. Smart. "A Faster, Cheaper and Safer Route to CE, *World Class Design to Manufacture*, Vol 2, No 2, pp. 10-16, MCB University Press, ISSN 1352-3074, 1995.
3. S. Johne, P. Snelson *Successful Product Development: Management Practices in American and British Firms*, Oxford: Basil Blackwell, ISBN 0-631-17448-6, 1990.
4. M. Hammer, J. Champy, *Re-engineering the Corporation: A Manifesto for Business Revolution*, Nicholas Breasley Publishing, 1993.
5. J. MacDonald, *Understanding Business Process Re-engineering in a Week*, Holder and Stoughton, 1995.
6. B. Brooks, N. Schofield, "Time to Market: Time Equals Money, but Where does It All Go", *World Class Design to Manufacture*, Vol 2, No.6, pp. 4-10. ISSN 1352-3074, 1995.

7. J.R. Katzenbach, D.K. Smith *The Wisdom of Teams: Creating the High Performance Organisation*, Boston, Massachusetts: Harvard Business School Press, ISBN 0-87574-367-0, 1993.
8. F.E. Lettice, "Concurrent Engineering: A Team-based Approach to Rapid Implementation", PhD Thesis, Cranfield University, The CIM Institute, 1995.
9. V. Newman *The Creative Manager: A Toolbox for Problem Solvers*, Cranfield University, the CIM Institute, 1994.

7

Design for Manufacture (DFM) of Electronic Products

Sammy G. Shina

University of Massachusetts-Lowell, USA

Abstract

The principles of Design for Manufacture (DFM) of Electronic Assembly are not new. Childhood toys such as Tinker Toys, Lincoln Logs and Legos are good examples of DFM as they have the same objectives as modern products: minimum parts types, standard components, the use of parts that snap together, minimize the use of fasteners, no assembly tools required and reduced assembly time and operator skills.

In this Chapter, the principles and origins of DFM will be explored as well as examples of DFM guidelines and case studies of world class products. The Axiomatic Theory of Design will be used to highlight this methodology. These design guidelines were based on common lessons learned while developing electronic products. Many similar checklists are being used in major electronic companies as a repository for the collective wisdom of their successful design engineers.

These design guidelines emphasize the design of electronic products using self locating and aligning parts, built on a suitable base part. The number of parts should be minimized, by using standard parts and integrating functionality and utility. Several features should be used, such as standard and automatic labeling, self diagnosis capability at the lowest level, and using symmetrical and tangle free parts designs.

The IBM Proprinter, which when introduced in the mid-1980's, was the state of the art in DFM, will be discussed as the prime example of DFM product, whose parts design and process development is well integrated, and whose assembly requires no tools or adjustments. A later product, the HP 34401A multimeter will be used to illustrate second generation DFM products.

Keywords: *Design for manufacture, axiomatics, proprinter, quality function deployment, activity based costing.*

1. Introduction

The axiomatic theory of design [1] is a structured approach to implementing a product's design from a set of functional requirements. It is a mathematical approach to design which differentiates the attributes of successful products and demonstrates designs that are not manufacturable. The design process is seen as the development of functional requirements, which then can be mapped into design parameters through a matrix known as the Design Matrix, then into manufacturing process variables. The functional requirements and the design parameters are hierarchical, and should decompose into sub requirements and parameters.

The design function is bound by two types of constraints: Input constraints, from the specifications of the product, and Systems constraints, which are dictated by the environment where the product is used. These constraints act on the design parameters to form the boundary for the implementation of the design into physical parameters.

This approach is quite similar to the Quality Function Deployment — QFD [2] approach, developed in Japan and popularized by the automobile industry. They share the structured concept of functional requirements, yet QFD is implemented earlier in the product lifecycle by focusing on customer inputs. QFD can be used as a guideline to design evolutionary products, where the customer is already familiar with the product functionality and its intended use, and the technology of design has reached a mature stage. Axiomatic design theory could be used in revolutionary products, where the design implementation is in the startup or growth stage. However, both methodologies must incorporate customer requirements, and translate them appropriately into design requirements.

There are only two axioms of design:

1. The Independence Axiom which maintains the independence of Functional Requirements (FR's).

2. The Information Axiom which minimizes the information content of the design. It is a mathematical version of the principle of KISS, (known in the vernacular as "Keep It Simple Stupid").

1.1. The axiomatic corollaries

The axiomatic corollaries are developed from the axiomatic theory of design and they bear strong resemblance to many design guidelines that were developed in companies. The design guidelines that follow in the next section were grouped in the same categories as the axiomatic theory corollaries.

1.1.1. Decoupling of coupled designs: No final assembly adjustments. Self diagnosis capability at lowest level.

1.1.2. Minimize functional requirements (fr's): Subsystem modular design. Build on suitable base and stack/layer assembly. Minimize level and direction of assembly.

1.1.3. Integrate physical parts: Minimize number of parts and fasteners. Apply labels automatically.

1.1.4. Standardization: Standardization of fasteners, components, materials, concentrics and finishes. Use modular and multifunctional parts.

1.1.5. Symmetry: Use symmetrical parts, whenever possible. Exaggerate unsymmetrical parts.

1.1.6. Largest tolerance: Use self locating features to eliminate tools and fixtures. Accommodate for errors, uncertainties, maximize compliance. Limit flexible items.

2. The Design Guidelines

The design guidelines presented below are a collection of guidelines specific for electronic products. These guidelines can be adopted in part or whole for different electronic products.

2.1. Decoupling of coupled designs

2.1.1. No final assembly adjustments: Assembly of modules at final assembly with no adjustment to achieve system functions. This will reduce assembly cost, enhance automation and facilitate maintenance and refurbishment

Many electronic products are eliminating the need for final assembly adjustment. This is best done by a more robust design with controlled variability that would not require adjustments. Other methods include making the adjustment at the subassembly level, such as the alignment of Cathode Ray Tubes (CRT's) prior to final assembly, or by having the customer perform the final assembly adjustments, such as the print head tension mechanism for the IBM Proprinter.

2.1.2. Self-diagnosis capability at lowest level: Provide capability to aid manufacturing in troubleshooting and self diagnosis of machine problems, and to identify in the field parts or assemblies that have worn, drifted or malfunctioned.

Examples of self diagnosis are the use of microprocessors for self diagnosis of the product each time it is turned on; the use of wear indicators, either mechanical or optical, to indicate time to replace worn parts, and the use of periodic monitoring of vital product subsystems to indicate problem areas. These techniques have been used widely in the electronic industry, with varying degrees of effectiveness.

One of the important options to new product developers is the level of problem identification for self diagnosis. There have been many attempts to isolate problems at the component level, most of which were not successful, because the cost of extra circuitry and logic for component fault isolation far outweighs the benefits.

Self diagnosis at the PCB assembly level is the most common method, with individual PCB's having indicators such as Light Emitting Diodes (LED's) monitoring the PCB's functional status.

Most electronic self diagnosis is activated by resident software on the PCB's microprocessor memory, or could be phoned in from a remote location, such as a regional or national service center. It is important that any diagnosis software for fault isolation be common for customers as well as the factory, to reduce the investment of new test software.

2.2. Minimize functional requirements

2.2.1. Subsystems modular design: A module is a discrete and self contained assembly with a defined set of inputs on its performance. Components should be grouped as discrete modules used for similar products in the same family. Products share the same power supplies, fans, front panels, housings and hardware.

Subassemble for use in final assembly. Multifunctional parts can reduce assembly complexity.

Typically it is more efficient to use the minimum level of assemblies. The ideal product structure is the one where all components go into subassemblies, which then plug into final assembly. This structure eliminates the need to make interim scheduling of assembly levels and line fabrication items, and enhances the use of Just In Time (JIT) production[3]

A good partitioning of electronic products into functional and modular subassembly makes it easier to test the modules in process, and enhance the turn on percentage at final test.

2.2.2. Build on suitable base and stack assembly: Orient in horizontal plain. Provide stable base position and support.

Place bottom part or base onto assembly fixturing.

Establish part position with guides or aids such as pins, recesses or insets. Stack parts vertically.

Assemble from above or divide into subassemblies.

Take advantage of gravity. Avoid rotating or orienting or regripping parts. If fasteners must be used, apply & orient vertically.

Use parts which are self fixturing and aligning. Use pick and place operations whenever possible.

Allow for ease of insertion and removal, but consider serviceability.

The ideal electronic product does not require any tools or special gadgets to assemble. Parts should drop in, self align and snap together. It is important that as the assembly of the parts and sub assemblies progresses, there is adequate direct access for production operators or service personnel for making adjustments, replacing or servicing subassemblies.

2.2.3. Minimize level and direction of assembly: Generate only those subassembly drawings that are either required as field spares or replacement by the manufacturing process. This results in reduced material handling and inventory control. Ideally assemble all parts in one direction: *down*. Unit not subjected to rotation and inertial loads during assembly.

Avoid multi motion insertion. Facilitate assembly by providing chamfers or tapers which will help to guide and position parts correctly.

The use of minimal directions of assembly facilitates the future automation of the assembly process. Since the pick and place motions required are much simpler and could be performed by the less complex robots. For manual operations, one directional assembly facilitates tasks by using only one hand to manipulate each new part.

Using the minimum amount of assembly levels and motions lessens the number of documents required to support the assembly process. When parts fit together using guides and chamfers, the need for assembly tools, diagrams and instructions to operators would be eliminated. This reduces the number of defects, as there is only one way to adequately assemble the product.

2.3. Integrate physical parts

2.3.1. Minimize number of parts: Eliminate excess parts by applying three criteria [4]:

1. Must the part move relative to others parts in performing its function?
2. Must the part be made of different material for strength or insulation?
3. Must the part be disassembled from the rest of the product for servicing or replacement?

Use value analysis tools to simplify designs:

1. Identify necessary functions performed by each part.
2. Find the most economical way to achieve function.
3. Use checklist for parts design simplification.

Brainstorm and identify designs that require less parts, integrate functionality by using plastics, sintered materials or powder metallurgy. Choose the design for the best assembly method consisting of base plus vertical stacking.

The number of parts is directly proportional to the cost of the product, in terms of direct purchasing costs. Support costs such as purchasing and inventory of parts, supplier qualifications, warranty and reliability estimates increase proportionally with the number of part numbers. Eliminating parts is one of the most important methods of reducing electronic product cost.

The costs of new parts is usually not identified to the design engineer. They include the cost of setting up the part, selection of the suppliers, qualification of

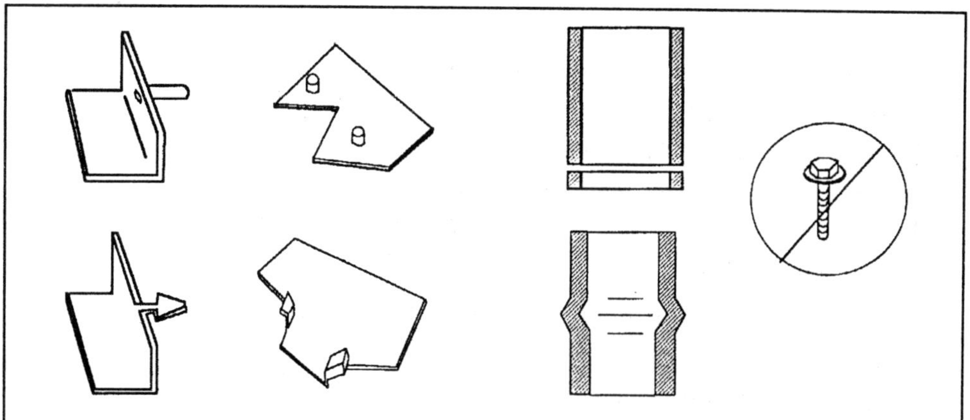

Fig. 7.1: Examples of Integrating Parts

the part and the supplier, the cost of purchasing and keeping adequate inventory, the risks of obsolescence, and the reliability ratings. Every additional part contributes to the increase of Mean Time Between Failures (MTBF) of the product [5], and the setup of a new part could cost in excess of $5,000.

Examples of integrating parts are given in Fig. 7.1. These examples show that extra parts could be eliminated using designs that would not only eliminate parts, but reduce assembly operation. As a result of these attempts at reducing parts, the suppliers and fabrication shops of electronic companies have been asked to make much more complex parts. The designers have to be careful when integrating new parts, because reducing assembly time can inversely affect the cost of fabricated parts.

2.3.2. Part design analysis checklist

1. What is the purpose of the part?
2. What is its location in assembly and use?
3. Can another part be substituted for it?
4. Can it be combined with another part?
5. Can you do without it?
6. Can you change the material?
7. Can you make it symmetrical?
8. It is available at a lower cost?
9. Is it quickly assembled or disassembled?

10. What does the competition do?
11. Is it safe to handle (no sharp edges)?
12. Is the assembly process compatible?
13. Can you use other operation sequence?
14. Are there interactions with other parts?
15. Is it used for long? Does it wear out?
16. Can it be repaired easily?
17. How does it work in field environment?
18. Can it be grasped easily?
19. Can it be distinguished easily?
20. Does it have the same finish, tolerance and material as the rest of the parts?

There are no rigorous guidelines for product design efficiency that can be applied across all products. The following checklist is intended to keep the part designers focused on reducing the number of parts, and if not able to do so; to integrate parts, make them more assembly efficient and compatible with the current manufacturing process. The checklist is intended as a self motivating guideline for development engineers to design more efficient parts and products.

2.3.3. Design for lowest cost fastening: Whenever possible, use snap fits, press fits, slot, tabs, screws, adhesives and welds in this order.

Snap fits: Advantages are tooling costs, tight tolerances, disassembly. However. disadvantages are low cost and the need to use Computer Aided Design (CAD) support packages.

Press fits: Can lose force over time (creep). Requires tighter molding tolerance than snap fit, though less tooling costs.

Slot/tab fits: Use two interlocking parts such as slot and tab, or bent tab.

Screws: If they must be used, then:

1. Minimize numbers and types used.
2. Use common head size, make room for drivers.
3. Orient for vertical insertion, allow space for automatic tools
4. Avoid flat washers, integrate with lock washers.

5. Use self tapping screws.

Adhesives and welds: They simplify design, but cause high assembly cost and difficulty of repair.

The elimination of screws and other fasteners is important in order to reduce the number of components, and therefore the time of assembly and cost of new products. However one important consequence is the increasing difficulty of disassembly of electronic products when snap fits are used. Sometimes this has led to using special tooling for disassembly in order to reduce possible damage to the products. New product designers should carefully balance the two issues.

The use of adhesives and welds is appropriate when there is minimum space available for assembly, or hermetic sealing is required. The setting of parameters for adhesives or welds is important in achieving proper assembly. For adhesives, the parameters are the proper amount of adhesive to apply, the cleaning of parts before and after the adhesion operation and the type of material to use. For welding, the setting of the weld equipment in terms of electric current level, dwell time and pressure are important. In both cases, the successful use of Design of Experiments and similar methods [6, 7] has been helpful in optimizing the manufacturing process.

*2.3.4. **Apply labels automatically:*** Mold, paint, stamp or engrave as part of assembly process. Avoid silk screen and detached metal labels. Use multi-purpose labels and combine information in one label. Program for serial markings and identification. Use bar codes or laser marking. Bar codes can be used for tracking and programming assembly.

The application of labels on the product is an important issue for registering the product through serial and model numbers for future warranty and repair history. Managing the labeling issue is critical, as label generation and application can be time consuming in terms of new parts creation and its associated costs of documentation, purchasing, inventory and storage. An additional benefit to applying automatic or bar code labels is that they can be used to set automatic routing and process parameters during the manufacturing of the product.

*2.3.5 **Cables:*** Avoid cables because they are difficult to route, connect and may require hardware. Use prewired fans or direct connect. Cables cause low reliability because they contain many parts, pins and wires. If cables must be used, then key the connectors, use positive latch mechanisms and lock with snap feedback. Route away from sharp edges, bends or pinching. Allow sufficient space to connect, and to service unit. Use dummy plug to safeguard connector during assembly.

Cables are one of the hidden elements contributing to poor quality in new products. The amount of components and assembly operations involved are large, leading to increased probability of defect creation. In many cases, final electronic testing of products will not cut out poor cable connections, which might eventually fail in the field. Many analysis of product defects in the field will show that this low technology problem is the cause of failures of many high technology electronic products. Connectivity could be accomplished by using flexible Printed Circuit Boards (PCB's), or by mounting outside connectors (front and rear) directly into the PCB's.

2.4. Standardization

Implementing a standardization program of fasteners, components, materials, concentrics and finishes means commitment to a standard parts program. A goal should be 90 per cent of parts used in a new design are *standard.* In addition, the reduction of setup of new parts can be substantial, as much as $5000 per part.

2.4.1. Use modular and multifunctional parts: Group components in self contained modules for similar products in same family. Modular parts reduce assembly time and improve inventory costs. Multifunctional parts combine several functions into one part at the assembly level and reduce complexity.

One of the main problems in controlling the number of standard parts is the lack of knowledge of designers as to the existence of parts of identical or similar functions in the company's data base. Although there are many part numbering systems used to identify common types of components and parts, most are inadequate. For example, it is much easier for a designer to create, specify and draw a new spacer bar than to go through many lists of existing product and part data bases to find out if a similar part is already used in the company.

The new concepts of Group Technology [8] help designers to increase the use of standard parts. There are many computer based systems that will retrieve the existing parts from the data base and present CAD drawings of the parts to designers. These systems use specialized data compression and information query and retrieval techniques to reduce the amount of time and computer resources necessary to electronically identify and retrieve parts from the data base for design engineers. These systems could be stand alone, or integrated into the CAE/CAD/CAM architecture of the company. They are quite expensive, but at a $5,000 cost of implementing a new part through its lifecycle, the rate of return on group technology systems makes investing in them seem reasonable in order to reduce overall development costs.

One of the interesting measures of DFM is setting an aggressive goal for new designs to use a specified number such as 90 per cent of existing and standard parts. This target seems unattainable, especially since technology is continuously providing updated electronic components. Upon close examination, many components of electronic products use standard basic parts such as resistors, capacitors, spacers, existing IC logic families components. Therefore the goal of using existing parts in 90 per cent of each new design is tenable. The advantages of such a plan is to significantly lower new component set ups and increase the quality of the new products. Older parts generate less defects, since their processes are well documented through previous use.

2.5. Symmetry

2.5.1. Use symmetrical parts, whenever possible: Easily handled parts promotes assembly efficiency, symmetrical parts minimize handling, making small changes can result in perfect symmetry.

2.5.2. Exaggerate asymmetrical parts: If parts are asymmetrical, they should have distinct polar properties by geometry or weight, so they can be separated, oriented and fed easily either manually or by automatic methods. Avoid nesting or tangling of parts. Change part designs to eliminate by using ribs, slots, close open spring ends, increasing dimensional thickness or angles or changing hole dimensions.

It is easier for production operators and automatic assembly equipment to grasp symmetrical parts for presentation to the next assembly operation. Therefore, the use of symmetrical parts whenever possible, or the addition of features to parts to make them one axis, two axis or fully symmetrical, is recommended. In many cases, when the part is stamped out of sheet metal or molded by plastic injection, the extra cost of making the part symmetrical by adding extra holes or features is relatively low. The only adverse effect on the development cycle is the increased length of time it takes to add these features to the drawing and the subsequent machining of plastic molds. Examples are given in Fig. 7.2.

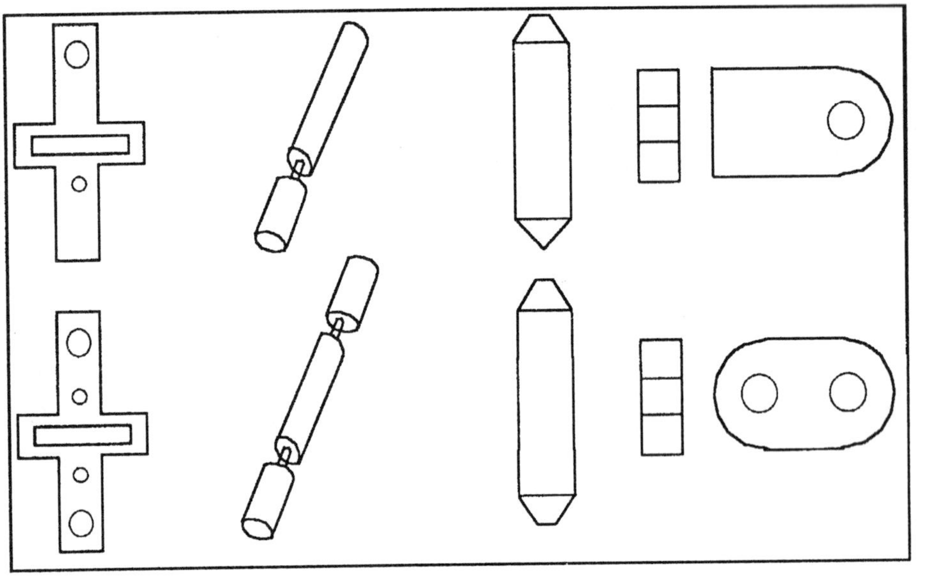

Fig. 7.2: Examples of adding symmetry

Another element in the reduction of the grasping time is the elimination of nesting or tangling of parts. The addition of design features to reduce tangling and nesting, such as closing open spring ends and washers and altering some of the dimension and features of parts that cause nesting, can very easily be achieved in the design stage at a minimum cost to the development cycle, and produce lower cost assemblies for new products. Examples are given in Fig. 7.3.

When symmetry cannot be achieved readily, or the cost of making the part symmetrical is too prohibitive, the asymmetry of the part should be exaggerated to make grasping of the part by manual or automatic means much easier. Examples of increasing asymmetrical designs are given in Fig. 7.4.

Another condition for using asymmetry is the exaggeration of a hidden feature that makes identifying the part orientation prior to grasping easier. Examples of such design features could be the addition of an underpin, or the addition of features that might identify a particular surface or position, such as adding a flat surface, a pin or a shoulder to a particular side. Examples of increasing asymmetry to orient hidden features are given in Fig. 7.5.

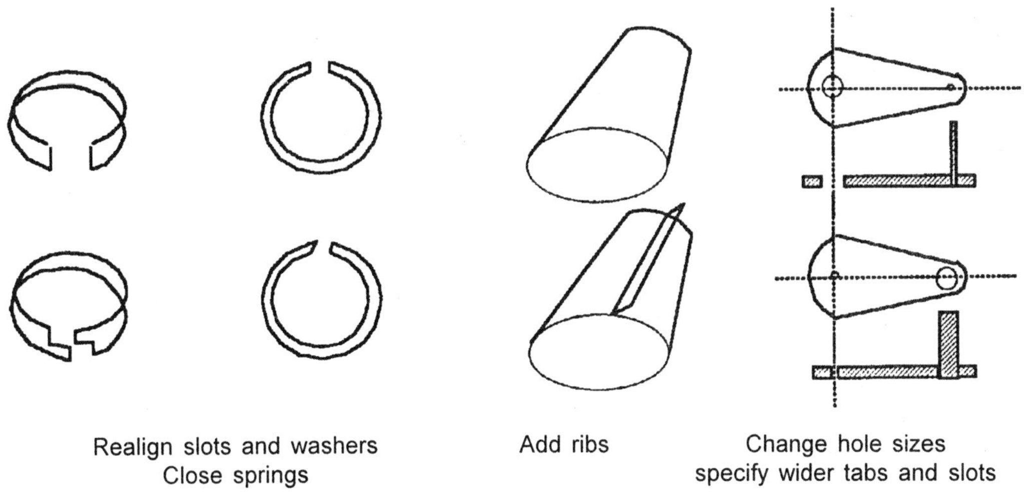

Fig. 7.3: Increasing part asymmetry

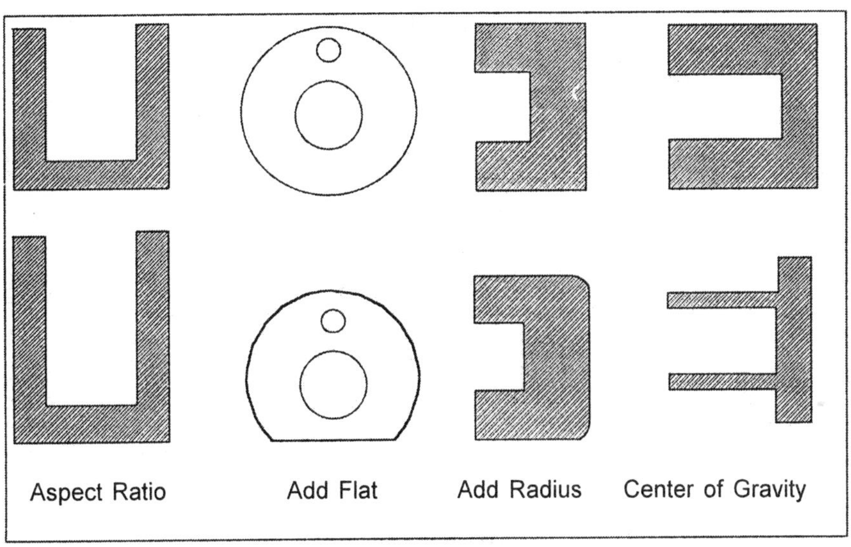

Fig. 7.4: Increasing part asymmetry

2.6. Largest tolerance

2.6.1. Self-locating features: Assembly of parts or modules to a precise location that eliminates the need for orientation or assembly adjustment. Examples include tab in slots, cutouts, d-shape holes, hard steps, molded in locators, guidepins, dimples, perforations. Design a rigid part to act as "base" to which other parts are added to reduce tolerance stackup.

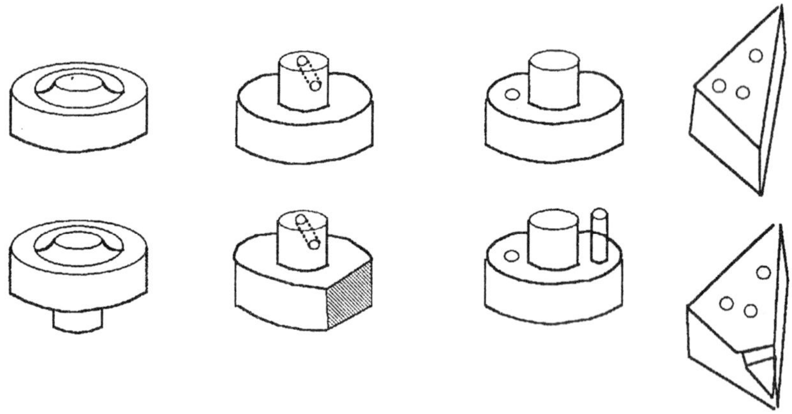

Fig. 7.5: Increase asymmetry to orient hidden features

The design tolerance of parts should include self locating features with the widest possible tolerance to help in assembling the parts. The features mentioned above are some of the techniques that can be used to guide parts into final assembly locations, with one base part used to stack the other parts onto it.

2.6.2. Accommodate errors, maximize compliance: Compliance, the accommodation of manufacturing error or uncertainty, should be designed into a product to avoid excessive assembly force, rework and scrap. Use only quality and therefore consistent parts and specify adequate tolerances on all part drawings. Accommodate for mechanical wear and use compliance techniques as well as guide features: chamfers, ramps and lead ins.

The relationship of the manufacturing tolerance to the part specification limits, called the Process Capability Index [9]. There should be a common goal for all engineers. Design engineers could increase the tolerance limits to the maximum that would still allow the proper functioning of the product, and manufacturing engineers should reduce the variability of the manufacturing process by using Statistical Process Control (SPC) and other quality enhancement tools, better equipment and tool replacement and maintenance schedules, and by using Design of Experiments to narrow the process variability. The ratio of their combined efforts is calculated in the Process Capability Index, commonly referred to as Cp.

Examples of self locating and guiding features are given in Fig. 7.6. These are simple design changes that could make the assembly of parts much easier, especially by eliminating the use of special tools or techniques.

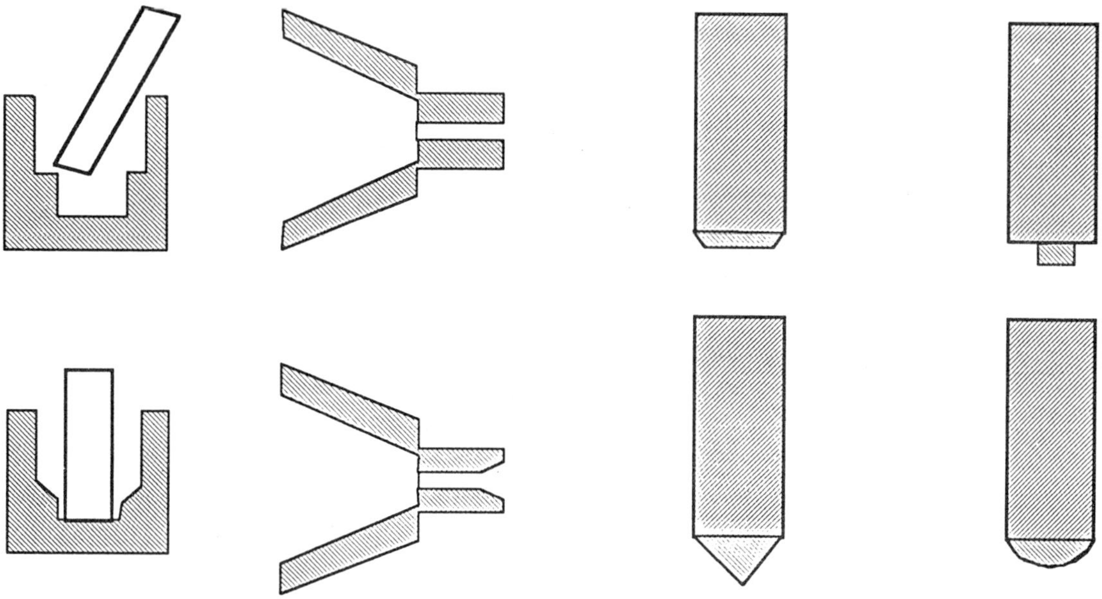

Fig. 7.6: Self locating and guiding features

2.6.3. Limit flexible items: Design parts with safety margins sufficient to prevent bending or collapsing under the force of assembly. Wires, cables and belts are difficult to handle, especially in automated assembly. Components should plug together, where possible. Use gears and shafts to substitute for belt drives.

Flexible items are difficult to grasp, especially using automatic feeders, and therefore should be substituted or replaced by different designs whenever possible. Examples are the use of drive shafts instead of belts and the use of flexible spacer materials instead of soft grommets to fit a large tolerance dimension.

3. DFM Case Studies

3.1. DFM case study 1: The IBM proprinter

The IBM proprinter is considered a prime example of an electronic product that was designed for flexible automated assembly [10]. By focusing on Concurrent Engineering and Design for Manufacturing, IBM has been able to use manufacturing as a strategic weapon to achieve and maintain a market share in the highly competitive personal printer market, dominated by the far east.

The early philosophy of the Proprinter was developed in 1982, when a high level task force of five engineers and managers was formed at IBM to develop the product and the process manufacturing strategy. The design engineering effort consisted of 60 engineers divided into 20 subsystem design teams, each focused on individual subassemblies. Each team was made up with a design engineer, a manufacturing engineer, a moderator and a technology expert, as needed.

The design goals were very simple and the design team developed a logo for the project [Fig. 7.7]. The criteria for design were very simple:

1. Develop a modular design
2. Minimize the total part count
3. All parts to be self aligning, for ease of assembly.

The design review cycle was updated to include mandatory DFM design reviews. Each DFM review took 4-8 hours to complete. A total of 50 design reviews were conducted, and the project took 6 months to complete.

Because of the DFM focus and review process, the design process took longer to be accomplished in the initial phases, but the project benefited in the long run from the increased manufacturability efforts. The manufacturing process was designed

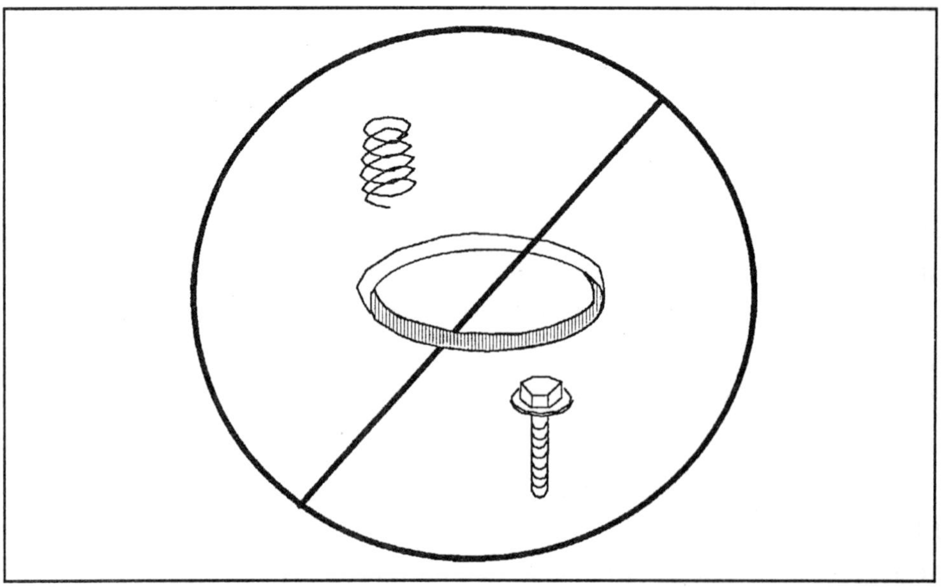

Fig. 7.7: IBM proprinter Logo

concurrently and implemented in a fully robotic plant built specifically for the IBM Proprinter.

The IBM Proprinter represented the state of the art in Design for Assembly, although the goal of full downward assembly was not totally accomplished. The number of parts counts was far lower than competing printers [Fig. 7.8].

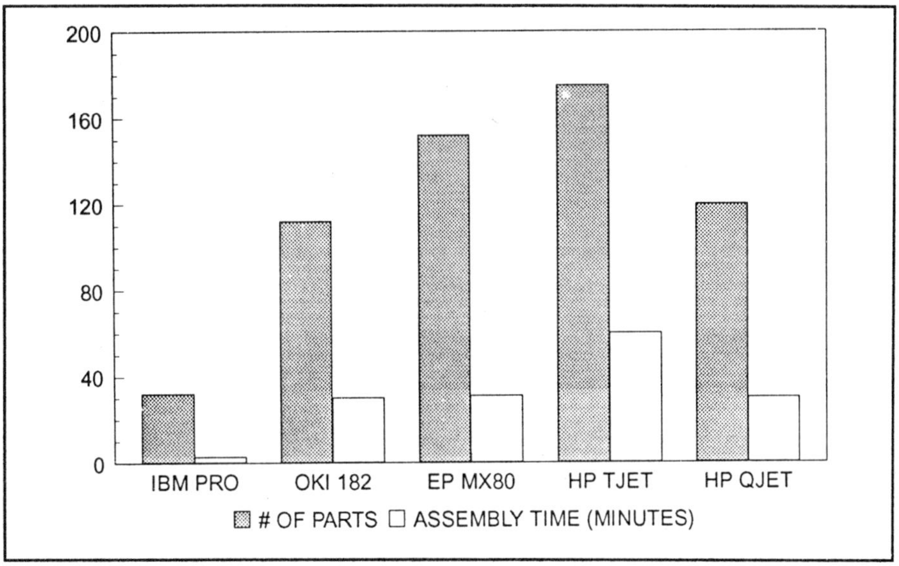

Fig. 7.8: Personal Printers Part Counts

Other principles of the Design for Manufacturing were successfully implemented, including:

1. no fasteners
2. no springs
3. no pulleys
4. no adjustments
5. no excess modules
6. no cables or harnesses
7. no paint
8. no labels
9. no extra parts
10. no multidirectional assembly
11. no location tools or fixtures
12. no external tests

13. no engineering changes (ECNs)
14. no custom builds or options
15. no manual assembly.

Several major companies were so impressed by the proprinter effort that they set about to understand and inform their engineers about the accomplishment and potential benefits of DFM to their products. They include XEROX Corporation, which prepared a report by their Automation Institute on the Proprinter design philosophy, and analyzed each subassembly. Westinghouse Corporation Center for Quality and Productivity prepared a video tape, which was made available to Westinghouse engineers and to other companies, outlining the benefits of Design for Manufacturing, and showing the manual assembly of a proprinter in about 3 minutes, without the use of any tools or fixtures, and with little prior experience.

3.2. DFM case study 2: The HP 34401A multimeter

The $5 billion test and measurement market is characterized by slow growth and increased competition from Europe and the Pacific Rim. Part of HP previous high volumes in this market had resulted from defense related activities, which softened since the demise of the cold war. The digital multimeter market is comprised about $300 million. Products in this mature market range from several hundred to several thousand dollars, depending on performance and capability. The 34401A development challenge was to deliver the performance of $3000-4000 instrument at a $1000 price. By accomplishing this task, HP would maintain its lead and growth in this mature market [11].

3.2.1. Design team formation: Several phases of the design team formation were made rather than an initial large team formation. Initial staffing included a project manager, one mechanical and two electrical development engineers, and one manufacturing engineer. The second phase involved the addition of several more manufacturing engineers and the addition of a manufacturing project manager. The third phase involved the addition of marketing and the co-location of the entire team. Communications were enhanced and barriers were removed. In addition, the team was allowed to challenge the existing financial systems and processes that were in place.

*3.2.2. **Tools and methods:*** The design team decided to use more than just the traditional DFM concepts and tools. The team took training in tools such as QFD, team development, conflict management and personality type analysis. They needed to understand how to handle conflicts arising in meeting product goals. The tools used were Quality Function Deployment (QFD), Activity Based Costing (ABC) and DFM.

I *QFD*

Extensive market research was conducted prior to team collection. Customer visits, focus groups and interviews with internal users of multimeters were conducted. The data were analyzed using QFD concepts. The benefits of QFD in design were as follows [12]:

1. As tool to allow the design team to focus on the voice of the customer and navigate through disagreements.
2. A method of translating the voice of the customer into product specifications and manufacturing requirements. For example, a specific customer objective was 24 hour delivery. This required the design of manufacturing process that can deliver orders to customers within that time period.
3. QFD was used as a common language allowing all functions to optimize the overall design into the business objectives.

II *ABC*

The traditional new product costing techniques was to design the product with customer goals in mind, then calculate costs and price by the accounting department [13]. The 34401A reversed that approach. With the QFD study, the team had a price goal set early in the design process.

ABC was used in the manufacturing floor with 15 cost drivers identified. However it assumed the use of the existing processes and allocations. A more enhanced financial model [14] was needed to characterize the 34401A as the only stand alone product in manufacturing.

Using this enhanced model, design tradeoffs decision were quickly evaluated. Product reliability was enhanced in order to reduce testing and quality costs. New methods were developed for Just In Time (JIT) manufacturing to reduce purchasing and part delivery costs. The team concentrated on selecting high quality materials, components and suppliers to minimize incoming inspection and implement Dock to Stock programs.

III *DFM*

Previously, there has been several effort in HP to use DFM concepts in redesigns of existing products. Improvement and cost reduction averaged in a range of 5-18 per cent. One to three manufacturing engineers were assigned to the design to perform DFM analysis and recommendations.

Every part in the HP34401A was analyzed for DFM. Many modifications were made, especially in the signal input connection scheme, which eliminated the soldering of ten wires. The entire front panel assembles with no screws. The key was significantly reduced parts count, as well as other enhancements, shown in Table 7.1.

3.2.3. Setting and measuring the design process goals: DFM goals for new product development usually take a historical progression in companies that are beginning to consider manufacturability and Concurrent Engineering as part of their competitive strategy.

Table 7.1: HP 34401A DFM Improvements

DFM Metric %	HP 34401A	Previous Generation	Previous Similar Generation
material $	80	100	200
Non material $	55	100	250
Assembly time	37	100	210
Average Repair time	33	100	400
No. of mechanical parts	30	100	190
No. of fasteners	31	100	172
No. of fastener types	8	100	85
No. of connects/disconnects	6	100	120
Final assembly part count	40	100	153
Total parts	68	100	190
Total part #'s	77	100	150
No. of suppliers	70	100	N/A
Inventory days	4	100	100
Throughput	100	100	100
1st Year engineering changes	0	100	58

The first attempt at DFM is the initiation of manufacturing, service and reliability plans that encourage manufacturing and other departments' feedback on new designs. These initial DFM goals are general in nature, and represent a commitment by the project team and their management to consider DFM as part of the design process. The DFM goals are not specific, and are usually "best effort" attempts to decrease manufacturing cost. The review for manufacturability becomes part of the design review process, as well as the review for testability, serviceability and reliability. Formal DFM goals should be set after the company has attempted some projects with DFM goals and experienced initial successes. These can be specific manufacturing targets which are measurable, and are in line with the other goals of the new product. However, the current levels of 'ilities' should be made available, either through existing databases and metrics or through actually measuring current products. These current levels should become the baseline from which achievable new product DFM goals could be targeted. Some of these specific goals could be in the following form:

1. Set minimum design efficiency values, based on design efficiency methodologies [15]. This percentage will be founded on baseline levels obtained from analyzing current designs.
2. Set the percentage of standard parts used in new products. The current percentage should be calculated from existing products, and the new product percentage should be set appropriately. A target of 90 per cent is achievable for new electronic products.
3. Set the product specification limits, based on a target process capability index for new product designs. The process capability index is a good methodology of getting both design and manufacturing engineering to achieve a common goal. A 100 ppm quality level is achievable from a Process Capability Index (Cp) of 1.3, and a six sigma level of 3.4 parts per million is achievable from a Cp of 2.
4. Set the target number of suppliers, part numbers and total parts, based on competitive analysis and current product levels. The reduction of the number of suppliers encourages closer relationship with the remaining suppliers, to improve quality, delivery and material costs. The reduction of part numbers lowers the cost of setting up new parts and inventory costs and increases product reliability. A typical scheme lowers the number of suppliers by a factor of 2 to 3.

5. Set the final product assembly and test times, at a level which is lower than comparable current products. This will encourage the design engineers to use parts that are easy to automate and assemble. Examples of these are modular assemblies, minimum part counts and symmetrical, easy to align parts. Set first pass yields at PCB automatic test Including functional tests) to 95 per cent, and the level of product first turn on at final assembly to 90 per cent.
6. Set the warranty costs of new products, normalized by either defects/K$ or defects per product at a level significantly lower than current products. Set the Mean Time Between Failures (MTBF) similarly. The quality goals of the company should be in line with the competition and their progress. Increasing the quality level by a factor of 2 for every product cycle (three to five years) is aggressive but achievable for the electronic industry.

These goals have the advantage of being measurable at different stages of the development cycle. Any combination of these goals will encourage the design team to use the design guidelines outlined in this chapter. Progress towards these measurable goals should be reviewed at the different milestones of the project. Formalizing the DFM principles in the project development phase will ensure that new products will be designed for manufacture.

4. Conclusions

This paper is intended to act as a model for developing design guidelines for manufacturing and field performance of the electronic products. These goals should be institutionalized in terms of setting very specific and measurable goals, rather than a 'best effort' attempt at implementing these guidelines. The performance of existing products in terms of these goals should be quantified, and act as baseline for setting new product goals. The new product development process should include design reviews for manufacturability and field performance. At that time, progress towards these goals should be quantified.

New product development project teams should focus on these strategies, by setting measurable and attainable goals for the product performance in factory and field. They should be set using current products' performance as the baseline with aggressive but achievable targets.

References

1. N. Suh, *Principles of Design,* Oxford University Press, New York, 1990.
2. J. Hauser and D. Clausing, "The House of Quality", *Harvard Business Review*, May-June, 1988, No. 3., pp. 63-73.
3. R. Hall, *Zero Inventories,* Dow Jones Irwin, Homewood, Illinois, 1983.
4. G. Boothroyd and P. Dewhurst, *Product Design for Assembly,* Boothroyd & Dewhurst Inc., 1991.
5. R. Mann, *Methods for Statistical Analysis of Reliability and Life Data,* John Wiley and Sons, New York, 1974.
6. M. Phadke, *Quality Engineering using Robust Design,* Prentice-Hall, New Jersey, 1989.
7. Taguchi, El Sayed & Hsiang, *Quality Engineering in Production Systems,* McGraw Hill, New York, 1988.
8. D. Bedworth, M. Henderson, and P. Wolfe, *Computer Integrated Design and Manufacturing,* McGraw Hill, New York, 1991
9. H. Mikel, *The Nature of Six Sigma Quality,* Motorola Incorporated Publications, 1987.
10. S. Shina, *Concurrent Engineering and Design for Manufacture,* Van Nostrand Reinhold, New York, 1991.
11. S. Shina, *Successful Implementation of Concurrent Engineering Products and Processes,* Van Nostrand Reinhold, New York, 1994.
12. L. Sullivan, "Quality Function Deployment", *Quality Progress,* Vol. XIX, No. 6, June 1986, pp. 39-50.
13. R. Kaplan, "Accounting Lag: The Obsolescence of the Cost Accounting Systems", *California Management Review,* Vol. XXVIII, Number 2, Winter 1986, pp. 174-199
14. L. Keys, J. Balmer and R. Creswell, "Electronic Manufacturing Process Systems Cost Modeling and Simulation Tools", *IEEE Transactions on Components Hybrids, and Manufacturing Technology,* Vol. CHMT-10, No.3, September 1987, pp. 332-358.
15. C. Poli, M. Graves and R. Gropetti, "Rating Products for Ease of Assembly", *Machine Design,* August 1986, pp. 45-57.

8

Product Realization Process in a Global Environment

Sammy G. Shina
University of Massachusetts-Lowell, USA

Abstract

Several recent developments have led to significant changes in the way new products are developed. The emphasis on core competency has resulted in having many companies discard their manufacturing capability, and hence becoming dependent on outside suppliers for manufacturing capability. At the same time, the cost of acquiring expensive modern manufacturing equipment has become prohibitive, and the pace of new manufacturing technology has quickened, making product companies reluctant to invest in their manufacturing plants, lest they become obsolete in a short time. In addition, the advent of global competition for quality and cost has increased the need for new product design teams to incorporate early manufacturing feedback into the design of the products.

The confluence of these issues have led to a set of unique problems and trends in modern industry. Manufacturing has become a worldwide commodity through the growth of contract manufacturing companies, which supply product companies with manufacturing expertise and capability. Their relationships with new product design teams is much more formal and subject to a contractual bidding process, without the benefits of detailed designs that can be bid on. The relationship is different than the traditional development methods of using internal manufacturing expertise to supply informal feedback on designs and the selection of the appropriate manufacturing processes.

This chapter addresses the conflicting issues raised above by identifying the changes required to the traditional methods of new product development and proposing a set of tools and metrics to address issues of manufacturing supplier selection, communications, cost, quality and capability in the new product development cycle.

Methodologies and tools discussed in this paper include the modification of the product development process to include the contractors' role in the timely execution of the project plans, the necessary identification of cost and quality at each manufacturing technology as well as volume levels, and the clear understanding of the tradeoffs involved in the design and manufacturing process selection. In addition, the paper will explore the issues of reduced manufacturing expertise within the parent company.

As manufacturing becomes a world wide commodity, a good understanding of these issues is very important to the future survival of the manufacturing contracting enterprise. Contract manufacturers need to balance their investments in maintaining the technological edge in the manufacturing process, successfully bidding on their customers' new products and clearly identifying their capabilities and levels of capacity, costs and quality without the risk of exposing their future strategy.

Keywords: *Product realization, subcontracting, teams, concurrent engineering, suppliers.*

1. Introduction

The product realization process has undergone several changes with the advent of concurrent engineering [1]. The change from a serial process of product development to a more parallel process has resulted in the need for new paradigms in product development.

Traditional product development required a top down control of the organizational activities of product creation [2]. Very formal organizational structures were developed and managed with a phase review process. The new product creation enterprise was managed in matrix projects with managers directing the activities of the project engineers drawn from functional and discipline centered departments, hence to be called functional silos. Plans and milestones had to be completed at the end of each phase of product development, and were subject to several levels of management reviews. After each review, the project was allowed to proceed and be funded until the next review. A general view of the process is given in Fig. 8.1.

The advent of concurrent engineering with its emphasis on quick new product realization, and the need for lower costs and higher quality has resulted in a shift towards shorter and less frequent milestones. In addition, the technology and the

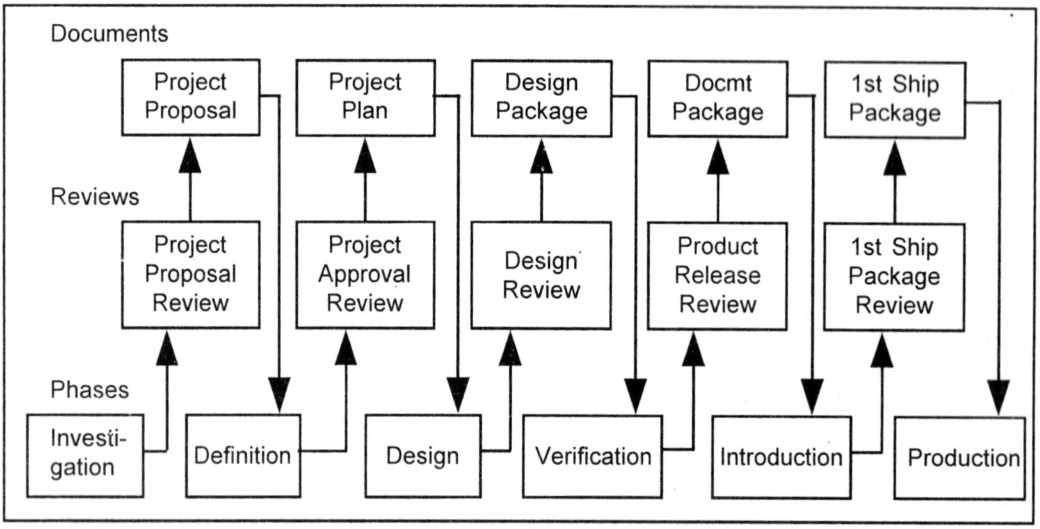

Fig. 8.1: General product development process

marketplace in certain industrial segments are moving much faster than before. An example would be the new product development process at Chipcom Corporation, a maker of computer networking equipment [3]. In this instance, all of the management review processes are performed early in the product realization process, and the development part of the process doesn't require any review [Fig. 8.2].

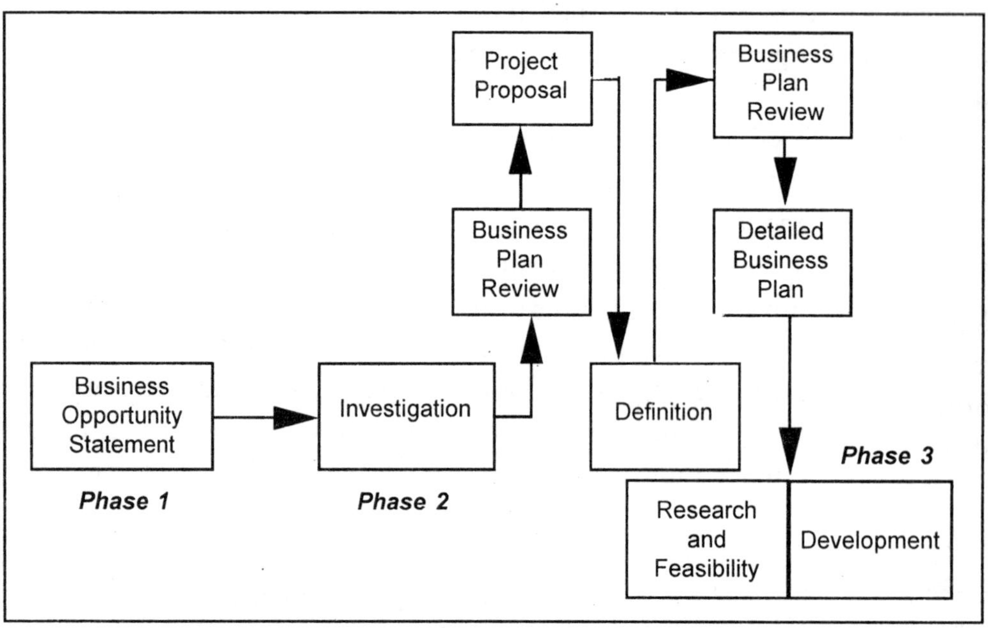

Fig. 8.2: New product development process at chipcom corporation

All of these changes have resulted in different types of organizational structures, centered on team processes. These teams might have a set of skills focused for different types of product realization. A review of these product types and organizations is given next.

1.1. New product types

There are three types of new products being created in today's global competitive environment:

1.1.1. Breakthrough products: These are technology based or core products, which are driven by basic research in the national or major corporate laboratories on new materials or technologies. The technology spawns product ideas which are brought over to the development organization through a process of *advance development,* where the product feasibility is determined both at the design and manufacturing stages, in a timeline that is usually 3-4 years before actual commercial production. This phase is outside of the tight new product development schedule (3-18 months), but has a definite set of requirements, budgets and timing goals to be met. The products are then scheduled for *development* through the product/project management process.

1.1.2. Follow on products: These are new products within the existing product families, which are introduced by industrial companies depending on the price/ performance characteristic of the marketplace. They are driven by changes in customer expectation, competition, technology, market development and opportunity. These products are defined internally by a combination of inputs from sales, product management and the line managers. They normally go through a regular development schedule with minimum interface to advance development or research laboratories. They can take the form of a new lower cost family of products, a new platform or architecture, or a new generation product that is using existing or modified technology.

1.1.3. Modified products: These are enhancements on existing products which are made essentially for cost reduction or specific customer inputs or options. They are very simple in nature and require little engineering effort. The modified products are usually handled by specially assigned departments. They sometimes require a thorough knowledge of the manufacturing process as well as the technology of the product and the material choices involved. In addition, there is the advantage of shielding the development engineers from current production problems and modified products. It has been estimated in some US companies that as much as 50 per cent of the development engineer's time is spent on handling current production problems. This could adversely affect the new product schedule.

Of the three types of products, the breakthrough products have the largest impact on the long term financial health of the company, as well as the greatest risk. The experience with breakthrough products at Hewlett Packard is typical: In the 1970's, the hand held calculator business was 1/3 of the company's sales and profits, which disappeared quickly as the competition reacted. In the 1980's the laser printer product family, which was originally developed by 3 engineers, made more money for the company than the thousands of engineers in the computer business [4]. The comparison of the two major product types are shown in Table 8.1.

Table 8.1: Two Major Product Types

Breakthrough Products	***Follow On Products***
- Complete development process Research - required advanced development-dev.	Mostly development phase
- Long total development cycle (3-4 years)	Short Cycle (3-18 months)
- Large impact on profits (home run)	Competitive positioning and market share protection (cash cow)
- Technology and innovation driven	Cost and market driven
- Thrives in uncoordinated processes (skunkworks)	Requires a systemic process
- Many competing designs (high development risks)	Dominant or proven design (risks are smaller)

The selection of the company product strategy is critical to its long term survival. The correct mix of product types and the timing of product introductions depend on many factors, including the maturity of the marketplace, the state of the competition, the customer trends and the state of the art and technology.

Clearly, the impact of new products is very critical, as indicated by typical vintage charts at different companies. In Northern Telecom, 70 per cent of the total revenues of the company come from products introduced during the last four years

[5]. The correct risk versus reward ratio in the new product creation process is what ultimately determines the future success of the company.

2. New Organizational Structures

For successful new product realization, technology and market inputs can be determined best by practitioners of both crafts. The inputs from marketing and sales organizations, the research laboratories, the advance development group and the current development organization should be evaluated and a collective decision reached for the timing of the next product rollout. A risk benefit analysis should be made of the tradeoffs between rushing a new technology or idea to market versus properly investigating the development and manufacturing problems [6].

Properly performing the traditional marketing functions in its entirety is critical. These activities include the following:

Strategic Market Analysis
Competitive Analysis
Product Planing and Positioning
Product Business Plans
Marketing Communications
Market and customer surveys.

2.1. Project management models

The project management model is directly connected to the organizational structure. Matrix organization tends to operate in *Management directed projects.*

In this model, the emphasis is on negotiating the project requirements by managers of the functions required to meet the project goals. The project is schedule driven, and the decisions are made by managers and acted through instructions to workers. Alternatives are left to the responsible manager to make a 'yes' or 'no' decision on meeting the project milestones. Concurrent engineering is best suited for *Team directed projects.*

In this model, the emphasis is on collective decision making. There is a core project team, which manages all project activities, and that is supported by sub teams of the different functions involved. The team members are the individual workers who are performing the specified tasks. The project manager is the *driver* of the project, making sure the schedule is on time and within budget. There is a strong technical component to this project management. Decisions made by the project manager are based on both technical and business evaluation of the project conditions. Tradeoffs are discussed collectively and decided upon to maintain the overall goals. These tradeoffs include project scope, resources, and schedule. The differences between the two types of project management is shown in Table 8.2.

Table 8.2: Project management styles

Management directed	***Team directed***
Project manager as *Scheduler*	Project manager is *Product Champion*
Workers operate many projects	Workers assigned to one project
Tasks negotiated by Managers	Team has a common vision
Long communication loops	Direct communication loops
Managers delegate responsibility	Workers agree on commitments
Workers shielded from other functions	They are exposed to total organization

This emphasis on new product realization has resulted in many organizations shifting to the team structure. The evolution to team structure from traditional project management organization has evolved into four distinct types of project management; which can be summarized into the following characteristics: (Fig. 8.3).

*2.1.1. **Functional silos:*** In these organizations, each discipline of engineering design activity such as mechanical, electrical or software engineering is collected under

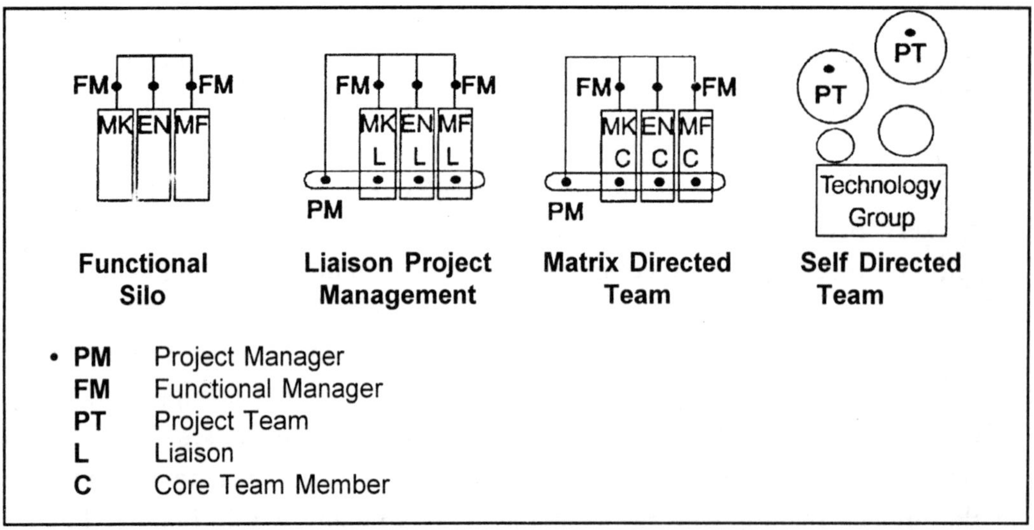

Fig. 8.3: Types of project management

an organizational function or department, and managed by a discipline specialist. In typical technical organizations, knowledge increases exponentially, and segregated functional organization tend to grow around discipline specialists. The advantages are that discipline resources and knowledge can be managed efficiently. Engineers of the same skill set can be trained and compensated easily. In addition, technology advances in the discipline can be monitored and exploited properly. Same skill engineers learn from each other.

Disadvantages of this discipline of specialist organizations are that specialization creates its own language and knowledge barriers between disciplines. There is a lack of breadth knowledge in competing technologies, as well as potential for competing on resources and power within the organization. There is always the danger of funding the organization long after the obsolescence of its mission.

The functional organizations can perform the task of advance development in new product realization. This would entail taking a new technology or basic research from the laboratory and making it ready for development and manufacturing. Functions would include finding applications for the technology into new products, including interfacing and control of the technology and determining manufacturing process requirements and design for manufacturing constraints.

*2.1.2. **Liaison project management:*** In this type of organization, a project manager is appointed to manage the different design and development functions through a liaison in each department. The liaison would provide functional expertise to the project as needed. The project managers maintain the budget and the project plan, and the liaisons help them in maintaining schedule through communications with the engineers from the different departments. This type of organization is best suited for modified new products and enhancements, because the knowledge base required to develop the product is scattered throughout the company, and the project does not have the complexity or critical mass needed to justify the assembly of full time members into a design team.

*2.1.3. **Matrix directed teams:*** This is the most common project management type organization. The project managers coexist with the discipline managers. They have full accountability of the project, including financial as well as technical responsibility. Individual engineers report directly to the project manager on product issues, schedules and expenditures. They report to their discipline managers on administration issues such as compensation, training, and general discipline problem solving. They work exclusively on the project at hand, which is not always possible. Some might work part time or full time during some of the phases of the project. This type of organization is best suited for follow on products, platforms or new architectures because of the importance of the project to the company strategy and its development complexity, which requires the assembly of full time members into a design team.

2.1.4. Self directed teams: In this model, this is the ultimate maturing of new product realization. In this model, product realization teams function as separate businesses with their own goals and operations. They would coexist with basic research and technology development groups. As each team finishes their project, they would disband and join new teams that are forming for new products.

The self directed teams have to be truly multi disciplinary, as they do not have a discipline organization to borrow part time resources during the operation of the project. Decision making resides within the team, with very little input from the management.

Disadvantages of self directed teams could be the focus on short term results, rather than investing in new technology. In addition, the integration of self directed teams within the organization might be difficult, since they will be competing for resources.

3. Concurrent Engineering and Product Realization

In order to create a concurrent engineering environment within the company, there should be a move *away* from the function based organization, towards self directed teams reinforcing the use of a standard model for efficient and specialized use of resources. This model is a good one for managing large and complex set of products and systems. In the current conditions of worldwide competition, the smaller more efficient organizations are the ones that are nimble and fast reacting to the market. They are successful because of their focus on their business unit products, and can make fast decisions by micro managing a smaller organization than by macro managing a large business entity.

Implementing concurrent engineering implies the understanding and valuation of several risks to product realization. These risks are generated by the desire to shorten product development cycle through reduction or elimination of project phases and milestones, as well as understanding the interface between the different stages of product realization: from concept to development then into manufacturing.

The risks can be divided into two categories, those of market risk, when the new product does not meet customer expectations in terms of functionality or features, and a technical risk that the design cannot be manufactured properly by current production technology. Usually, these risks have been solved by the use of specific tools. Quality Function Deployment, QFD [7] has been recognized as a good tool to bridge customer inputs into the product realization process. Design for Manufacture, DFM [8], Design for Quality, DFQ [9], and Design for Profit [10] have been recognized as good metrics for evaluating designs very early in the concept stage. Tools such as technical cost modeling [11], robust design [12] and six sigma [13] have also been used successfully by many companies to bridge the development to manufacturing risks in terms of estimating cost and quality.

An important element of the successful use of concurrent engineering in new product realization is the use of communication tools for achieving quick and correct team decision. Since there is a lack of many phases and milestones in concurrent engineering, design decisions have to be made correctly and early in the product creation cycle. Communication can be made easier through the use of regular team meetings and short periodic report by team member to update their colleagues, as well as the management. An example of such a report in shown in Fig. 8.4.

In this monthly report shown, each member updates their team to the extent of meeting their previous month's commitments and their planned activities for

Project________	Manager________	Date________
Previous Month Goals:		**Current Month Goals:**
Complete Layout Rev #2	✓	Release Prototype
Complete Material List	✓	Purchase Pre-production Material
Schedule Design Review	→	Schedule Design Review
Accomplishments		**Decisions**
MFG Efficiency Score > 50%		Build prototype outside
Previous Concerns		**New Concerns**
		Memory IC's obsolete/'96

Fig. 8.4: Periodic team member report

the next period. In addition, any accomplishments, decisions or concerns can also be noted. In the case of concerns, they will stay documented on the periodic reports until they have been addressed by the team. The update is limited to a maximum of five minutes.

3.1. Sub-contracting and the intellectual capital of the enterprise

The trend towards subcontracting parts of the product realization components or outsourcing have increased in recent years. Starting with manufacturing capability, and extending recently to contracting product development. This is due to the fact that companies are giving attention to their core competency: What is the distinguishing technology that clearly identifies their core business?

The advantages of contracting or outsourcing are many: The enterprise does not have to keep abreast of non core manufacturing or development technologies, saving engineering resources, capital equipment and large payrolls. The enterprise can easily expand and contract due to business conditions and product introductions, without the burden of hiring or firing, and the enterprise is free to seek the lowest cost contractor versus being shackled by an inefficient in-house organization.

Outsourcing can take from in many different directions depending on the amount of intellectual property deemed necessary to the continued growth of the company. Relationship with supplier(s)/partner(s) can be developed as the trend for more outsourcing continues [14]. These contractors are usually called supply chains. Examples of an outsourcing continuum are:

1. Develop new products based on the current in house design, development and manufacturing model currently used in the company.
2. Develop new products with active participation of the in house design and development teams, but outsourcing the manufacturing contribution to the supply chains.
3. Develop new products with active participation of the in house design, but outsource the development and manufacturing contributions with the help of the supply chains.
4. Develop new products with active participation of the in house marketing and conceptual design teams towards fixing the specifications of new products, and outsource the design, manufacturing contributions to the supply chains.

As each outsourcing scenario is embraced by the enterprise, their is no need to maintain parallel inhouse organizations. For example, as more manufacturing is outsourced, there should be a comparable reduction in the manufacturing staffing and expertise within the company. Manufacturing knowledge should be substituted by systems for measuring Design for Manufacturing (DFM) efficiency.

3.2. The supply chain axioms

An important issue is the protection of the company's intellectual capital in order to determine the proper amount of outsourcing. This protection can be in the form of either patenting current technology, or in the proper understanding of the system approach to designing its products.

This systems approach helps in properly decomposing the new product system in to components and specification that can be easily outsourced in design and manufacturing.

The issues in outsourcing can be summed up in the following axioms:

1. The amount of outsourcing is dependent on the amount of protected intellectual property either in patents or in the systems engineering knowledge of the product realization process. Good systems engineering can lead to partitioning the new product into segments that can be outsourced easily to the supply chains.
2. The interface between the supply chains and the remaining company's core elements is the same as in house capabilities. The supply chains should provide for guides to their manufacturing capabilities and constraints, very early into the product realization process.
3. The selection of the supply chains should occur at the concept stage of the product. The selection and bidding process should be based on historical relationships. Contractors could be initially qualified and then bid their cost model for the design and manufacture of the product.
4. The communication links between the supply chains and the enterprise should be available as easily as the in house accessibility. This element has become much easier to discern considering the advent of electronic communications and video teleconferencing.

The supply chain qualification process is dependent on industry standards in practicing world class principles in cost, quality and timeliness. Cost should be well quantified through a cost model based on activity based costing [15]. Quality should be quantified in one of the Process capability indices such as six sigma. Timeliness should be measured in terms of turn around time of order and shipment, especially with a manufacturing contractor practicing JIT principles [16]. The supply chain should also supply the company with their technology and equipment acquisition plans.

4. Product Realization Case Study

Mercury Computer Systems, Inc., a producer of high end floating point attached processors, typifies the small company agility, with responsive local subcontractors and procedural innovation conducive to product design and development. This case study refers to the MC860VM, an add on board that utilizes the Intel 40MHZ i860 microprocessor. It is a 16 Mbyte memory subsystem, with a local high speed direct l/o bus [17].

4.1. The product realization process at Mercury Computer

Original research and development is performed by the Advanced Product Planning group (APP) which is a long range technical group chartered with new concepts and technologies. Once a product opportunity is identified, the marketing department takes over through the Product Management (PM) function. PM assumes the coordination between all the other departments and makes sure that the time lines and critical paths are all negotiated and defined. Each contributing department will fill out their portions of the project plan and fold it into the overall product roll out schedules as labeled.

The traditional line between engineering and manufacturing in the development cycle is nonexistent, and was planned in this manner. Engineering is very proficient at developing architectures, circuit designs and solutions for technical problems. They are inherently less interested in performing tasks that require a high level of control and repeatability, which happens to be the very elements that makes a manufacturing organization successful. It is best to dovetail both of those capabilities and strengths together so that the combined result is greater than any individual effort.

The direct and tight coupling between new product development and manufacturing resulted from a discussion that occurred early in the company's history. Manufacturing suggested that the purchasing department, which was comprised of one person at the time, buy all prototype materials and components. Both parties benefited: development received good service and the benefit of purchasing experience with marginal suppliers, and manufacturing got an insight of what parts will be purchased for the next set of products. Since then, there has been a constant evolution and improvement of the new product introduction process. Currently, manufacturing continues to do all the purchasing for prototypes in research and development, as well as perform and support all mechanical design.

Throughout all new product development projects, manufacturing personnel work along with the designers who specify integrated circuits and architecture, and decide with the CAD operators where the parts should go and how best to manage air flow, mechanicals and cooling mechanisms. Issues and tradeoffs in such topics as packaging, manufacturability, testability, time to market, cost of introducing new products, risks, and how to go to ramp to full production and producible quantities as quickly as possible are discussed and agreed upon.

This new product introduction process methodology can be presented from the following functional perspectives (see Fig. 5.7):

1. *Material Acquisition* — including material control, logistics, and acquisition.
2. *Manufacturing Engineering* — including how the product is designed, through full production.
3. *Test and Diagnostics* — how will the product be tested, what is the confidence level, and how will testability, quality and reliability be imparted to the design.

4.1.1. Material acquisition: This task is initiated once engineering feels that they have assembled a preliminary Bill of Materials (BOM). The BOM is sent to manufacturing in two forms: one for a specific source of supply and the other specifies a generic manufacturer. The BOM is reviewed first with the specified suppliers: are they approved? Does the company have any history of difficulties either of a technical or a business nature with any of the supply sources? If such issues are raised, manufacturing will get back to engineering and suggest that they find another source if possible.

For components that do not have sources of supply, suppliers are identified for parts which are technically compatible for the application and engineering sign off is obtained, including part numbers. There might be more than a dozen products being designed simultaneously and costs are estimated for direct materials, labor and engineering so that on going development costs are measured.

The next phase is the acquisition of the material from the preliminary BOM, after enough suppliers and components are identified. The timing depends on the scope and the status of the project. Shortages and availability problems will always exist and purchasing will have to either expedite or substitute parts supplied from engineering. At this point, the manufacturing and engineering functions determine the kiting schedule which is the number of prototype boards that are going to be built. The materials organization will assemble kits for those specific quantities.

*4.1.2. **Manufacturing engineering:*** Manufacturing engineering activity starts when there is enough product concepts, architecture and sense of the package size from the marketing group. Some initial working drawings are created either by the design engineering or manufacturing, which would record the size and location of major components, as well as any special/unique mechanical features. Initial BOM's are messaged, while the drawings are continuously updated. At some point a stake is driven in the ground and the product concept is frozen: *"That's it! We are ready to go out and have this particular configuration designed".*

An outside subcontractor is used for all formal CAD layout and post processing. It allows for the ability to perform many designs simultaneously. Close working relationship have been established with several of the local design houses, with good success. Typically, the design engineers will have to spend some time with the CAD layout engineers before manufacturing gets involved to make sure that all of the components, documentation and net lists are accurate. At the same time, manufacturing will start transferring inputs such as design rules, device placement, footprints and mechanical dimensions and add that to the overall design within the first few days.

When the CAD operation is complete for the prototype, the schedule is updated to ensure that everyone in the project understands the hardware issues from the software and documentation perspective. When the prototype tools have been approved, a package is prepared including manufacturing fabrication guidelines, the photo tools themselves and associated magnetic media information. They are delivered to a previously approved quick turn around Printed Wiring Board (PWB) fabrication house.

Assembly subcontractors are used to build the prototype PWB's. Again, these suppliers have been carefully selected so that Mercury has the option to build boards at the subcontractors facility very rapidly with only the minimum documentation necessary. This arrangement also allows the subcontractor to move up the warranty curve quickly, as well as be integrated into the Mercury process. One example of this is the integration between the CAD house and the contractor assembly process: components are layed out by the outside CAD house so they can be automatically placed by the subconractor's automated machinery as much as possible. In addition, the CAD house has most of that manufacturing data on line and can have the data transferred electronically, if required, to the other subcontractor to produce the production tooling. An example would be the solderpaste stencils and the assembly contractor who does the component placement. The assembly can be achieved typically in less than two days. In some instances an arrangement has been made to allow Mercury manufacturing engineering to personally assemble the prototype boards using the subcontractor's equipment and being assisted by their employees.

After delivery of the assembled PWB's, a complete visual and manufacturability audit will be performed by the manufacturing engineers and rework technicians and the production team will audit the boards. The audit will use the same guidelines as the production PWB's: *"If you can build it right the first time, you can build it right all the time"*.

Manufacturing engineering will complete a part producibility review. This is a formal report that includes inputs for the next revision of the PWB, if one is required and includes the status and usability of the current documentation for fabrication and assembly.

4.1.3. ***Test and diagnostics:*** The test and diagnostic process begins at the very early stages where test engineering, diagnostic engineering and hardware design engineering all discuss the kinds of tradeoffs in the design and what each group would like to see accomplished. Depending on the tradeoffs of resources, schedules and desired performance level, a task list is generated. The diagnostic engineers are responsible for writing tests to exercise the product. The hardware design engineers assist them in achieving that task. The test engineers take the input of both groups, investigate the design, report back on the test coverage, test efficiency and what steps are needed to improve both. All of these events are scheduled to be completed as early as possible in the design cycle.

4.2. Supplier partnerships

Supplier partnerships are an important part of the overall Mercury competitive strategy. The development of a coordinated plan of action to locate, evaluate and maintain supplier partnerships is of critical importance to the success of the company and shorter time to market. Several steps have been identified to ensure success in supplier partnerships [18]. They are described in the following sections:

4.2.1. Utilize a supplier evaluation team: A team is formed with representation from materials, manufacturing, engineering, and quality. The technical and materials expertise is necessary to assess and form a technological as well as a business alliance. The quality representation is important with the growing emphasis on SPC, formal inspection criteria and other upcoming regulations such as ISO 9000. The quality organization is best qualified to communicate the company's quality requirements and expectations to prospective suppliers. The purchasing department, in coordination with the supplier evaluation team, should determine a relevant supplier rating, which is a key factor in maintaining and improving supplier relationships. The rating could vary with the level of supplier competency.

4.2.2. Use a defined process for supplier evaluation: A process approach was developed for the supplier evaluation team. The process begins with the determination of Mercury's own needs and expectations. These include examining the processes, technology, materials, volumes and costs required to develop new products successfully. Once this process has been consummated, the evaluation criteria for each potential supplier is determined, with each member of the team completing the portion of the evaluation related to their own expertise.

A list of potential suppliers is then accumulated, with information coming from various sources: sales representatives, trade journals, purchasing, trade shows and directories and recommendations from associates, both from within and outside of the company. Proximity of the supplier plays an important role since quick turnaround and personal communications are important.

Site evaluations and inspection by the team then follow. The purpose of such activities is to determine criteria for judging potential suppliers in: 1) their technological competence, 2) their management fit into the company's procurement strategy, and 3) their financial stability.

Intangibles such as the supplier equipment inventory, their processes and procedures, and their adherence to world class manufacturing and quality standards can be quickly ascertained. Evidence of SPC, JIT and other quality methodologies should be readily available. Handling of Engineering Change Orders, segregated customer storage areas and coordination of shortages are critical issues to be examined at site visits.

A Request for Quotation is then issued to potential supplier candidates. All necessary documentation is supplied, and if possible, applicable issues for manufacturability review are included. Realistic quantities, delivery times and tooling charges are itemized, and premium conditions are determined.

Supplier selection is determined after careful analysis of the issues of technical competence, quality, pricing and delivery. A trial job is contracted, and the supplier team purchasing representative assumes the role of the project manager during this phase of supplier evaluation. Good communication is the key to success during this initial trial. The purchasing representative should also assume the role of the communication "traffic cop" between the various experts working from both the company and its supplier, even for technical issues. In this manner the severity of problems and their resolution can be examined after the job is completed. Corrective action could be taken at the next design revision.

The team holds a meeting with the supplier after the completion of the trial job to discuss the initial results, such as which elements went smoothly and which need improvement. The level of commitment and expertise shown by the supplier, as well as their quality level and their communication channels are examined and discussed for future enhancements.

4.2.3. Help supplier exceed expectations: After the supplier has successfully completed the trial job, the business relationship with the supplier can be maximized by helping him exceed expectations. Some of the "help issues" can be in the following areas:

- Material and documentation are prepared and maintained correctly: examples are maintaining and delivering to the supplier the latest information regarding engineering changes and bill of materials changes.
- Delivery dates and pricing are expected to be reasonable and correct. The volume and frequency of order variability should be kept to a minimum.

- Feedback is provided to the supplier on their performance, by communicating inspection results in a timely, accurate and useful manner. This allows the supplier to correct process variations as early and cost effectively as possible and to review them before next shipment.
- Official and regular communication links are established. These links are minimized in number to a few key individuals to reduce misunderstanding, while unofficial links are eliminated. Regular feedback meetings are held with clear agendas. A proactive posture is important to avoid problems before they occur.
- Expectations are set jointly, especially in regard to the quality, workmanship, and inspection standards. Official standards such as IPC or MIL specifications are referenced clearly.

These procedures have helped Mercury Computer establish a strategy of mutually beneficial long term relationships with their suppliers, for quick introduction of high performance, superior quality and low cost products.

5. Conclusions

This paper has examined the different product realization processes, and their different product classes and organization structures to create them. In addition, the amount of enterprise activities to be contracted and role of the contractors' in fulfilling their customer needs have been explored. The relationship of the enterprise with its supply chain should be formalized in the following areas:

1. Develop the proper system engineering knowledge base to decompose the design, development and manufacturing phases into components that can be individually evaluated as to be outsource in design, development or manufacturing.
2. Develop procedures for transferring design information between the enterprise and its supply chain. The design information should include quality, reliability requirements and proper level of manufacturing standards and specifications
3. Ability of the supply chain to convey their own strengths as well as limitation and constraints. This could take the form of Design for

Manufacture (DFM) guidelines, cost models, quality standards and technology roadmap.

4. Establish a well developed channel of communications to quickly resolve problems.

This trend toward the virtual factory will continue as long as the need for global competition and customer satisfaction are growing.

References

1. S. Shina, *Concurrent Engineering and Design for Manufacture*, Van Nostrand Reinhold, New York, 1991.
2. S. Wheelwright and K. Clark, *Revolutionizing Product Development*, The Free Press, New York, 1992.
3. S. Shina, *Successful Implementation of Concurrent Engineering Products and Processes*, Van Nostrand Reinhold, New York, 1994.
4. Hewlett Packard *Annual Reports*, 1990-1995.
5. J. Dransfield, "DFM at Northern Telecom", *Concurrent Engineering*, Volume 1, Number 2, March-April 1991, pp. 24-30.
6. Stalk and Hout, *Competing against Time*, Detroit Press, New York, 1990.
7. R. King, *Better Designs in Half the Time*, GOAL/QPC, Methuen, Massachusetts, 1989.
8. G. Boothroyd and P. Dewhurst, *Product Design for Assembly*, Boothroyd & Dewhurst Inc., 1991.
9. D. Clausing and H. Simpson, "Quality by Design", *Quality Progress*, January 1990, pp. 41-44.
10. R. Dunlop, "Design for Profit", *Proceedings of the National Electronic Packaging and Production Conference*, 1992, Anaheim, CA, pp. 139-147.
11. S. Arnold, "Technical Cost Analysis Using Discrete Event Simulation: A Case Study Analysis of Materials Substitution in Automotive Systems", *AMSE PED-Vol.59*, Concurrent Engineering, 1992, pp. 267-280.
12. M. Phadke, *Quality Engineering Using Robust Design*, Prentice-Hall, 1989.
13. H. Mikel, *The Nature of Six Sigma Quality*, Motorola Incorporated Publications, 1987.
14. C. Fine and D. Longo, *Effective Joint Development Projects with Equipment Suppliers*, MIT Sloan School Research report, 1995.
15. E. Kroll, "Towards Using Cost Estimates to Guide Concurrent Engineering Process", *ASME PED-Vol.59*, Concurrent Engineering, 1992, pp. 281-293.
16. R. Hall, *Zero Inventories*, Dow Jones Irwin, Homewood, Illinois, 1983.

17. Dozier and Yacovitch, "From Specification to Beta Site in Three Months", *Surface Mount Technology,* April 1990, pp. 45-52.
18. G. Koslosky, G., "A Contractor Selection Checklist", *Surface Mount Technology*, August 1992, Vol. 6, No. 8, pp. 62-63.

9

Economic Justification in a Concurrent Engineering Environment

Hamid R. Parsaei
Department of Industrial Engineering
University of Louisville, Louisville, Kentucky, USA

Abstract

Concurrent engineering has recently been recognized as a viable approach in which the simultaneous design of a product and all its related processes in a manufacturing system are taken into consideration, ensuring required matching of the product's structure with functional requirements and the associated manufacturing implications.

Traditional economic and cost justification techniques are not considered adequate to measure the economic desirability of products and processes within a concurrent manufacturing environment, particularly, if these products are produced in advanced and highly automated facilities. The majority of these techniques fail to measure the multitude of costs and benefits, both quantitative and qualitative, and their trade-offs.

Keywords: *Concurrent engineering environment, economic justification, qualitative variables, traditional economic analysis.*

1. Introduction

The introduction of microprocessors and computer controlled production tools into industry has given a new perspective to manufacturing processes both in the US and abroad. Computer Aided Design, Computer Aided Manufacturing, Group Technology and Computer Integrated Manufacturing, which is now called Computer Integrated Enterprise, are considered by many as viable tools which can reduce direct and indirect manufacturing costs, improve product quality and increase the variety of products offered. Although these technologies are considered to be highly beneficial, only a few companies in the US have attempted to implement them.

Among the various road blocks to implementation of these technologies which have been cited include the inability of traditional engineering economy and capital budgeting techniques procedures, to measure the effectiveness of new technology implementation [1-13].

The majority of the recognized benefits of these advanced manufacturing technologies are considered to be "intangible" or "non-monetary", and often hard, if not impossible, to quantify and translate into values which can be easily included in say, traditional discounted cash flow analysis methods.

This paper is intended to present a classification model to categorize the so-called traditional discounted cash flow-based methods and non-traditional economic analysis methods which either have been, or may be, used for product and project justification in advanced automated manufacturing systems.

2. Background

Some of the larger US manufacturing companies are investing in advanced manufacturing technologies such as Flexible Manufacturing Systems (FMS), Group Technology (GT), etc. in an effort to become more competitive with other industrialized nations in the global marketplace. This is because such advanced automated manufacturing systems have the potential for improving manufacturing performance in terms of productivity, quality, flexibility and low cost of production. Some of the cost of production. Some of the often-cited benefits of the FMS are listed in Table 1 [14].

A recent survey of five FMS installations indicates that the overall manufacturing cost decreased by about 30 per cent due to the implementation of FMS [15 - 16]. However, the implementation of FMS is an expensive, time consuming, and complex process. The evaluation of the multitude of costs and benefits involved, both qualitative and quantitative, and their trade-off with competing investments is complex. The process of initiating advanced automated manufacturing projects involve the following steps:

- Develop and establish a strategic plan based on the firm's long term and short term goals and objectives.
- Study existing manufacturing processes in order to understand where automation may be most beneficial.
- Develop and establish a tactical plan to obtain an estimate of the eventual form of the company, and of the immediate funding and activities necessary to reach the firm's strategic goals.
- Select projects based upon the identification of the appropriate technology.
- Consider and evaluate the various costs and benefits which may be tangible and/or intangible, financial and tactical.
- Proceed with implementation only following the justification phase.

Since manufacturing companies will become more frequently faced with the challenge of proper analysis of advanced manufacturing technology, various issues have to be considered in the economic justification procedure. These include:

- Initial costs
- Quantification of indirect benefits
- Prediction of benefits over project life time
- Performance uncertainties of new technology
- Lack of long-term commitment to technology innovation
- Reliance on inappropriate economic analysis methods.

Due to the high level of investment involved in implementing advanced manufacturing technologies, it is imperative that economic evaluation be done using efficient techniques that incorporate qualitative benefits as well as quantitative ones in the evaluation process. However, the economic and financial justification analysis of advanced manufacturing technology projects are all often performed using only traditional economic analysis methods such as net present value, internal rate of return, payback period etc.

3. A Proposed Classification Scheme

A review of the literature indicates that a few classification approaches have been proposed by researchers in the past. For example, Meredith and Suresh [1] categorized economic analysis methods into three major classes. Their classes are methods which are suitable for stand alone manufacturing systems, methods which are appropriate for linked systems, and methods which are more strategic in nature and can be applied to integrated systems. Another classification scheme, which was recently proposed by Soni *et al.* [6], categorizes existing economic justification methods into four groups. These are:

1. Single objective deterministic methods
2. Single objective non-deterministic methods
3. Multiple criteria deterministic, and
4. Multiple criteria non-deterministic.

Swamidass and Waller [17] present a classification of the literature on the acquisition of new manufacturing technology. the literature reviewed is divided into planning and financial justification categories. Each of these categories is sub divided into various other themes.

The classification scheme proposed in this paper categorizes existing justification methods into two major groups: single criterion and multiple criteria methods. Each major group is then divided into two subgroups termed deterministic and non deterministic methods.

4. Single Criterion Methods

The justification methodologies falling in this category employ a single economic objective to justify investment in advanced manufacturing technology. Various authors have used traditional financial justification methods in their justification procedure [18-20]. Traditional financial methods including net present value (NPV), internal rate of return (IRR), benefit/cost ratio (B/C, payback period, mathematical programming, and minimal annual revenue requirement (MARR), belong to this category. This category also includes certain optimization methods and the productivity model as well as non-deterministic methods such as sensitivity analysis, decision trees, optimistic/ pessimistic analysis, and Monte-Carlo simulation.

4.1. Single criteria deterministic method

4.1.1. Net present value: The net present value (NPV) can be defined as the sum of the net cash flows discounted at some minimum acceptable rate of return to time zero. Theoretically, an investment is economically justified if the NPV ≥ 0. The benefits of investment in advanced automated manufacturing projects are generally realized over a long period of time. This has the effect that when a high hurdle rate (discount rate) and short recovery period are used in the analysis to compute the NPV, as is often done in justifying investments in traditional economic analyses, high technology projects are many times rejected. Therefore, the proper choice of a discount rate and recovery period is very important. Krinsky and Miltenburg [19] review the expected-NPV and stochastic-NPV and present a new technique called the state-price NPV.

An example illustrating the effect of high hurdle rates on the selection of a project using NPV is presented in Table 2. Project 1 requires low initial cost and has a life of 6 years; whereas, Project 2 is a capital intensive automated manufacturing project with a project life of 10 years. For a discount rate of 15 per cent, NPV analysis indicates that the automated manufacturing project is the more desirable alternative. But, for a higher hurdle rate of 30 per cent, the automated manufacturing project is not desirable. The results of the example indicate that the choice of the discount rate should be made carefully.

*4.1.2. **Internal rate of return:*** The internal rate of return (IRR) is that interest rate which makes the sum of the discounted cash flows equal to zero. Investment in a project is considered to be economically acceptable if the internal rate of return is greater than, or equal to, a selected hurdle rate (minimum attractive rate of return, MARR) [22]. This method of economic evaluation of projects is similar to the net present value method, and has similar benefits and shortcomings in that, since the acceptability of a project depends on MARR, it is important to choose an appropriate value of MARR based on certain considerations such as risk of the project. Terichow *et al.* [23] investigated the decision making procedure for accepting or rejecting investments based on internal rate of return and discounted present value.

*4.1.3. **Benefit/cost ratio:*** An investment is considered to be economically justifiable if the ratio of benefits to be derived from the investment to the costs associated with the investment is greater than, or equal, to 1. This method is particularly popular for evaluation of large, government projects and in organizations concerned with public service, welfare or defense projects. This method is highly dependent upon the proper definition of benefits and costs and provides no advantage over the net present value of the internal rate of return methods [23].

*4.1.4. **Payback period:*** The payback period is the time required to recover the initial investment, or, in other words, to balance the incoming cash flows and the cash outflows. A project is considered acceptable if the payback period is equal to, or less than, a predetermined payback period. The simplicity of this analysis tool has made it the most prevalent method used in industry to justify investments.

However, there are certain disadvantages with this method. A project judged acceptable based on the payback period may not be acceptable by the NPV or IRR methods, and vice versa. This is because the payback period does not consider the time value of money (interest). This method also fails to incorporate the benefits resulting from strategic issues involved in the investment (Soni *et al.*, 1992).

*4.1.5. **Modified minimum annual revenue requirement:*** The minimum annual revenue requirement is simply the minimum income required to cover all incremental costs, including capital recovery on the incremental investment, return on the incremental investment, incremental costs of goods sold, and the incremental taxes inherent in an investment alternative. This approach was modified by Soni, *et al.* [7-8] to consider the possibility of a firm facing a declining market share, and, consequently, declining gross incomes, in the event that an investment in advanced manufacturing is *not* undertaken.

This methodology compares a series of minimum annual incremental revenue requirements to a corresponding series of annual incremental gross incomes. If the discounted value of the difference between the incremental gross income and the incremental revenue requirements is greater than, or equal to, zero, the project is judged acceptable [6].

*4.1.6. **Mathematical programming:*** This approach attempts to use a mathematical programming formulation to choose a subset of interrelated projects for investment from a given set of projects. The objective function is to maximize the net present value subject to various constraints of interdependence, *e.g.*, mutual exclusivity, multi-project budget, labor and material restrictions. There are certain drawbacks with this approach [6]:

- It ignores a potential cross-correlation of cash flows between the projects, and
- The discount rate must be estimated by the analyst under an assumption of perfect and complete markets. The analyst must also provide all the information regarding future cash flows, interdependency, etc. [24].

4.2. Single criterion non-deterministic methods

4.2.1. Sensitivity analysis: Sensitivity analysis is one of the most important parts of any decision making process. In the economic evaluation of investment in projects, a decision maker must consider uncertainty and risk. A sensitivity analysis can be performed to handle the issue of uncertainty and risk. This analysis is done when there may be inherent errors in the estimation of the values of parameters in the problem, or when preferences associated with the various projects change. Graphical and tabular methods are available to aid in the performance of sensitivity analyses. Moerman [20] discusses about sensitivity analysis and monte-carlo simulation in the economic evaluation of investments in new production technologies. Miltenburg and Krisky [21] propose a methodology for evaluating flexible manufacturing systems using traditional financial justification methods. A framework for conducting sensitivity analysis is presented.

4.2.2. Decision trees: The drafting of a decision tree is a diagrammatic procedure useful in modeling complicated problems involving risk, sequential decisions and outcomes. The decision tree approach in justifying automated manufacturing technology is a appropriate for situations wherein the analyst is making several similar decisions over a period of time. A number of commercial software packages are available to assist in decision tree analysis, such as SUPERTREE, Decision Programming Language, etc. All offer graphical capabilities to reduce the otherwise time-consuming calculations required.

A related approach to decision trees is the influence diagram approach [25]. A problem modeled as a decision three can be converted to an influence diagram. A combination of these two approaches is computationlly efficient.

4.2.3. Monte-Carlo simulation: This technique, also called the 'method of statistical trials' is used to analyze situations involving risk. This method is useful when other analytical approaches are difficult or not feasible to use. an outcome for each variable of interest (element) is randomly selected from a probability distribution assumed to represent each criterion of interest, and these outcomes are then combined. A certain number of trials are conducted and the combined outcomes are checked for some prescribed degree of accuracy. The important requirement of the technique is that the outcomes of all variables of interest be randomly selected [10, 26]. This method can also be used for problems with more than one criterion.

5. Multi-Criteria Methods

Like many real world problems, the decision of investing in advanced manufacturing technology frequently involves multiple and conflicting objectives, *e.g.*, minimizing costs, maximizing flexibility, minimizing machine down times, maximizing efficiency, etc. The decision maker has to consider a number of criteria and may assign certain priorities for each criterion so that the most important criterion is satisfied first. Since certain criteria are not quantitative, efficient methodologies are needed to evaluate AMT benefits that are non-financial and non-quantitative in nature [27]. Mathematical models have been developed to quantify performance measures such as productivity, quality, and flexibility for justifying investment in AMT [28, 29]. Many multi-criteria techniques have been developed and applied to the problem of justifying advanced manufacturing technology [30]. Sullivan [31] discusses various models such as scoring, expert systems and AHP for automation decisions. Some of the deterministic methods for solving multi-criteria problems are multi-objective mathematical programming, scoring models, the analytic hierarchy process (AHP), outranking methods and goal programming. Non-deterministic, methods include fuzzy techniques, expert systems, game theoretic methods, and multi-attribute utility and value analysis.

5.1. Multi-criteria deterministic methods

5.1.1. Multi-Criteria 0-1 Integer programming: This is a simple approach to modeling and solving the problem of selecting the best project from a given set of projects. Given a set of projects

$$X = \{X_1, X_2, \ldots, X_n\}$$

where X_i, i = 1,2,..., n represents the project and

X_i=1, if the Ith project is selected 0, otherwise.

It is assumed that the minimum acceptable values of each attribute, such as NPV, payback period, work in process inventory, flexibility, competitive advantage, etc., is known and available. If qualitative factors are considered in the problem, a weight on a scale from 0 to 1 is used for each factor. The values of each of these attributes for each project form the coefficients of the decision variables in the constraints and the objective function of the model. The main advantage of this method is that it can solve a problem with a large number of alternatives in a short time.

A drawback of the problem is that the decision maker must know, or be able to determine, the 'b_j' values in the constraints (the minimum acceptable values of each attribute). Then, a multi-criteria 0-1 integer programming problem can be formulated as following:

Minimize or Maximize $\{f(X_1,..., f(X_k)\}$ subject to

$a_{ij}x_i \geq b_j$
$\Sigma x_i = 1$
x_i is 0 or 1, 1 = 1,2,...,n

Here, the $f(X_i)$ refer to the various objective functions such as minimizing payback period, work in process inventories, etc., and maximizing net present value, competitiveness, etc. Various multi-criteria decision making techniques are available in the literature to solve these models, many of which have been incorporated into computer software to run interactively and/or non-interactively.

5.2. Scoring models

Scoring models feature the ability to accommodate the consideration of intangible, or economically non-quantifiable, elements involved in an investment decision in an analytical fashion. Scoring models can be classified into:

- unweighted 0-1 factor models
- unweighted factor scoring models
- weighted scoring models
- constrained weighted factor scoring models.

Input data for scoring models are subjective 'guesses' rather than sophisticated forms of the same guess required by other models.

Among common scoring models, the linear additive model is widely used by researchers for scoring competing alternatives. Parsaei and Wilhelm [4] proposed a methodology which is based on a linear additive model developed by Klee [32]. This methodology aids decision makers in evaluating the desirability of a firm's long-term and short-term advanced automated manufacturing technologies.

The methodology is implemented in two phases.

Phase I

In Phase 1 of this methodology, a list of the firm's mutually exclusive strategic investment proposals is structure. The independent, but common set of benefits (attributes) resulting from these strategic proposals are weighted, based on corporate long term objectives, using ordinal weights like those provided in Table 9.1. The performance of each strategic proposal is then evaluated with respect to each priorizied, resulting benefit (attribute). To evaluate the performance of each strategic proposal with respect to a given attribute, the methodology uses ordinal weight values like those provide in a Table 9.2.

The liner additive model employed in Phase 1 to select the best strategic proposal can be expressed mathematically using the previously cited formulation as follows:

$$\underset{j}{Max} N_j = \sum_{i=1}^{m} P_i' X_{ij}, \text{ for } j = 1, 2, \ldots, n;$$

where

N_j = the total score earned by the jth strategic proposal in satisfying the corporate goals for factory automation,

P_i' = a ratio scale variable created by dividing the weight, pi, (ordinal weight from Table 9.1) assigned to the ith strategic decision attribute, which expresses the relative importance of the corporate automation goals achieved by implementing each proposal, by the sum of the weights assigned, assuming 1 < 1 < m,

X_{ij} = the weight (ordinal value) assigned to the ith strategic decision attribute, which reflects the anticipated performance of the jth strategic proposal with respect to strategic decision attribute *I*,

m = number of independent strategic attributes common to all strategic proposals,

n = number of mutually exclusive strategic automation proposals under consideration by the corporate decision maker.

Table 9.1: Benefits of Advanced Automated Manufacturing Systems [14]

Strategic
Better competitive advantage
Ability to adjust to varied product life cycles
Development of engineering and management expertise
Lower exposure to labor unrest
Ability to introduce products faster in the market
Being viewed as the leader in the use of new technologies
Improvement in Return on Equity
Improvement in Overall Productivity
Tactical
Lower work in process inventories
Reduced setup time
Reduced throughput time
Reduced variability in throughput time
Lower fixtures and jigs costs
Improved manufacturing control
Improved quality
Reduced scrap rate
Reduction of floor space used
Reduced labor costs
Reduced tooling costs
Reduced rework
Better status monitor of machines, tools and material handling devices
Improved data management
Improved control of operations
Improved control of parts
Improved response time to demand variations
Improved ability to adjust to machine breakdowns
Improved working conditions
Improved ability to respond to design or process change

Table 9.2: The net present values for two proposed projects at MARR = 15% & 30%

Project #1 low-initial cost		***Project #2 Automation project***	
End of year	***Annual cash flows***	***End of year***	***Annual cash flows***
0	-600,000	0	2,500,000
1	250,000	1	200,000
2	250,000	2	200,000
3	300,000	3	400,000
4	350,000	4	500,000
5	100,000	5	800,000
6	50,000	6	1,000,000
		7	1,000,000
		8	1,200,000
		9	1,200,000
		10	1,500,000
NPV (15%)	275,165	NPV (15%)	759,880
NPV (30%)	36,610	NPV (30%)	-860,45

Phase II

The objective in Phase II of this methodology is to evaluate the various alternatives associated with the strategic automation proposal selected in Phase I. For example, if one concludes that the most desirable proposal in Phase I is to install industrial robots, the decision maker in Phase II will concentrate on the evaluation of different models and/or manufacturers of industrial robots, each of which, in turn, possesses its own unique set of characteristics (attributes), such as size, drive system, degrees of freedom, controller memory capacity, etc. Extending the method of Phase I, the components of the linear additive model used in Phase II of this methodology may be described as follows:

$$\underset{j}{Max} V_j = \sum_{i=1}^{p} W_i' Y_{ij}, \text{ for } j = 1, 2, \ldots, q;$$

where

V_j = the score representing the ability of the jth tactical alternative to achieve the goals of the strategic proposal,

W'_i = a ratio scale weight computed by dividing the ordinal scale weight, W_i, assigned to the ith characteristic (or attribute) to reflect its importance in the strategic proposal by the total of the weights assigned to all attributes, assuming | ≤ | ≤ p,

Y_{ij} = the ordinal scale weight assigned to the ith characteristic, which reflects the anticipated performance of tactical alternative j with respect to the ith characteristic (or attribute),

P = the number of independent characteristics (or attributes) common to all alternatives under consideration,

q = the number of mutually exclusive alternatives under consideration.

Illustrative example

A company has decided to study the feasibility of adopting a number of different automation proposals as part of their strategy for improving productivity, better controlling inventories, improving their responsiveness to customer orders, and to be known as a technological leader in the industry. However, since the financial conditions extant prohibit the capital investment necessary to implement all of the automation proposals available, the decision has been made to proceed with implementation of the automation strategy in a piecewise fashion. Accordingly, mutually exclusive proposals have been forwarded to corporate decision makers who will begin the phased implementation of the strategic goals of the company. The proposals include such state-of-the-art systems as industrial robots, automatic guided vehicles, computer aided design and drafting systems, automated storage and retrieval systems, etc. These were reduced to the top three strategic proposals for final, detailed analysis.

Decision makers agreed that every proposal considered should possess, to some degree, each of a common set of attributes. These common attributes are reduced lead times, reduced work-in-progress, improved product quality, direct cost reductions, flexibility to accommodate product changes, flexibility to accommodate schedule changes, and improvement in safety practices.

In applying the decision methodology proposed herein, first the importance, P_i, of each attribute in achieving corporate strategic goals is assessed by using the ordinal weighting scale in Table 9.3. Then, these weights are converted to ratio scale, P'_i, by summing them and dividing each individual rank by the total. The performance, X_{ij}, of each of the three strategic automation proposals with respect of each of the attributes is assessed using the ordinal scale values from Table 9.4.

Table 9.3: Example ordinal scale weights for ranking the beneficial attributes of available strategic proposals or tactical alternatives

Very important	1.00
Important	0.75
Necessary	0.50
Unimportant	0.25

Table 9.4: Ordinal scale used to evaluate the performance of each strategic proposal or tactical alternative with respect to each attribute

Superior	1.00
Good	0.80
Above average	0.60
Average	0.40
Below	0.20
Poor	0.00

Table 9.5 summarizes the calculations required in Phase I of the methodology. As can be seen from the last row of Table 9.5, after normalizing the N_j scores for each strategic proposal, proposal 2 yields the maximum value. Therefore, proposal

2 is the one selected for further consideration in Phase II of the methodology.

Table 9.5: Phase 1 - Selection of the best strategic automation proposal

i	*A'i*	*Attribute*	*Proposal 1* X_{i1}	A'_iX_{i1}	*Proposal 2* X_{i2}	$A'X_{i2}$	*Proposal 3* X_{i3}	A'_iX_{i3}
1	.125	Flexibility in production mix	.80	.100	.60	.075	.60	.075
2	.187	Flexibility in scheduling	.80	.149	.60	.112	.80	.149
3	.25	Cost reduction and savings	1.00	.250	.80	.200	.60	.150
4	.25	Product quality improvement	.40	.100	.80	.200	.60	.150
5	.181	Reduction in WIP	.60	.108	.80	.145	.40	.075
		Kj		.707		.732		.599
		Normalized Kj		.965		1.000*		.818

* The most desirable strategic proposal (Max Kj = * AiXij)

The procedure in Phase II is very similar to that described above in that the decision maker identifies common set of independent attributes required for each mutually exclusive tactical alternative for achieving strategic proposal 2. Each of these alternatives are weighted using the ordinal scale values in Table 9.4 with respect to their importance, W_i, in implementing strategic automation proposal 2. Each Wi rank is converted to a ratio scale weight, W_i. Then, assuming that there are three alternatives, the performance, Y_{ij}, of each of these three tactical automation alternatives with respect to each of the attributes is assessed using the ordinal scale values from Table 9.3. Table 9.6 shows the calculations required to select alternative 2 as the one which maximizes the normalized V_j score.

Table 9.6: Phase 2 - Selection of the best tactical alternative

i	*B'i*	*Attribute*	*Proposal 1* X_{i1}	B'_jX_{i1}	*Proposal 2* X_{i2}	B'_jX_{i2}	*Proposal 3* X_{i3}	B'_iX_{i3}
1	.266	Capital recovery cost	.80	.213	.60	.160	.80	.213
2	.133	Floor space required	.60	.080	.80	.106	.60	.080
3	.133	Expandability of system	.80	.106	1.00	.133	.60	.080
4	.266	Compatibility	.80	.212	1.00	.266	.40	.106
5	.202	Ease of operation	.60	.121	.60	.121	1.00	.202
		Lj		.732		.786		.681
		Normalized Lj		.931		1.00*		.866

* The best available alternative (Max Lj = * BiYij)

*5.2.1. **Total productivity model:*** This method is used to assess the impact of the proposed equipment investment on profitability from the standpoint of productivity. If a project has a total productivity. If a project has a total productivity level greater than, or equal to, a predetermined productivity level, it is accepted. This approach is appealing to manufacturers because one of the prime reasons for considering investment in advanced automated manufacturing systems is the potential payoff in increased productivity.

The total productivity model suggested by Sumanth and Pino [33] considers five productivity measures related to personnel, material, capital, energy and other measures. Projects are evaluated based on their ability to score at acceptable levels on these productivity measures. This method is computerized, and the software package offers features such as easy modification and the ability to conduct 'What -If' type analyses approach to solve the problem of selecting an FMS. The first phase involves a screening of the alternatives using the analytic hierarchy process implemented in the EXPERT CHOICE software. A variation of the analytic hierarchy process for multiattribute evaluation of AMT with a present value framework is discussed by Boucher and MacStravic [34].

*5.2.2. **Deterministic outranking methods:*** Outranking methods are used in multi-criteria decision making to rank various alternatives based on the decision maker's preferences [35]. These techniques for decision analysis were developed, and are in wide use in Europe. Various methods such as ELECTRE, ORESTE, PROMETHEE and MELCHIOR belong to this family.

The advantages of these methods are simplicity, clarity and stability. They have been extended to include specialized features such as fuzzy set aspects. These methods have been successfully applied in making public policy decisions and other decisions involving large capital investments. The applicability of outranking methods for the multi-attribute evaluation of advanced manufacturing systems is suggested by Kolli and Parsaei [36].

5.3. Multi-criteria non-deterministic methods

*5.3.1. **Fuzzy linguistic methods:*** The use of fuzzy linguistic variables to evaluate investment in advanced automation technology was proposed by Wilhelm and Parsaei [14]. This method involves the use of linguistic variables from the theory of fuzzy sets to support the phased implementation of a computer-integrated manufacturing (CIM) strategy. Fuzzy linguistic models permit the translation of verbal expressions into numerical ones, thereby dealing quantitatively with imprecision in the expression of the importance of each strategic goal (*e.g.*, enhanced competitiveness, high product quality, low product cost, etc.) and the enabling technology involved in implementing CIM systems (*e.g.* CAD, CAM, group technology, computer-aided process planning, etc.).

Wilhelm and Parsaei [14], in their proposed methodology for the evaluation of CIM system investments, defined two fuzzy linguistic variables: importance and capability. The use of these linguistic variables allows the analyst to specify the importance associated with each of a set of strategic goals which impact the CIM strategy, and the tactical capability of each available CIM technology to meet the strategic CIM goals of the organization. Their study developed a heuristic algorithm based on the use of fuzzy linguistic variables to characterize the capability of available enabling technologies, and to select the best technology at each phase in the implementation of the CIM plan.

*5.3.2. **Expert systems:*** An expert system is a computer program that has capability of solving complex problems by certain rules and logical reasoning mechanism. These rules represent the problem solving approaches of experts. The main feature of expert systems is the ability to handle problems with inexact data [10].

An expert system consists of a knowledge base, inference engine, control mechanism cache or working memory and the user interface. Expert systems can be developed with various computer languages and expert system shells. They can also interact with other computer software.

Expert systems have been developed for handling the problem of evaluating investment in advanced automated manufacturing systems. Sullivan and LeClair. [37] developed an expert system for IBM PCs called XVENTURE. XVENTURE is used for solving investment justification problems quickly and consistently [24]. XVENTURE sets company survival as it's primary objective during the decision. The decisions from the expert system could be:

*GO — Venture is justifiable
*DEFER — do not venture now
*NO GO — reject/abandon the venture

Another expert system developed by Padmanabhan (1989) combines the knowledge based system with analytical techniques. This expert system is developed using the PCPLUS expert system shell and can be used for the justification of flexible manufacturing systems. Zhang and Lu, [38] developed an expert system framework for economic evaluation of machining operation planning. The operation plan derived from the integrated manufacturing and management system ensures that the required specifications are met and economically utilizes labor, material and working capacity. Choobineh [39] discusses a procedure of using MYCIN, an expert system in economic analysis.

Boubekri *et al.* [40] developed an expert system designed to assist management in the selection of industrial robots based on functional, organizational and economic criteria. Fisher and Noff [41] developed a knowledge based expert system for the selection and replacement of manufacturing facilities. This expert system combines the heuristic decision making techniques of human expert and economic analysts in quantitative models.

5.3.3. Decision support system: A decision support system refers to a computerized approach to establishing an information system for managerial analysis. It typically includes a model which may be a set of financial, simulation, and optimization techniques, a database and a terminal through which the user interacts with the model for solutions to a managerial problem. A decision support system focuses on a decision process rather than data processing. Decision support systems are developed for middle and top management. A 'What-if' kind of analysis is possible with the DSS, which provides the manager with necessary information for making better decisions.

Monahan and Smunt, [42] developed a multi-level Decision Support System for evaluating the overall performance of automated flexible manufacturing systems. Kassicieh and Shultz, [43] also introduce a decision support framework for evaluating computer-integrated manufacturing systems.

The application of traditional economic evaluation methods, simulating, mathematical programming or accounting techniques for the evaluation of advanced manufacturing systems suffer from limitations when used alone, but good analysis is possible when all the techniques are combined. With a combined decision support system several alternatives can be studied in less time. Also, modifications are possible during the decision process, and sensitivity analysis can be performed.

Stam *et al.* [44], use a visually interactive decision support framework involving multi-criteria analysis designed to aid the decision maker, particularly top management in selecting the most appropriate technology. Badiru, *et al.* [45] present a spreadsheet model containing modules for AHP, utility model, and system value model developed with LOTUS 1-2-3 macro language. This spreadsheet model is useful in handling multiple attributes encountered in the economic evaluation of advanced automated evaluation of advanced automated manufacturing technology.

5.3.4. Non-deterministic outranking methods: The outranking methods mentioned before have been extended to incorporate special cases such as fuzziness and uncertainty. D'Avignon and Vincke, [46] present an outranking method to incorporate uncertainty of consequences. Martel *et al.* [47] present a fuzzy outranking relation for multi-criteria decision making. This fuzzy outranking relation is characterized by a degree of credibility obtained from a confidence index and a doubt index.

6. Conclusion

In this paper, a classification model to categorize the traditional discounted cash flow based methods and non-traditional economic analysis methods for investment justification in advanced automated manufacturing systems is proposed. This classification categorizes the existing justification methods into two major groups based on:

(a) Single criterion
(b) Multiple criteria

Each group is then branched into two subgroups of deterministic and non-deterministic methods. This article then attempts to survey analytical techniques which can be used by practitioners for evaluation and justification of advanced manufacturing technology systems. Purely subjective methods are not included in the proposed classification model since these methods are not quantitatively oriented and often used in concert with some quantitative methods.

References

1. Meredith, Jack R. and Nallan C. Suresh. (1986), "Justification Techniques for Advanced Manufacturing Technologies", *International Journal of Production Research*, Vol. 24, No. 5, pp. 1043-1058.
2. Primrose, P. L. (1985), "The Use of a Conceptual Model to Evaluate Financially Flexible Manufacturing System Projects", *Proceedings of the Institute of Mechanical Engineers*, Vol. 199, No. B1.
3. Primrose P.L. (1985), "Evaluating the Intangible Benefits of Flexible Manufacturing Systems by Use of Discounted Cash Flow Algorithms within a Comprehensive Computer Program", *Proceedings of the Institute of Mechanical Engineers*, Vol. 199, No. B1.
4. Parsaei, Hamid R. and Mickey R. Wilhelm. (1989), "A Justification Methodology for Automated Manufacturing Technologies", *Computers and Industrial Engineering*, Vol. 19, No. 3, pp. 363-373.
5. Parsaei, Hamid R., Waldemar Karwowski, Mickey R. Wilhelm, Angela Walsh. (1988), "A Methodology for Justification of Flexible Manufacturing Systems", *Computers and Industrial Engineering*, Vol. 15, Nos. 1-4, pp. 117-122.
6. Soni, Ramesh G., Hamid Parsaei and Donald H. Liles (1992), "Economic and Financial Justification Methods for Advanced Automated Manufacturing: An Overview", *Economics of Advanced Manufacturing Systems*, Hamid R. Parsaei and Anil Mital (Editors), Chapman and Hall, 1992.
7. Soni, Ramesh G., Hamid R. Parsaei and Ali Khosravi-Kamrani. (1990), "Economic Justification Methods for Advanced Automated Manufacturing Systems", *Proceedings of the 1990 IIE Conference*, pp. 146-151.
8. Soni, Ramesh G., Hamid R. Parsaei and Donald H. Liles (1990), "A Methodology for Evaluating Computer Integrated Manufacturing Technologies", *Computers and Industrial Engineering*, Vol. 19, pp. 210-214.
9. Canada, John R. (1986), "Annotated Bibliography on Justification of Computer Integrated Manufacturing Systems", *The Engineering Economist*, Vol. 31, No. 2, pp. 137-150.
10. Canada, J. R. and W. G. Sullivan. (1989), *Economic and Multiattribute Evaluation of Advanced Manufacturing Systems*, Prentice Hall, Englewood Cliffs, New Jersey.
11. Canada, John R. and W. G. Sullivan. (1990), "Persistent Pitfalls and Applicable Approaches for Justification of Advanced manufacturing Systems", *Engineering Costs and Production Economics*, Vol. 18, pp. 247-253.
12. Chandra, Jeya and Susan O. Schall. (1988), "Economic Justification of Manufacturing Systems Using the Leontief Input-Output Model," *The Engineering Economist*, Vol. 34, No. 1, pp. 27-45.

13. Wilhelm, Mickey R. and Hamid R. Parsaei. (1991), "A Fuzzy Linguistic Approach to Implementing a Strategy for Computer Integrated Manufacturing", *Fuzzy Sets and Systems*, Vol. 42, pp. 191-204.
14. Choobineh, Fred, (1986) "Justification of Flexible Manufacturing Systems", *Flexible Manufacturing Systems: Current Issues and Models*, Fread Choobineh and Rajan Suri (Eds.), pp. 269-281.
15. Meredith, Jack R. (1987), "Managing Factory Automation Projects", *Journal of Manufacturing Systems*, vol. 6, No. 2, pp. 75-91.
16. Meredith, Jack R. (1987), "Implementing the Automated Factory", *Journal of Manufacturing systems*, Vol. 6, No. 1, pp. 1-13.
17. Swamidass, P. M. and M. A. Waller. (1990), "A Classification of Approaches to Planning and Justifying New Manufacturing Technologies", *Journal of Manufacturing Systems*, Vol. 9, no. 3, pp. 181-193.
18. Azzone, Giovanni. (1989), "Measuring the Economic Effectiveness of Flexible Automation: A New Approach", *Int. J. of Prod. Res.*, Vol. 27, No. 5, pp. 735-746.
19. Krinsky, I. and J. Miltenburg. (1991), "Alternative Method for the Justification of Advanced Manufacturing Technologies", *Int. J. of Prod. Res.*, Vol. 29, No. 5, pp. 997-1015.
20. Moerman, P. A. (1988), "Economic Evaluation of Investments in New Production Economics", *Engineering Costs and Production Economics*, Vol. 13, pp. 241-262.
21. Miltenburg, John G. and Krinsky Itzhak. (1987), "Evaluating Flexible Manufacturing Systems", *IIE Transactions*, Vol. 19, No. 2, pp. 222-233.
22. Stevens, G. T. (1989), *The Analysis of Capital Expenditures for Managers and Engineers*, Ginn Press, Needham Heights, Massachusetts.
23. Terichroew, Daniel, Alexander A. Robichek and Michael Montalbabo, (1965), "An Analysis of Criteria for Investment and Financing Decisions Under Certainty", *Managements Science*, Vol. 12, No. 3, pp. 151-179.
24. Reeve, J. M. and William G. Sullivan. (1988), "Strategic Evaluation of Interrelated Investment Projects in Manufacturing Companies", Cost Management Systems Research Report Submitted to CAM-I, International.
25. Call, Hollis J. and William A. Miller (1990), "A Comparison of Approaches and Implementation for Automating Decision Analysis", *Reliability Engineering and System Safety*, pp. 115-162.
26. Sullivan, William G. and R. Gordon Orr. (1982), "Monte-Carlo Simulation Analyses alternatives in an Uncertain Economy", *Industrial Engineering*, pp. 43-49.
27. Sullivan, William G. (1991), "A New Paradigm for Engineering Economy", *The Engineering Economist*, Vol. 36, No. 3, pp. 187-200.
28. Son, Young K. (1991), "A Cost Estimation Model for Advanced Manufacturing Systems", *Int. J. Prod. Res.*, Vol. 27, No. 3, pp. 441-452.

29. Park, Chan S. and Young K. Son. (1988), "An Economic Evaluation Model for Advanced Manufacturing Systems", *The Engineering Economist*, Vol. 34, No. 1, pp. 1-25.
30. Falkner, Charles H. and Saida Benhaijla. (1990), "Multi-attribute Decision Models in the Justification of CIM Systems", *The Engineering Economist*, Vol. 35, No. 2, pp. 91-114.
31. Sullivan, William G. (March, 1986), "Models IEs Can Use for Strategic, Non-Monetary factors in Automation Decisions", *Industrial Engineering*, pp. 42-50.
32. Klee, A. J. (1971), "The Role of Decision Models in the Evaluation of Competing Environmental Health Alternatives", *Management Science*, Vol. 18, No. 2, B52-B67,
33. Sumanth, David J. and Lourdes Del Pino. (1986), "Equipment Selection and Justification Through Total Productivity Model", *Proceedings of the 8th Annual Conference on Computers and Industrial Engineering*, pp. 91-94.
34. Boucher, Thomas O. and Elin L. MacStravic (1991), "Multiattribute Evaluation with a Present Value Framework and its Relation to the Analytic Hierarchy process", *The Engineering Economist*, Vol. 37, No. 1, pp. 1-32.
35. Goicoechea, Ambrose, Don R. Hansen and Lucien Duckstein. (1982), *Multiobjective Decision Analysis with Engineering and Business Applications*, John Wiley and Sons, New York.
36. Kolli, Sai and Hamid R. Parsaei. (1992), *Multi-Criteria Analysis in the Evaluation of Advanced Manufacturing Technology using PROMETHEE*, 14th Conference of Computers and Industrial Engineering. Cocoa Beach, Florida.
37. Sullivan, William G. and S. R. LeClair, (1985) "Justification of Flexible Manufacturing Systems Using Expert Systems Technology", *Conference Proceedings-AUTOFACT 1985*, Society of Manufacturing Engineers, November 1985, pp. 7-13
38. Zhang, Guangming and Stephan C. Lu. (1990), "An Expert System Framework for Economic Evaluation of Machine Operation Planning", *Journal of Operational Research*, Vol. 41, No. 5, pp. 391-404.
39. Choobineh, Fred. (1989), "Modeling Uncertainty in Economic Justification of Manufacturing Systems", *Proceedings of 1989 IIE Integrated Systems Conference*. pp. 605-611.
40. Boubekri, Nourredine, Majid Sahoui and Chabane Lakrib. (1991) "Development of an Expert System for Industrial Robot Selection", *Computers and Industrial Engineering*, Vol. 20, No. 1, pp. 119-127.
41. Fisher, Edward L. and Shimon Y. Nof (1987), "Knowledge-Based Economic Analysis of Manufacturing Systems", *Journal of Manufacturing Systems*, Vol. 6, No. 2, pp. 137-150.
42. Monahan, George E. and Timothy L. Smunt. (1987), "A Multilevel Decision Support System for the Financial Justification of Automated Flexible Manufacturing System", *Interfaces*, Vol. 17, No. 6, pp. 29-40.

43. Kassicieh, Suleiman and Carl R. Shultz. (1987), "Decision Support Flexible Manufacturing Systems", *OMEGA Int. J. of Mgmt. Sci.*, Vol. 15, No. 6, pp. 495-502.
44. Stam Antonie and Markku Kuula, (1991), "Selecting a flexible Manufacturing System Using Multi Criteria Analysis", *Int. J. prod. Res.*, Vol. 29, No. 4, pp. 803-822.
45. Badiru, Adedeji B., Bob C. Foote and Joseph Chetupuzha. (1991), "A Multiattribute Spreadsheet Model for Manufacturing technology Justification", *Computers and Industrial Engineering*, Vol. 21, Nos 1-4, pp. 29-33.
46. D'Avignon, Gilles R. and P. Vincke. (1988), "An Outranking Method Under Uncertainty", *European Journal of Operations Research*, Vol. 36, pp. 311-321.
47. Martel, Jean-Marc, Gilles R. D'Avignon and Jean Couillard. (1986), "A Fuzzy Outranking Relation in Multicriteria Decision Making", *European Journal of Operations Research*, Vol. 25, pp. 258-271.

10

Product Data Requirements in Concurrent Engineering

Imad Moustapha and John Driscoll

Advanced Manufacturing and Technologies (AMMT)
Department of Mechanical Engineering
University of Surrey, Guildford, Surrey, UK

Abstract

This paper investigates special data requirements within the context of concurrent engineering. It covers the information technology needed to support product data and product data management to facilitate CE practices. Discussion is primarily focused on product data representation, exchange, supporting infrastructure, and management throughout the whole lifecycle of the product. Current research work at AMMT as regarding a non proprietary solution to a concurrent engineering system is presented.

Keywords: *Concurrent Engineering, Data Exchange, Product Data Management, STEP*

1. Introduction

The American Advanced Research Projects Agency (ARPA)[1] interest in concurrent engineering (CE) was a direct response to the US's need for higher quality weapon

---

1. ARPA is the new name of the Department of Defense Advanced Research Projects Agency previously known as DARPA.

systems, developed in less time and at lower costs. While recognizing the importance of organizational and cultural change to concurrent engineering practice, ARPA's initiative in Concurrent Engineering concentrates on the computer technology and information management methods that integrate design perspectives and applications. This paper is primarily concerned with data and information management requirements for concurrent engineering. It takes into account ARPA's adoption of the open environment, and discusses data requirements and needs that provide for a "virtual team" environment, thus enabling effective concurrent engineering practices.

Concurrent Engineering has three domains of information problems: communication, management and synchronization. These problem areas are outlined in this paper and a discussion of best practices is presented. The communication problem is related to the integrated access to data by all parties involved in the product development cycle. Key elements to this problem domain are databases, computer networks and a thorough set of design/process documents. The first two elements will be discussed later in this paper, the third has become increasingly important due to ISO 9000's emphasis on documenting all aspects of the processes and quality systems. Documentation facilitates the transfer of know-how and archives all aspects of design, processes and operations. Furthermore, it motivates the people involved in all these activities to review, check and verify all information pertinent to their work, it facilitates intercommunications between different disciplines, and provides solid basis for the implementation of an ISO 9000-based quality system. Resultant documents can also be used to extract useful information in the master schedule plan that is considered a major element in the synchronization problem. The management problem is concerned with project management, multidisciplinary teams, quality control/management and DFX issues. Synchronization is more concerned with optimizing the processes and important is the elimination of bottlenecks in the product development cycle production chain. Project management techniques are used to minimize delays, manufacturing resource planning systems are used to streamline the production schedules, and Just-In-Time (JIT) techniques are borrowed to achieve a high level of inter-tasks synchronization.

CE depends on the existence of a communication infrastructure which facilitates the exchange of product, process and business-related information. The enterprise model investigated here is of a multidisciplinary team working concurrently in an electronic product development project and also working with a number of external business partners and subcontractors. The product data will encompass all phases of the product life cycle from conceptual design, through prototyping, developing, engineering, procurement, production, maintenance, recycling and disposal. In this case, information is needed to communicate components database, library of functional designs modules, completed designs, printed circuit boards, artwork documents, and others. Information will also be related to the concurrent activities of determining the viability of designs from the DFM viewpoint, tasks allocation, scheduling plans, and finally management of the whole project.

It may be useful to mention here that the standing subcommittee of ISO working in the area of product data is TC184/SC4. The committee works into three areas of product data technology, namely: STEP, PLIB, and MANDATE. STEP is a standard for Product Data Representation and Exchange, PLIB is a standard for Parts Library Data Representation, and MANDATE is a standard for Manufacturing Management Data.

2. An Open Model for Concurrent Engineering

Most published research work on CE ignores the importance of developing a virtual model for the enterprise in which CE practices will take place. A virtual enterprise is the natural incubator of the virtual team as proposed by ARPA. The multidisciplinary team will need to have access to a computerised global model of the enterprise to facilitate monitoring and analysis of interactions between different divisions and departments, and to develop the workplan for the new product across all functional organizational and support divisions. The European project ESPRIT provides a frame work for such a model known as Computer Integrated manufacturing Open Systems Architecture (CIMOSA). CIMOSA provide a reference architecture for enterprise modelling, and an integrated infrastructure for the integration of heterogeneous systems. CIMOSA separates the different activities of the enterprise into general and specific functions in an attempt to allow the enterprise's operational system to be easily reconfigured and extended. General functions include: management of information, management of communication, integration of resources and control of workflow. Specific functions include all production related activities (including among others: design, engineering, process planning, scheduling, production, services, accounting).

The Reference Architecture and integrating infrastructure suggested by CIMOSA are illustrated in Fig. 10.1.

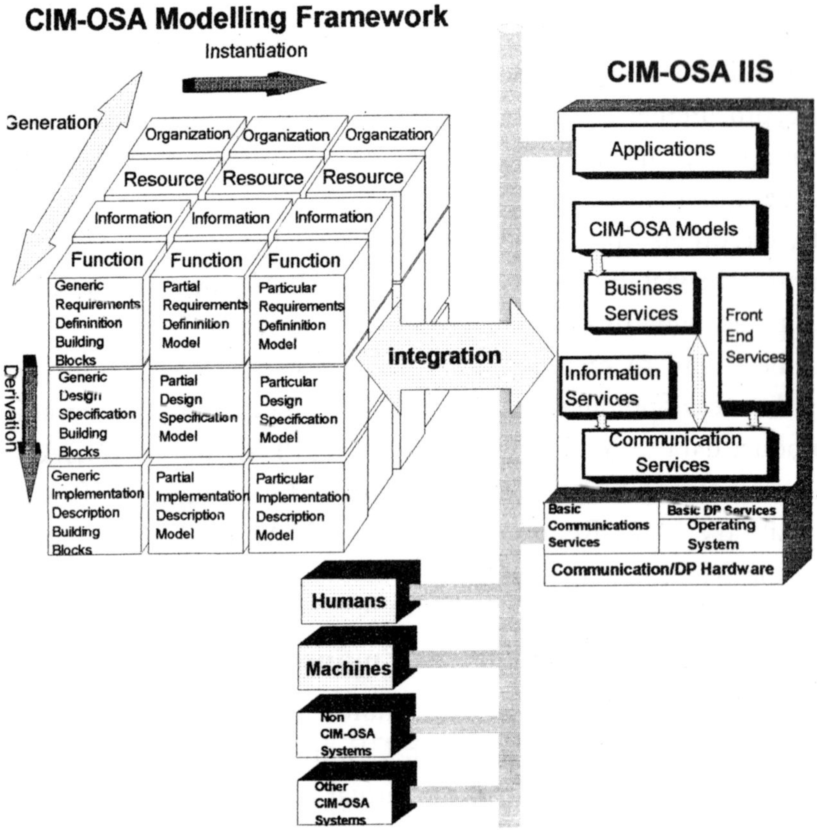

Fig. 10.1: CIMOSA Reference Architecture and Integrating Infrastructure

The Reference Architecture [AMICE} provides architectural constructs and guidelines to help the CIM-based enterprise to develop a structured model of CE requirements. Furthurmore, this model standardises the communication network that will constitute the backbone which enables almost all CE practices to take place. The underlying computer network will be separately discussed later in this paper. The CIMOSA Modelling Framework allows the creation of models in which the separation between general and specific functions is facilitated, while the CIMOSA Integrating Infrastructure (IIS) supports the execution of general functions and establishes a link to the specific functions. On each modelling level in the Generation process the enterprise is modelled by CIMOSA using four Modelling Views:

1. The Function View describes the work flow of the Enterprise Functions.

2. The Information View describes the Inputs and Outputs of the Enterprise Functions.
3. The Resource View describes the structure of resources.
4. The Organization View defines authorities and responsibilities in the previous three model views.

The Derivation Process has three modelling levels: starting with Requirement Definition in which the enterprise business requirements are defined, and next comes Design Specification where requirements are specified and streamlined, leading to the Implementation Description of the actual implementation methods.

From the viewpoint of abstraction (generic *vs.* particular) CIMOSA defines three levels of abstraction in order to reduce modelling effort: the first is purely generic and the last is highly particular. The first Generic Level is a reference catalogue of basic CIMOSA architectural constructs (building blocks) for components, constraints, rules, terms, service functions and protocols. The second Partial Level contains a set of partial models applicable to a particular category of manufacturing enterprises. The third Particular Level is related to one particular enterprise and is defined in the instantiation process by the CIM designer who has completed his building blocks from the General and Partial Level and is developing new particular enterprise components.

Once the CIMOSA model is completed it can be released for the execution of the Integrating Infrastructure (IIS) environment, this is called the Integration Process. naturally each enterprise will have its different set of specific requirements, which leads to different CIMOSA systems, nevertheless some blocks will be generic enough to be shared by different enterprises. The Integrating Infrastructure provides the basic functionality in form of set of services that operate in a distributed data processing environment thus allowing the execution of the CIMOSA model in such an environment. These services are the following: The Business Services which define an Interpreter for the Function View, and allows the control of workflow and other modelled operations as defined in the Function Model. The Information Services which define a set of general functions for the handling of the information defined in the Information View, this includes data access, data integration, and data manipulation. The Front-End Services for the integration of enterprise resources (machines, humans, applications). The Dialogue Services which define an interpreter for dialogue control programs that make the link between the Function Model wgich is being executed in the Business Services and the heterogeneous set of resources defined in the Resource View. The Communication Services for communication handling providing the location transparency required for the interactions of other IIS Services. And finally, the System Management Services which provides general functions to allow system managers to intervene as defined in the Organisation View (modify, release, activate, and deactivate models). The CE team will not only use this model as basis for their planned concurrent activities, but also to analyse and suggest improvements and changes to the structure and functionality of the enterprise to meet the needs and requirements of CE practices.

3. The Nature of Data in a CE Enterprise

Two types of data exist in the CE enterprise: product-related and management-related. The product related data comprises all data necessary for the design, modelling, analysis and manufacturing of the product. Management data encompasses all data that contribute to the management and general aspects of the product life cycle. Product-related data can be further subcategorised into design data, process data, and production plant data. It should be mentioned here that there is a growing awareness of the importance of integrating product data with the paper documentation describing this product. Moving the standards for documentation towards the standards for product data will result in a better support of product lifecycle data. Research efforts in this area are mainly focused on STEP and the SGML family of standards. SGML is the Standardised General Markup Language adopted by ISO for document description or structure. STEP will be elaborated upon later in this paper. The goal for such a research work is to manage SGML entities within STEP as product data. This involves finding a solution for the modelling, storing, and retrieving of SGML entities in STEP. This means that STEP may evolve in the near future to include product documentation, which implies representation of the information structures involved in product documentation, including classification and identification of types of documents or information, and support of all types of character code sets [SWEDCALS-95].

3.1. Design Data

Design data contains standardised electronic components library, and standardised mechanical parts. Additionally, it contains a library of design submodules that can be reused in the new product development process. The standardised representation of data allows different 'islands of technology' to represent, communicate and exchange all product data information smoothly and reliably. The process and manufacturing data are needed to use well established DFM techniques from the onset of the design phase. Spooner and Hardwick [Spooner 93] pointed that exchange of product data is essential for the integration of life-cycle activities and the realisation of concurrent engineering. Concurrent engineering cannot be fully implemented unless knowledge is modelled and standardised to allow communications among all computerised systems [Carver 91]. Standardisation efforts in this area should be directed to the following aspects of product data: representation, coding, querying and retrieval. Representation and coding standardisation has attained a high level of maturity due to the concentrated international efforts in the field of STEP (Standard for the Exchange of Product Model Data, ISO 10303). The much talked-about shared database in a CE environment can only materialises by the use of such a thorough and rigorous data standard not only for the neutral file exchange (the physical file format) but for the modelling, implementation, sharing and archiving of product databases. The formal data specification language used to develop STEP models is called EXPRESS (ISO 10303 - Part 11] which the object oriented technology to model shape, layout logical relations, rules, tolerances, assemblies and configurations (Driscoll).

STEP is such a large data standard that different disciplines of engineering and manufacturing need only to use well defined subsets of this standard called Application Protocols (APs). Since the enterprise investigated in this paper is primarily concerned with electronic products, product data will belong mainly to AP 210 which describes printed circuit boards (PCBs) and printed circuit assemblies (PCAs). Wire harness and interconnectivity can be described using AP 201 and AP 202 (explicit and associated draughting), Part 204 for the boundary representation of the mechanical design of the case containing the PCBs, and Part 208 for life cycle product change process and Part 211 for electronic systems tests, diagnostics, and remanufacture.

Each AP includes three types of models: an application interpreted model (AIM), an application activity model (AAM) and an application reference model (ARM). The AAM describes the processes and information flows of the industrial activities within the scope of the application. The ARM model lists the entities required to model the content of these information flows, and it has to be validated to ensure that it completely specifies all essential data. The AIM covers the rest of the information of the application that are necessary to satisfy the requirements and constraints of ARM, and is assembled from resource constructs in the integrated resources.

The Application Protocol 201 specifies an AP for explicit draughting, it scope is the representation for the purpose of exchange of individual technical CAD drawings. This AP supports the presentation of product shape by explicit 2D geometry and of product properties by explicit 2D annotation without association between geometry and annotation.

The Application Protocol 202 specifies an AP for associative draughting, its scope is the information requirements to unambiguously exchange, access, and archive drawings. This part of ISO 10303 is applicable to the inter-company exchange of computer-interpretable drawing information and associated product-definition data. The Application Protocol 204 specifies an AP for mechanical design using Boundary representation. Its scope is the use and exchange of boundary representation models in the computer aided engineering design context, together with appropriate data models and a physical file implementation form. The data represents all geometric and topological aspects of a complete description of the external form of a mechanical engineering part.

The Application Protocol 208 specifies an AP for life cycle product change process, and the management of change of configuration-worthy items. It includes the identification of a product anomaly, and its cause, the approval and performance of the resulting changes (repairs) to the anomalized product and/or process definition, and the authorization of corrective actions to prevent anomaly recurrence. The identified information provides change-management support for activities the life cycle of he product such as technical-publication generation, retrofit planning, change-proposal coordination, supply interface, and material-requirements planning.

The Application Protocol 210 specifies an AP for the exchange of electrical printed circuit board design information. It defines the information shared between design and manufacturing process planning engineers for transforming a PCB detailed logical design into a manufacturable description. It identifies the PCB components and interconnections between these components. The manufacturing description include the physical realization of that logical design. This AP also provides support for configuration management of the printed circuit assembly (PCA) product data. But AP 210 does not include analysis tools, process plans, procurement data, and cost data of the PCB. Fig. 10.2 illustrates the structure of AP-210. The AAM displays the flow of information through the design and manufacturing processes, ARM presents the constituent entities of the PCB and the inter-relationship among them, AIM provides the formal EXPRESS definition of these entities and draws all generic entities from the available integrated resources.

The Application Protocol at the level of electronic integration represented by PCBs and line-replaceable modules. The AP will encompass the test, integrated diagnostics, and remanufacture functions associated with this level of electronic integration.

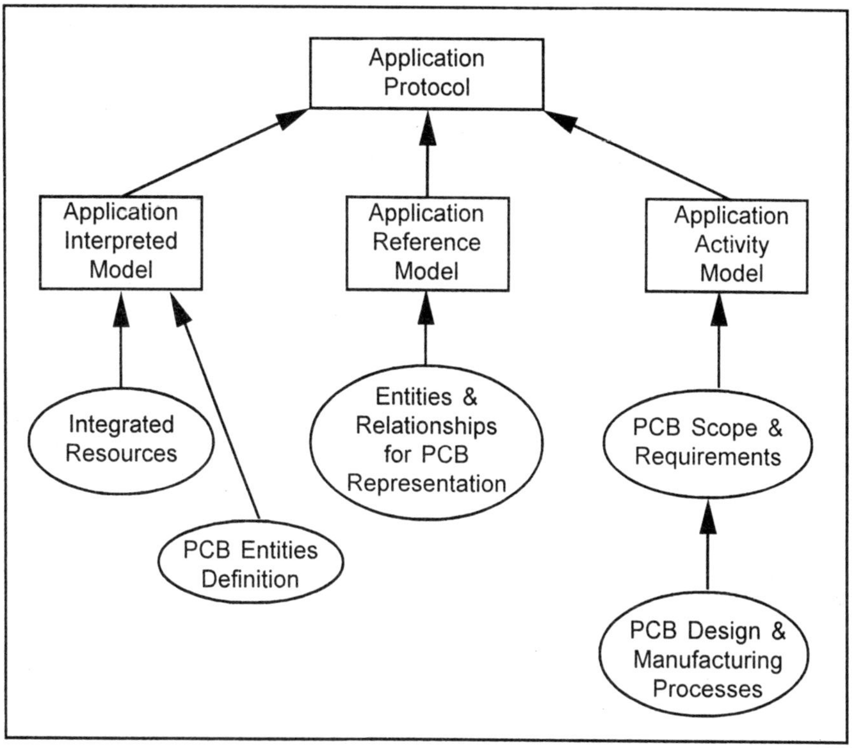

Fig. 10.2: The Structural Components of Application Protocol 210

3.2. Components library

A sister standard to STEP is the ISO 13584 which is aimed at the capability for sharing of parts library information. This is particularly relevant to applications in design and engineering where the end product includes the assembly of components procured from different sources, such as electrical, electronic, and mechanical assemblies. The ISO 13584, known as PLIB, is not only limited to the representation of part library information, but it also covers the exchange mechanisms that enable different applications to exchange components and parts, and use shared databases. The scope of the parts library is the complete lifecycle of products, including design, manufacture, maintenance, and disposal.

3.3. Process data

The multidisciplinary team will face a variety of design decisions that are considerably affected by the existing manufacturing processes. The team will need to access process information in order to be able to select design parameters matching the existing process capabilities, it also has to decide which set of process tools to select among alternative options, and to be sure that selected processes will meet required product specifications. This clearly indicates the essential role of process data in concurrent engineering. Process data will not only describe the manufacturing capability of the enterprise but actually help translating manufacturing information of the product into manufacturing processes. Naturally process data is plant-specific (non-generic) and it directly corresponds to the existing technology (machines, equipment, and resources) used in the enterprise and its extended partnerships. To give a specific example of process data in concurrent engineering of electronic products, the PCB process can be described. PCB process data will cover the following processes: cutting tools used in cutting PCBs to size, which must be a factor taken into consideration when designers have to decide the optimal size of the PCB, drill machines used in drilling holes which will have impact on earlier stages of design when pad and hole sizes have to be determined, and other processes that are generally called mechanical processes of image transfer, plating, and etching. In the important following stage of bare board testing data will need to be downloaded from the CAD system to the ATE (automatic test equipment) system, the process data of testing equipment should be provided from an early stage since designers must take into account DFT (design for testability) considerations. The last stage will normally be the assembly process wherein component leads are clinched, soldered and finally inspected. Capabilities of all these processes must be modelled and stored in the distributed database to form the process data of a partial electronic product life-cycle data model.

3.4. Production plant data

The manufacturing plant model will be very useful in selecting which process to apply and what yield can be expected from the selected process. Process performance depends on the existing equipment model information will include machine type, model, specifications, manufacturer, the list of processes the machine can perform and the processes constraints imposed by this specific machine. Constraints include resolution, accuracy, repeatability, speed, acceptable part sizes and shapes, machine power, and cut or drill depth limits.

Since lead-times are a major element in the concurrent engineering environment, lead time data is an important aspect of the overall scheduling plan and plant model, especially when the product development cycle is short and there is very little slack in the cycle of processes leading to the finished product. Finally, the plant model may include costing factors related to yield, set-up and tear-down times, auxiliary materials cost, processing cost, tooling cost, labour cost, and other overhead costs.

3.5. Management data

The Industrial Manufacturing Management Data (MANDATE) project is developing a series of standards for the data (other than product data) which is shared within an industrial manufacturing plant or which is exchanged between different manufacturing plants. Three project areas are being actively worked upon in MANDATE:

- Data exchanged between an industrial manufacturing company and its environment of manufacturing managements activities.
- Data able to describe an industrial manufacturing company's resources database.
- Data for controlling and monitoring the flow of materials within an industrial manufacturing company.

4. Production Data Management

In the previous section the nature of data have to be modelled, generated, accessed and processed was discussed. The question of managing this data is of vital importance since the product in its entire life cycle will have an enormous amount of data related to different aspects, operations and descriptions of this product.

The definition of the term "Product Data" is given in ISO 10303-1, Overview and Fundamental Principles:

"product data: a representation of information about a product in a formal manner suitable for communication, interpretation, or processing by human beings or by computers."

According to TC184/SC4, the term Product Data denotes the totality of data elements which completely define a product for all applications over its expected life cycle. Product data includes the product description, configuration, geometry, topology, tolerances, materials, along with the relationships necessary to completely define a component part or an assembly of parts for the purposes of design, analysis, manufacture, test, inspection and product support.

Product data management in concurrent engineering requires: control of engineering data, quality assurance of engineering data, reuse of engineering data, security of engineering data, availability of engineering data, control of engineering workflow, and support for new engineering strategies [Stark 92].

PDM provides at least the following features: electronic vault (storage bank), process control (workflow), structure management (relationship), and configuration management (complex relationships). In addition to conversion of paper to electronic format combined with optical character recognition and full indexing. Common key elements of PDM systems would include: a distributed database management system (DDBMS), a bill of materials (BOM) mechanism, configuration management, data search engines, engineering changes management, project management, message handling, access control, document status monitoring, and a long term archiving system.

The PDM system will maintain product structure relationships and issue history via a bill of materials file (BOM). The BOM can automatically extract information from CAD and it must be compliant with the ISO 9000 traceability requirement, this will involve maintenance if historical information corresponding to the completion of every engineering change order. Fig. 10.3 illustrates the concept of product data associativity.

Document status monitoring use flags to indicate the current status of each document: draft, submitted for checking, checked, approved, and finally issued. Activities, messages, and warnings will be flaged via the electronic mail system. This will allow the CE team members to determine and track the current system status and to interact to any message they receive.

Configuration management will link all files and documents necessary to describe, specify, develop, prototype, install, operate, test, maintain and dispose of

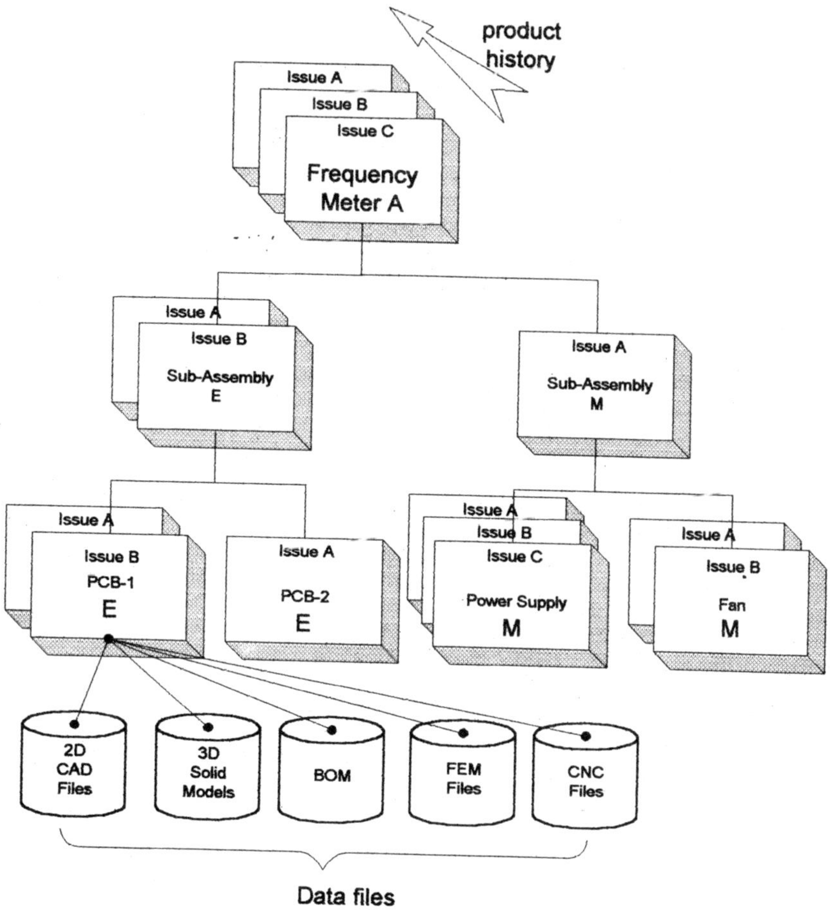

Fig. 10.3: Product Data Associativity

the product throughout its entire life cycle. Configuration management will provide accurate and updated record of the actual configuration of a given particular product during its different lifecycle phases, offering distinction between as-designed, as-built, as-installed, and as-maintained configurations of the product. This includes relating components, boards, subassemblies, and assemblies, while maintaining a complete history of the product throughout its life cycle.

The status of all engineering workflow information is monitored by configuration management. In the electronic example it will maintain information related to the physical/logical definitions of used components and materials, sub-assemblies, interconnections, wire-harness, CAD drawings and models, design-rules checking results, artwork photomasks, process plans, NC data files, and quality assurance results. Additionally, configuration management tracks exact configuration information on each release of the product, thus supporting multiple versions of data, and maintaining all information related to engineering changes.

4.1. Metadata

DBMS will provide the elementary requirements of product data management in concurrent engineering, namely: provision for physical data independence, provision for explicit data validation rules and standards, provision for controlled access, security and recovery, reduction of data redundancy, and enabling data sharing between different users with different requirements [Stark 92]. But while ordinary databases will provide all these functionalities, they will fall short on the capabilities of storing and managing all types of engineering data: they can only handle characters and numbers, while engineering data is a mixture of types and structures including graphical data. This, and other minor differences, exclude the concept of putting all engineering data in a single repository and using one single DBMS. Instead, the concept of metadata is implemented. This involves leaving the data physically were it was originally created, and only putting data about this data in the DBMS. So metadata stored in the engineering DBMS instead of data. This metadata will include information related to the project, directory and file names, file location, underlying creator program, ownership, privileges, status, creation and updating dates, release number part name, data type, data format and structure, references to other files and projects, log information, among others.

Original engineering files are maintained in their respective locations and native formats, but the engineering DBMS automatically tracks any changes occurring in the system, spontaneously modifying the metadata. Metadata is not restricted to computerised forms of information, it can be extended to include any kind of information relevant to the engineering process, such as the physical location of an archive magnetic tape, or the cabinet in which a punched paper tape may be stored.

4.2. Types of PDM systems

Conventionally, systems that address the management of engineering data and workflow were classified into [Stark 92]: engineering drawing management systems, engineering data management systems, engineering document management systems,

CAD/CAM management systems, and configuration management systems. On the other hand, recent trends have shown a growing tendency to integrate all aspects in one PDM system. Williams *et al.* [Williams 94] expect that by the year 2000 the entire information management industry will align along new, solution defined lines. Even new generations of computer operating systems may soon offer some or all of the document management features bundled with their operating systems.

4.3. PDM systems architecture

A PDM system should provide: a) an intuitive and friendly user interface, b) code to perform management functions and operations such as launching applications and initiating data translation, c) electronic vault concept as a repository to managed product data, and d) a meta-database containing data pointers and correlating different data clusters and files, and access and interface capabilities to other systems and databases. Naturally, PDM systems will require local area networks,

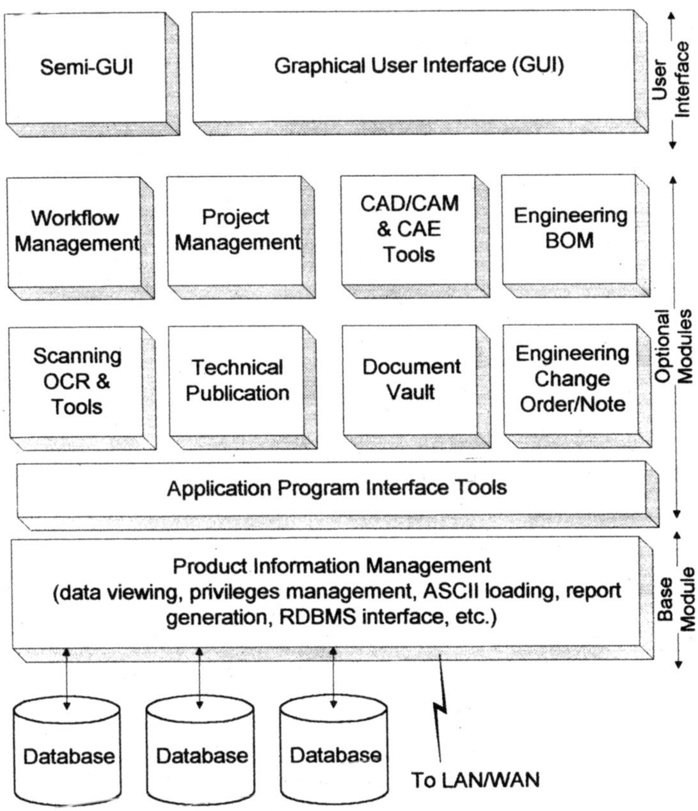

Fig. 10.4: PDM Systems Architecture

and an internet protocol such as TCP-IP for successful communication. And finally the PDM system should be able to communicate with any of the major RDBMSs that support SQL (Structured Query Language). A recent trend is to support object oriented databases and API (Application Program Interface) that achieve seamless integration within the PDM system, so that members and environments. Fig. 10.4 illustrates an optimal architecture of a modern PDM system in concurrent engineering.

5. A Database for Concurrent Engineering Applications

Earlier in this paper the concept of metadata was discussed within context of PDM systems. It has been noted that distributed RDBMS is a must for concurrent engineering. Object oriented databases have met considerable success recently in the domain of product modelling and product data. A particular example is the ROSE database management system that was designed and implemented specifically for concurrent engineering applications [Spooner 94]. ROSE uses EXPRESS as its data definition language and produces C++ Class definitions by compiling specifications for entities written in EXPRESS. Objects created in EXPRESS classes are considered persistent. ROSES main features are listed below:

1. Concurrency control by using a special tool called delta files which detects differences between files and versions and facilitates the process of merging versions.
2. Data translation between STEP and other industry and de facto formats such as IGES and DXF.
3. Schema management allowing persistent objects to be mapped to different application programs via casting and saving/addition of instance variables.
4. Portability across a wide variety of platforms (UNIX and Windows NT) and interface with many programming languages such as C++, Lisp, and SmallTalk.

Current research work is focusing on building links between the product database and metadatabase systems [Spooner 94].

6. The Communication Network

As mentioned earlier in this paper, a computer network in the backbone for the enabling infrastructure in concurrent engineering. All activities of sharing and accessing distributed data resources can only take place with the installation of a proper network interconnecting all machines, resources, functional departments and team-members. Initially, any local area network (LAN can do the job provided it enjoys a suitable bandwidth and all services required in a distributed data environment.

The network protocol adopted by ISO under the name Manufacturing Automation Protocol (MAP offers an application services element called MMS (Manufacturing Message Specification) that has lately gained wide acceptance in the manufacturing enterprises. MMS is an internationally standardised messaging system for exchanging real-time data and supervisory control information between networked devices and/or computer applications in a manner that is independent of both the application function being performed and the developer of the device or application. MMS is an international standard (ISO 9506) that is developed and maintained by Technical Committee Number 184 (TC184), Industrial Automation, of the International Organization for Standardization (ISO).

Almost all familiar network links are supported by MMS, namely RS-232, Ethernet, TCP/IP, MiniMAP, and can connect to many more types of systems using networking bridges, routers, and gateways. MMS provides much more than TCP/IP which essentially offers a mechanism to transfer streams of bytes. MMS transfers commands with parameters between machines. Three major effects of using MMS that can contribute a successful concurrent engineering environment are: interoperability among different platforms, independence from any proprietary solution, and access to distributed data and information required by an application.

Communications related applications in CE can quite benefit from the adoption of MMS in an open CIM architecture. The functionalities of MMS and its VMD (virtual Manufacturing Device) services can facilitate the implementation effort considerably. The VMD object uses a standard view to represent the structure and behaviour of a manufacturing device from the point of view of the communication processs. This makes controlling and monitoring manufacturing devices through the network much easier. Actually, MMS is the only communication standard adapted for CIMOSA, and it is a powerful integratic.. tool among heterogeneous systems.

7. A Case Study Reviewed

Texas Instruments has designed a concurrent engineering working environment to support PCB design from concept to manufacture [Amundsen 90]. The Texas

Instruments concurrent engineering system has the structure illustrated in Fig. 10.6. Amundsen and Hutchinson listed the objectives sought-for in such a concurrent engineering system for electronic design and manufacture, namely:

- A standardised user interface to facilitate all levels of engineering expertise;
- Information capture from all specialty applications and disciplines into a knowledge base;
- Data integrity and consistency across the system;
- A single design representation that can be shared by all disciplines and tools;
- Intelligent use of the knowledgebase to guide the design process towards the optimal configuration;
- Integrated tool suite to facilitate productivity and efficiency of the design team; and
- Finally, the capability to accommodate for changes in circuit technology and complexity without the need for redesign or reprogramming.

The Texas Instruments (TI) CE environment enjoys a single common representation which implies that all parameters can be accessed by any of the tools.

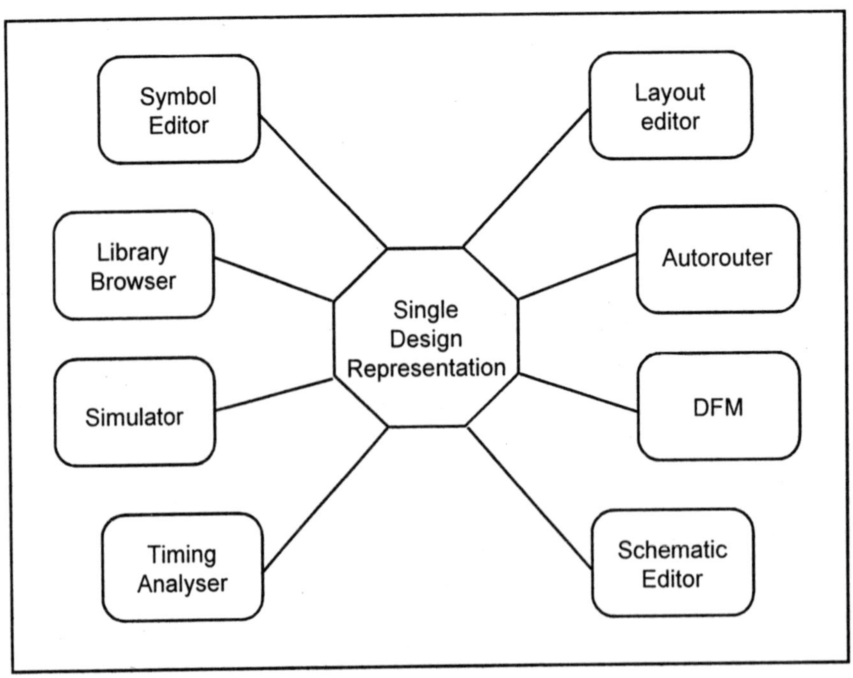

Fig. 10.5: Texas Instruments Concurrent Engineering Environment

Any change to a parameter is immediately reflected in all applications. Nevertheless since this is an in-house environment, all solutions are proprietary.

If we decide to re-design a similar concurrent engineering system using the concepts, principles, and tools discussed earlier in this paper, the following important questions will have to be answered: a) what existing tools to use, b) which tools and functions should be developed, and c) how to seamlessly integrate the whole set of tools and techniques to achieve the guidelines set by Amundsen *et al.* Current research work at the AMMT group is using the STEP standard and its affiliated Application Protocols to develop a non-proprietary design for such a system as compared to TI proprietary solution.

This involved using a set of exsiting CAD software packages, and evaluating potential problem areas for a seamlessly integrated CE system. The printed circuit design package used is CADSTAR from Zuken-Redac, with an EDIF output format, the 3D solid modeller is AutoCad Release 13 from Autodesk with a DXF output format, the simulator and timing analyser is Work View from View Logic which also supports an EDIF format.

Components library are being redefined in compliance with the ISO 13548 standard (PLIB) in order to obtain a part library independent from any particular CAD system. The existing components were all defined using the EDIF format, and are currently being redefined according to PLIB as part of the overall design of the non-proprietary system. DFM rules are being described using the object oriented description language EXPRESS and stored in the ROSE object-oriented database management system which was originally designed to support concurrent engineering applications, and as a part of the DARPA initiative in CE. A DXF and EDIF bidirectional translator to/from STEP is being partially used, and partially developed, and C++ is used as the development environment of this research project. An earlier SIMSCRIPT model of the enterprise was developed, but this has to be remodified according to the CIMOSA model, and its code re-written. Further work still have to be done in the areas of data management. Supporting LAN infrastructure has already been modelled and implemented using an Ethernet protocol, but MMS has still to be introduced into the model, this is projected for the next phase if this research project.

Accessing CAD data and integrating it with the STEP-based ROSE database is achieved using either of the following methods:

1. Using the DXF translator available with the Auto CAD package, and the DXF-to-STEP translator available in the ST-Developer development tools.
2. Using an EDIF-to-STEP translator (which has yet to be implemented).
3. Sharing CAD data via the standard data access interface (SDAI) : the database based on the STEP data model is shared among AutoCAD, CADStar and other application programs via a SDAI interface program.

The last method is the most convenient because it allows nonproprietary application programs to the developed and used. But since an essential part of the product data is being generated via existing CAD systems that do not support the STEP physical file format as yet, then the first two methods will continue to be used in the foreseeable future. The AMMT group depends on all three methods for its current research work, since each has its own merits.

8. Conclusions

This paper emphasised the importance of data and information control and management in concurrent engineering. Requirements for design data, process data and management data were evaluated with special emphasis on the STEP standard and its companion standards. A model for the manufacturing enterprise based on the CIMOSA architecture, and for the communication network with emphasis on MMS, and the object-oriented database management system ROSE were presented.

Finally, research work currently undertaken by the AMMT group at the University of Surrey was outlined, this involves a standardised solution for a concurrent engineering system for the design and manufacture of electronic products and encompasses a wide variety of tools and platforms with one common goal: the ability to share and exchange data using non-proprietary solutions.

References

1. [AMICE] ESPRIT II Project 2422 AMICE Consortium, CIM-OSA Reference Base I and II.
2. [Amundsen 90] Amundsen M. and Hutchinson, K. 1990, "Concurrent Engineering for Electronic Circuit Design", *Proceedings of Second National Sumposium on Concurrent Engineering*, Morgantown, WV, USA, February 7-10.
3. [Driscoll 96] Driscoll J., Moustapha I., and Cziulik C. 1996, *Data Exchange Standards for Computer Integrated Engineering.*

4. [Gu 95] P. and Chan K., 1995, "Product Modelling Using STEP", *Computer Aided Design*, Vol. 27, No.3, pp.163-179.
5. [McIntosh 95] McIntosh K., 1995, *Engineering Data Management*, McGraw-Hill, UK.
6. [Bogdanowicz 94] Bogdanowicz L., 1994, *MMS Applications Under MS-Windows for CIM-OSA Demonstrator.*
7. [Candadi 94] Candadi A., Champati S., Herrmann J.W., Minis I. and Ramachandran V. (1994) *Information Needs in Agile Manufacturing, Engineering Data Management: Integrating the Engineering Enterprise,* ASME 1994.
8. [Spooner 94] Spooner D. L., 1991, "An object-oriented product database using ROSE", *Journal of Intelligent Manufacturing*, Chapman & Hall.
9. Braithwaite, K.S., 1993, *Object Oriented Database Design: Concepts and Application.* Academic.
10. [Nakamura 93] Nakamura I., Kojima T., Kugai Y. and Kimura F. 1993, "A CAD Database Interface Based on STEP", *Interfaces in Industrial Systems for Production and Engineering*, Rix and Schlechtendahl (editors), Elsevier Science Publishers.
11. [Spooner 93] Spooner D. L., and Hardwick M., 1993, "Using Persistent Object Technology to Support Concurrent Engineering Systems", *Concurrent Engineering,* Gu P., and Kusiak A., eds. Elsevier Publishing.
12. [Stark 92] Stark J., 1992, *Engineering Information Management Systems, Beyond CAD/CAM to Concurrent Engineering Support*, Van Nostrand Reinhold, NY, USA.
13. [SWEDCALS 95] *Interoperability between STEP and SGML, SWEDCALS Whitepaper*, Swedish Association for CALS, 1995.

11

Concurrent Product Planning and Development Using Quality Function Deployment (QFD): A Case Study

D. J. Gonzales[a], and A.A. Aswad[b*]

[a]Manager Mid-Lux Car Division, General Motors Corporation, USA

[b]Professor, Department of Industrial & Manufacturing Systems Engineering The University of Michigan-Dearborn, Dearborn, USA

Abstract

The Quality Function Deployment methodology is adapted for use in the concurrent product planning, design, and development of an automotive door controls component. A systemic methodology is presented incorporating the voices of the customer and the producer, design concepts selection, design for manufacturability and assembly techniques. Concurrent Engineering concepts are expanded beyond design and manufacturing, to incorporate risk and cost justification analyses, in order for the product to satisfy demanded quality, at a target cost, and in a short cycle time.

Keywords: *Concurrent Engineering, Quality Function Deployment, Product Development System, Product Risk Assessment, Concurrent Management.*

---

* Presenting Author.

1. Introduction

The continued competitive pressures to be first to market through reduced design cycle times led to the application of concurrent engineering concepts in the design and development of products, where engineers and managers must balance all product and process requirements concurrently and satisfy customer and market demands of quality, cost, and delivery.

This paper adapts and extends the quality function deployment (QFD) methodology to implement the concepts of concurrent engineering in a systematic manner. systematic manner. Specifically, it prescribes a master plan to be followed by a product development project team in order to realize their objectives effectively. The systematic development process is illustrated by applying it to the design and development of an automotive door controls component. While the market information and technical specifications conform to demanded quality requirements, the design, test, and cost target values were coded to protect proprietary information.

The concurrent design and development master plan is illustrated in Fig. 11.1. Steps (1) through (4) in the figure outline the processes used to construct the product planning matrix, (phase I in the simplified QFD methodology). The market survey process, the Kano multidimensional quality model [7], and the KJ affinity method, which were used to structure and weight customer demands and the substitute quality characteristics methodically, are described in the following sections.

It is a common and unfortunate practice in the simplified QFD methodology to proceed directly and construct the parts planning matrix (phase II). This implicitly assumes that a given design concept has been finalized, limits the creativity of the development team, and generally leads to uncompetitive product designs. Thus, in our master plan in Fig. 11.1, we interjected a series of steps, namely context usage analysis — step (5) — and function analysis — step (6) — in order to relate the voice of the customer (VOC) to functions rather than parts that realize the demanded requirements. The parts are later specified after a design concept is selected — steps (8) and (9) — the risks are assessed in step (10), and a design for assembly (DFA) study is conducted in steps (11) and (13). Although product design and process reliability studies are not presented in this paper, these are indicated in step (14) and can be incorporated in the future as part of our proposed master plan. The parts planning matrix is thus constructed in step (15) of the diagram.

Also, in the generic QFD process in phase III, which details process planning, we have divided this phase into two parts. Manufacturing processes are specified in the first part, and related assembly processes are specified in the second part. However, we believe that these processes must be planned concurrently, and thus we have juxtaposed them together as illustrated in step (16).

Manufacturing planning (phase IV) in the QFD methodology is described in the section that corresponds to step (17).

Additionally, we have incorporated in the master plan a step that provides the opportunity for making the "business case" for a proposed new product. Although we have not discussed this step in this paper, the business case could easily be formulated to demonstrate the profitability of the selected design while satisfying the collective voices of the customer, the design engineers, the manufacturing engineers, and the business organization.

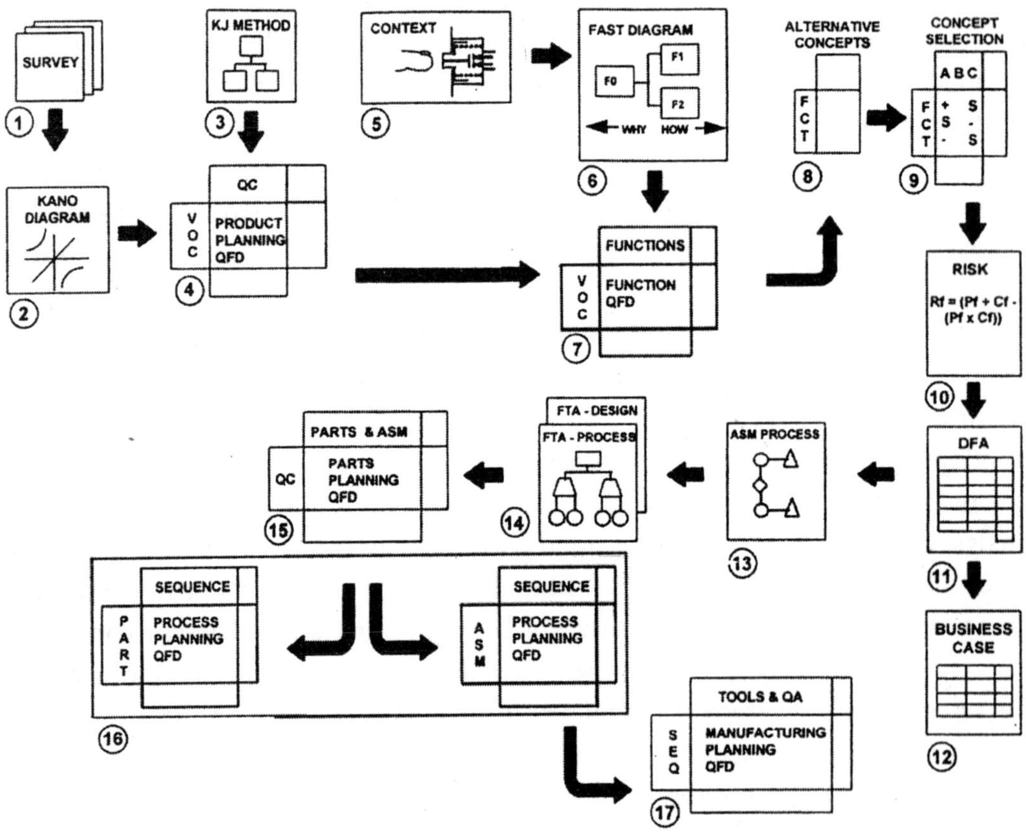

Fig. 11.1: The concurrent design and development process using QFD

2. Description of a Typical Automotive Controls Component

Automotive controls are customized designs accommodating the specific needs of the automotive vehicle's market segment, equipment, and financial restrictions. A relatively simple control mechanism common to many vehicles is a passenger's window and door lock control. Activating the window or door lock varies from pressing a button to pushing a rocker. In our case, a highly stylized switch is required with a "soft touch" feel, a short travel button, and low-effort actuation.

The components of a typical switch to meet these needs are detailed in Fig. 11.2.

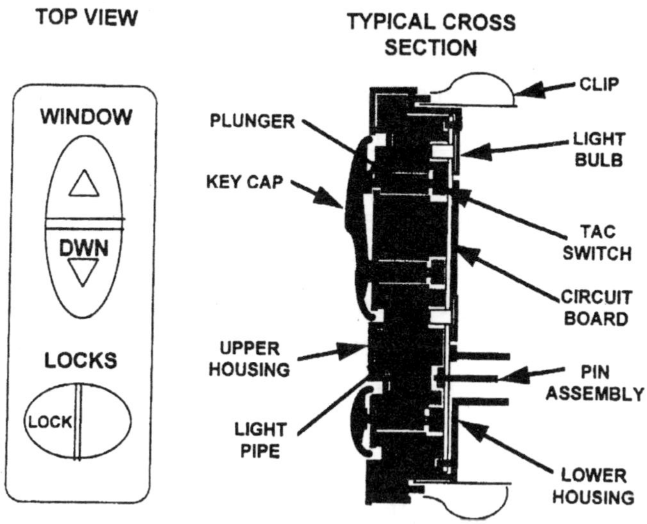

Fig. 11.2: Door lock and window control

The components of the control with their basic functions are:

1. Plunger: A plastic extension of the key cap that activates the tac switch when the key cap is depressed by the operator.
2. Key Cap: A soft-touch painted cover that the operator pushes to activate a switch function. The key cap is painted with a white base coat and a soft-touch black top coat. Graphics are laser etched by burning off the black paint to reveal the white graphics underneath.
3. Upper Housing: A clear plastic part painted white as a base coat and black as a top coat. Graphics are laser etched by burning off the black paint to reveal the white graphics underneath. The housing provides sealing, water management troughs, and a mounting surface for the key caps.

4. Light Pipe: A clear acrylic part that disperses light evenly from the bulbs to the upper housing and key cap graphics.
5. Clip: A metal formed part that retains the control into the door trim to mount the part and provides a removal force to prevent rattles.
6. Light Bulb: An incandescent source of light to backlight the graphic during night-time driving. The light bulb is mounted to the circuit board and twisted during assembly to be locked into place.
7. Tac Switch: A tactile switch that turns current on and off to the window and lock motors for operation. The switch provides driver feedback that is closed by initially resisting the finger push and "snapping" away from the finger after peak travel force is obtained.
8. Circuit Board: A fiber part that routes current from the vehicle's wiring harness to the tac switches and light bulbs and back out to the window and lock motors.
9. Pin Assembly: A series of tin-plated copper pins held in a row by a plastic base. The pin assembly is soldered to the circuit board and engages the vehicle wiring harness connector to conduct current into and out of the circuit board.
10. Lower Housing: A plastic part that provides sealing and mounting of the switch's internal parts to form a control. The housing provides mounting for the clips.

3. Determining the Voice of the Customer (VOC)

Customer wants and needs, which we will hence call the voice of the customer (VOC), were gathered using the survey method described in step (1) below. The information was then structured in step (2) using the Kano technique [7] in order to prioritize customers' demands. Next, we determined substitute quality characteristics (QCs), i.e. technical design requirements, that satisfy customer demands and classified them using the KJ affinity grouping method in step (3). These inputs were subsequently used for determining the product planning QFD matrix of step (4).

3.1. Customer survey — step (1)

A questionnaire was constructed to determine the VOC as follows:

1. A preliminary questionnaire was drawn up from the automotive company's market segment study [6], augmented with questions relating to reliability,

sound, and service. Each question as posed in a pair of forms: a positive from (functional) and a negative form (dysfunctional). The initial draft was comprised of 20 questions.

The questions were checked for appropriate wording following the advice of S. Shiba *et al.* [11] to:

(a) Avoid statements in the negative form, i.e. "does not break when dropped" is reworded to "provide strength." It is better to design for strength than avoid weakness.
(b) Avoid two valued concepts that inhibit flexibility in tradeoffs, i.e. use "temperature" not "hot or cold."
(c) Avoid abstract words like "reliable" or "durable." Use clear wording specific to the product and its use, i.e. "last 10 years."
(d) Do not state solutions; it prematurely limits the design options, i.e. use "actuator" not 'rocker."
(e) Avoid premature detail; it limits the design options, i.e. use "provides sealing" not "fog-, salt-, and waterproof."
(f) Avoid auxiliary verbs like "should" and "must"; they prejudge that the requirement is a necessity before all the customer requirements are known. Use present tense terms, like "is" or "are."
(h) Avoid intangible concepts. Use terms that are more concrete, i.e. use "evenly lit" not "the lighting is aesthetically pleasing."

2. A pilot study was administered to a cross-section of product users, with a sample size of ten. The respondents were requested to answer each question pair, choosing from five possible responses:

   (a) I like it that way
   (b) I expect it that way.
   (c) I am neutral.
   (d) I can live with it that way.
   (e) I dislike it.

   An excerpt from the questionnaire is reproduced below:

   12a. If the switch is scratch proof, how do you feel?
   12b. If the switch is not scratch proof, how do you feel?

Furthermore, the respondents were requested to suggest reworded questions in the event that some of the pilot questions were unclear to them. Based on the pilot study, two additional questions were added relating to abuse and accidental operation of the controls, and one redundant question was eliminated. The final questionnaire now contained a total of 21 pairs of questions and was administered to a larger sample of forty-four potential users. The Results were tabulated and analyzed in order to determine the primary response mode and the relative importance of each response from the customers' viewpoints. The Kano model methodology, which is described next, was used to accomplish this task.

3.2. The Kano methodology — step (2)

Professor Noriaki Kano [7] proposed that customer requirements are multidimensional and fall into three groups: one dimensional, attractive, and must be. These groupings are illustrated conceptually in the Kano diagram of Fig. 11.3, where the vertical axis represents customer satisfaction and the horizontal axis the degree to which product functionality is achieved. The diagram illustrates the relative importance of various functional quality characteristics for the customer. This permits product engineers and marketing personnel to jointly design-in product features that provide the greatest customer satisfaction levels.

The straight line in Fig. 11.3 represents "one dimensional" performance requirements. Increasing functionality yields a linear increase in customer satisfaction, *e.g.* the cheaper a television is the better — the customer likes it. Some requirements do not behave in a linear fashion. The "must be" curve in the figure represents basic requirements, which if not present cause customer dissatisfaction. Increasing the functionality in this case does not appreciably increase the amount of satisfaction, it only eliminates dissatisfaction. The Customer expects to have these requirements met, and they are typically unspoken by the customer. However, they must be included as the "price of entry" into the marketplace, i.e. a television must have good reception. The curve in the quadrant of Fig. 11.3 represents requirements that are attractive to the customer. Thus, the producer needs to discover and incorporate these into innovative designs in order to attract and excite the customer, *e.g.* automatic color control incorporated into the station signal that adjusts the television's color without viewer intervention.

The model is dynamic, and requirements change with time. As more producers add attractive features, such features become commonplace and no longer excite the customer. The features migrate to the linear performances curve and eventually become expected and end up the fourth quadrant curve of unspoken basic requirements. Thus, producers must continually incorporate new exciters in their product designs in order to satisfy the changing demands of customers.

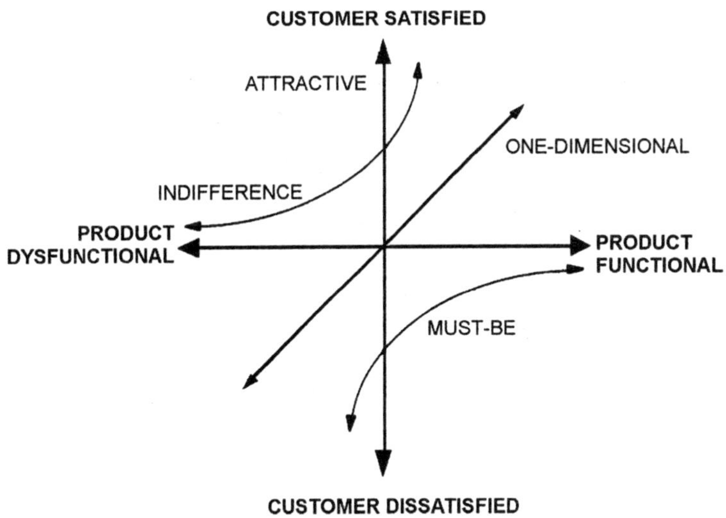

Fig. 11.3: The Kano diagram

In our study, the survey question paired responses were evaluated to determine the type of customer requirement that is being met. The Kano matrix enables the survey paired responses to be classified into one of six categories as illustrated in Table 11.1 below.

Table 11.1: The Kano matrix

Customer Requirements	Dysfunctional Response	1. Like	2. Must be	3. Neutral	4. Live with	5. Dislike
Functional Response	1. Like	Q	A	A	A	O
	2. Must-be	R	I	I	I	M
	3. Neutral	R	I	I	I	M
	4. Live with	R	I	I	I	M
	5. Dislike	R	R	R	R	Q

Where: A = attractive
O = one dimensional
M = must be
Q = questionable response
R = reverse
I = indifferent

Responses that are classified as A, O, or M easily plot into the corresponding quadrant of the Kano Diagram. Responses that are questionable (Q) indicate poor wording. Indifferent responses (I) mean the customer does not care. Reverse responses (R) mean that the customer changed his position for the same requirement and should be not be used.

The primary answer mode of each question (requirement) needs to be determined. The mode is determined by the most frequent response. In some cases, the survey might not clearly indicate a primary response mode. In other cases a tie may be found. Judgments by the project team members, increasing the sample size, or rewording the question and conducting another survey are the only actions available to resolve ties. In this case, judgment was used to select the basic "Must be" requirements. None of our survey responses were found to be questionable or reverse, and only two questions, *i.e.* "if the switch knobs color match" and "if the switch snaps when you push it," had indifferent responses. The requirements that correspond to these questions were thus ignored. The results of our survey are illustrated in Fig. 11.4.

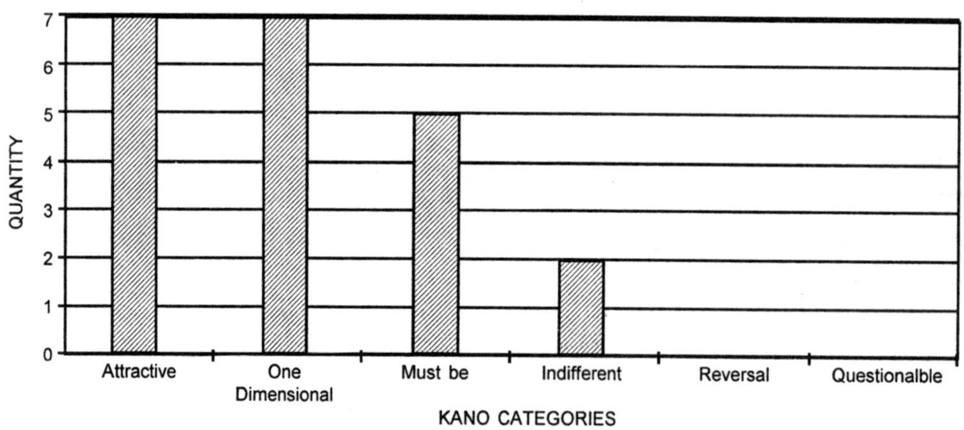

Fig. 11.4: Controls Kano model questionnaire results

The response frequencies above were used to determine the relative importance of each requirement for input to the QFD product planning matrix. The responses to each question pair were counted as one, and only the functional question response scores were tallied. The respective responses to the dysfunctional part of each question were used to group customer requirements into the basic, one dimensional, and attractive quality categories.

Next, the results were plotted as illustrated in Fig. 11.5. The diagram separates customer requirements into the corresponding categories of the Kano model.

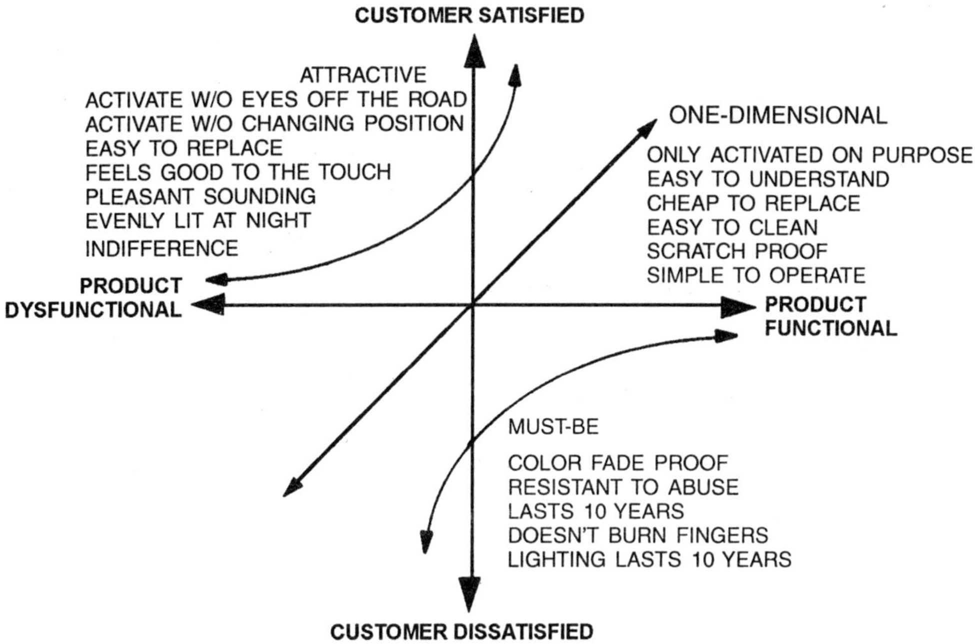

Fig. 11.5: Automotive controls multidemensional customer requirements

3.3. Classifying Quality Characteristics (QC by the KJ Method — step (3)

The project team, after obtaining customer demands, has the responsibility of determining the product design technical requirements, or substitute quality characteristics (QC). These are technical requirements that must be measurable and verifiable. The process is creative, and the product planning experts on the team must take the lead. Brainstorming for ideas is generally the customary approach. The KJ method is used to identify existing affinities among information entities for classifying them into similarity groups.

The KJ method was used in this case to group the quality characteristics (QC), as proposed by the team of experts, and organized them as the input "Hows" in the QFD product planning matrix. The process was as follows:

1. Brainstormed in order to determine the QCs for the automotive controls.
2. Wrote down QCs on "post-it" notes.
3. Grouped the quality characteristics into similar groups.

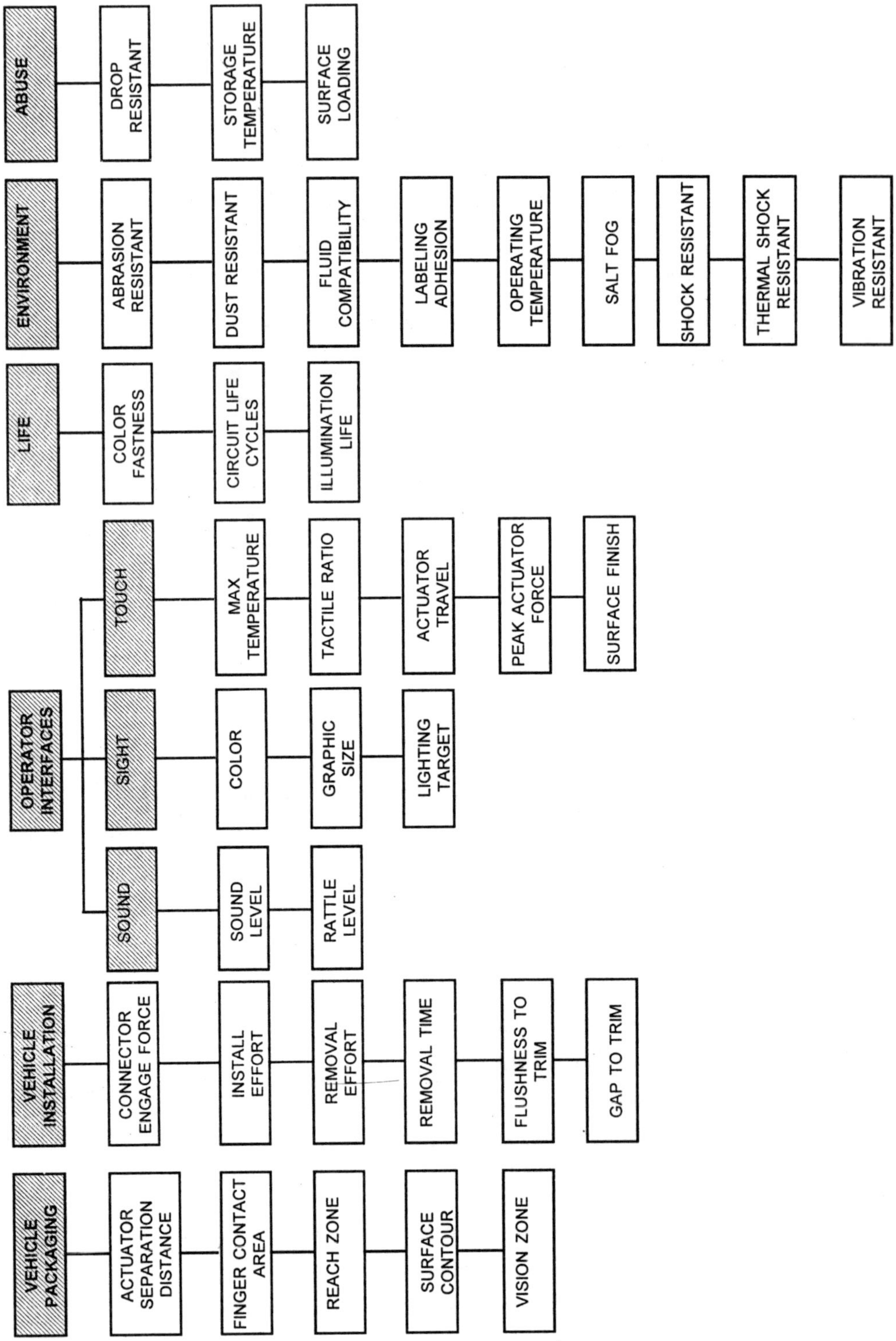

Fig. 11.6: The KJ affinity grouping of the automotive controls quality characteristics

The resultant groupings were: vehicle packaging, vehicle installation, operator interfaces, life, environment, and abuse. These are illustrated in Fig. 11.6. It is important to note that these characteristics are not the traditional technical specifications describing the physical attributes of parts and components, but the functional attributes of the planned product. This is a crucial distinction, and this step must be observed in order to develop innovative design concepts and not be limited to a preexisting fixed design.

4. The Product Planning (House of Quality) Matrix — Step (4)

The purpose of the product planning matrix is to relate the customer demands (VOC) to a measurable set of technical design requirements or substitute quality characteristics (QC), summarize the competitive benchmarking data, and establish a product quality plan. The conceptual elements are illustrated in Fig. 11.7, and the actual matrix for the controls case is reproduced in Fig. 11.8. We used the computational techniques of the QFD methodology, and as such we will not elaborate on the details in this paper. The interested reader can consult the QFD literature, *e.g.* see Aswad [3, 4].

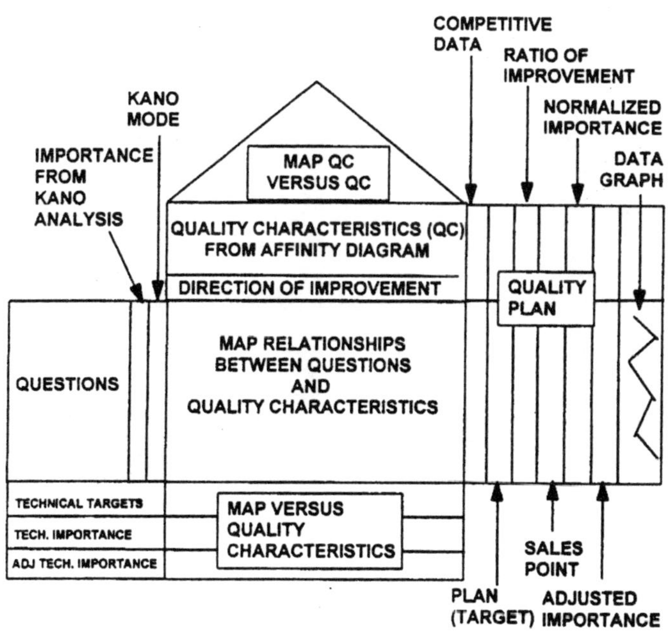

Fig. 11.7: Conceptual Product Planning House of Quality

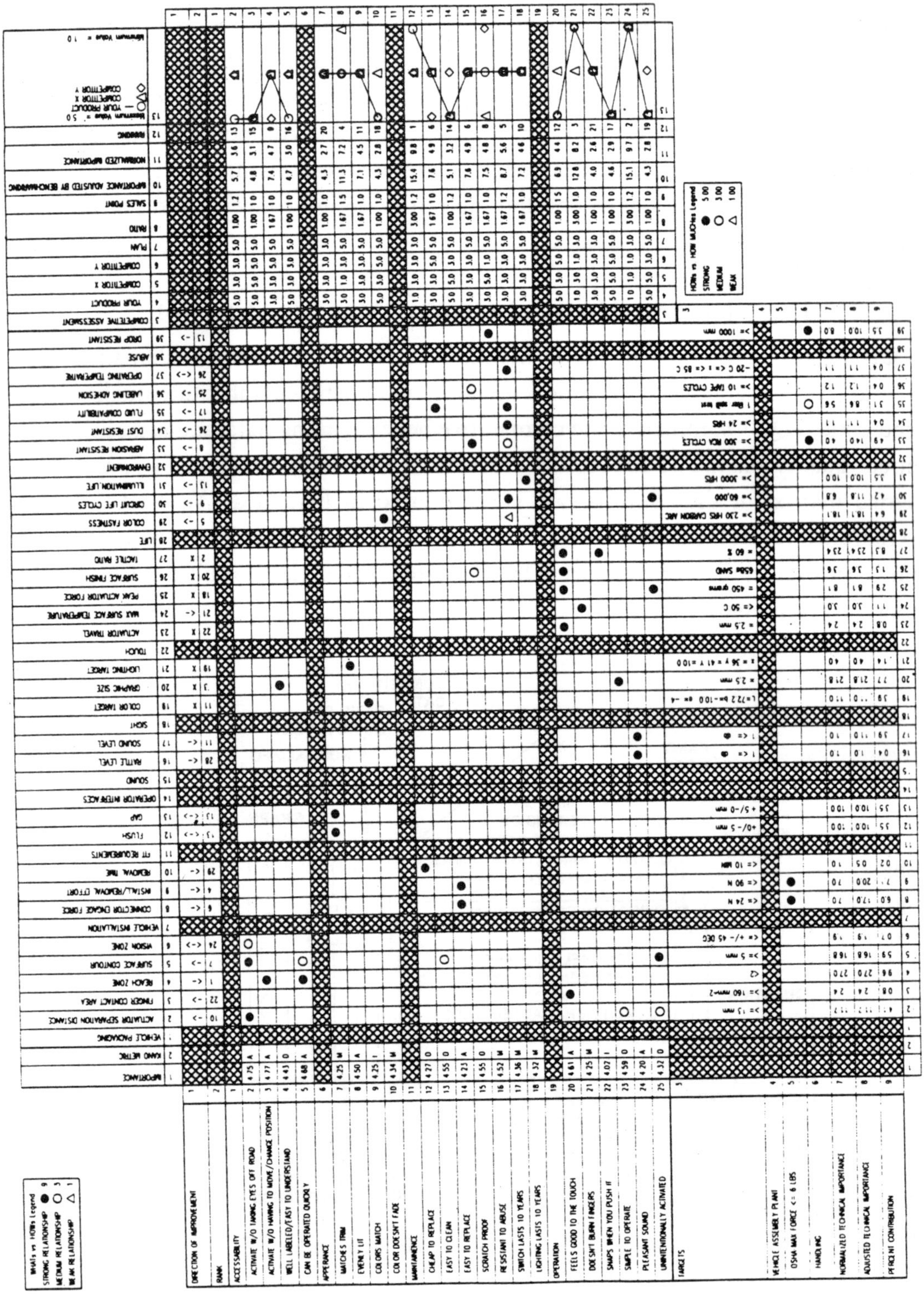

Fig. 11.8: Automotive Controls Product Planning Matrix

However, it is noteworthy to mention that the benchmarking activity was conducted by a questionnaire directed at customers in the market segment who are familiar with the competitive products, in addition to those who owned our product. Once the comparative capabilities of the competitors were determined, a design quality (target) plan for our product was established. The new product capabilities must at least meet but preferably exceed those of the competition. This is typically a strategic concurrent managerial decision which is to be taken by senior management based on the inputs of the development team.

5. Function Analysis: Context and FAST Diagrams — Steps 5 & 6

Cost and quality tradeoffs are often ignored in the simplified QFD methodology. On the other hand, value analysis studies typically omit relating demanded quality when striving to reduce cost. We will use function analysis to incorporate such tradeoffs at an early stage of the product development process.

According to Akiyama [2], functional analysis is the breaking down of the whole to reveal the various components, elements, and aspects of which it is composed. The breaking down process is a systematic decomposition of functions from the product's goal down to primitive functions that support this primary goal. The organization of functions into a horizontal diagram where the product's goal is charted on the left and primitive functions on the far right is known as a Function Analysis System Technique (FAST) diagram. FAST diagrams are used in value engineering to identify necessary and unnecessary functions with their associated costs. Reducing costs while maintaining all demanded functions increases the product's value to the customer. Reducing the number of components through Design for Assembly (DFA), while maintaining the original functionality, reduces the cost of assembly and the final cost.

The functional analysis process consists of four steps:

5.1. Understand the object of analysis through data collection

The scope of the project needs to be defined to determine the boundaries of the product and its functions. For example, it is not sufficient to specify the scope as "use the switch in an automobile," because the functions required for assembling and servicing the controls are not captured. A context diagram is required to set a more comprehensive scope. Fig. 11.9 illustrates the context diagram for our controls case. The scope as redefined by this context diagram is "assemble, use, and service the controls in an automobile." This scope statement captures the life cycle of the controls in a more expressive way.

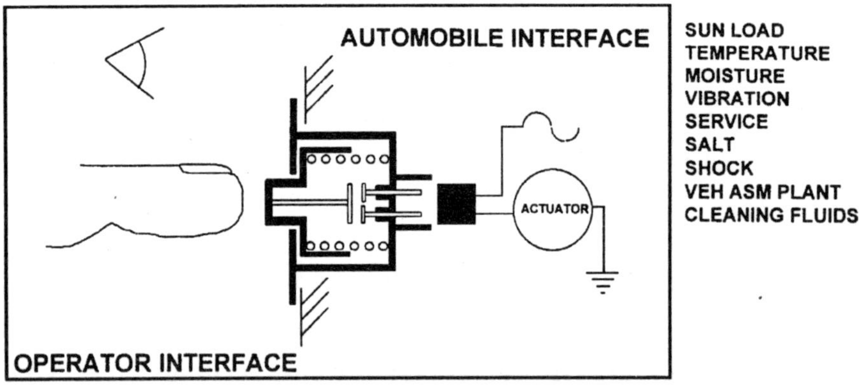

Fig. 11.9: Context Diagram for the Controls Case

5.2. Defining the functions using noun-verb phrases

Defining functions using noun-verb phrases makes it possible to identify each function clearly. Care should be exercised in formulating these phrases such that product functions are described rather than part designations. For example, the phrase "switch current" predefines a solution, while the preferred "control current" phrase allows the consideration of design alternatives ranging from solid state transistors to mechanical switches.

All such functional phrases were obtained through a brainstorming session of the product development team, and subsequently classified using the affinity grouping (KJ) method.

5.3. Systematize the functions

Functions exist in relationships to each other. To understand the relationships, the functions are organized into a FAST diagram. The principal function of "Control Windows & Locks" is positioned on the far left,, while supporting functions are placed to the right. As you move across the diagram the principal function is decomposed into supporting functions. Each supporting function to the right on a common branch answers "how" the function to the left is accomplished, while moving to the left answers "why" the function is accomplished, as shown in Fig. 11.10.

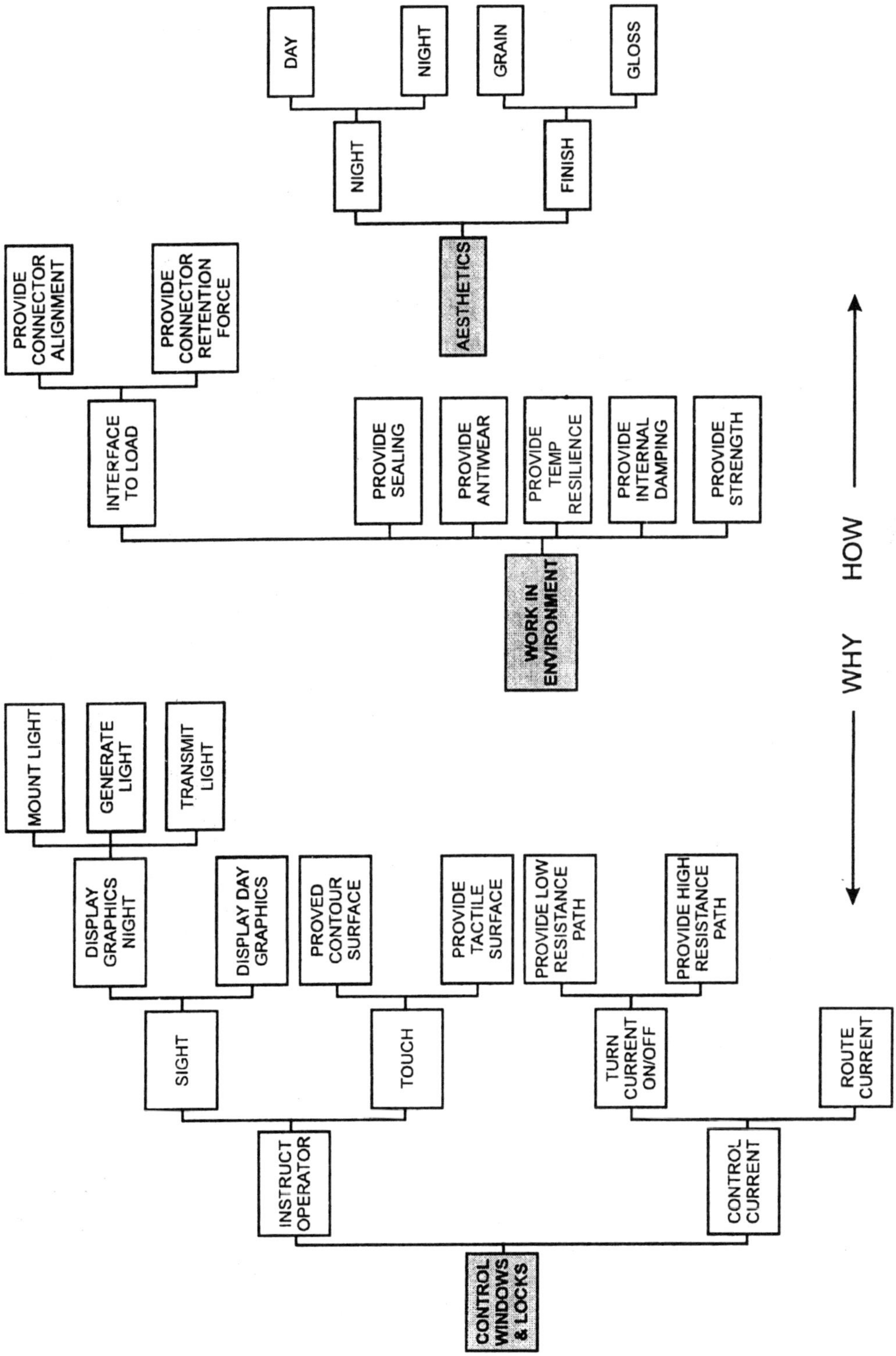

Fig. 11.10: FAST diagram for Automotive Controls functions

The decomposition process ends when the last supporting function represents a basic entity achieving a singular goal; in our case, a primitive function that is executed by a simple rudimentary part.

The FAST diagram is checked by moving along each branch to ensure the "how" and "why" questions are answered consistently. The branch end point is also tested to ensure that the function could not be decomposed further and is a primitive function.

5.4. Identify functions in the FAST diagram as basic and secondary

Functions are classified from a variety of perspectives. Two basic classifications are *use* and *esteem* functions. Use functions involve the purposes or goals of why a product is used. Esteem functions relate to the sensory attributes of a product like color, texture, and smell. Use and esteem functions are composed of both basic and secondary product functions. Basic functions give the product its reason for existence, while secondary functions assist in the realization of the basic function. The esteem functions are grouped together and labeled "Aesthetics." Furthermore, all principal functions are decomposed into basic functions.

6. The QFD Function Matrix — Step (7)

The simplified QFD methodology proceeds directly to phase II, i.e. the parts planning matrix. This jumps directly to dealing with physical parts that pertain to a specific design and does not explicitly explore alternative concepts. The capabilities of alternative designs to satisfy the required functions must also be evaluated. The FAST diagram, developed in the previous step, enables such evaluations. By staying in the functional realm, the concurrent engineering team is thus not restricted by preconceived parts concepts, and the generation of new concepts becomes easier.

Not all customer demands are equal, as illustrated by the relative importance column in the product planning house of quality matrix. It follows that the functions which meet these demands must also be weighted accordingly. A function matrix is created by mapping functions from the FAST diagram to the customer demands. This mapping thus weights the relative importance of each function and provides the ability to evaluate various design concepts effectively. Thus, referring back to customer requirements in this step ensures that all demanded functions are incorporated in a design or are eliminated if they do not map into any customer demands. Fig. 11.11 illustrates such a function matrix, illustrating how mapping the functions to customer demands assigns relative importance weights to each function.

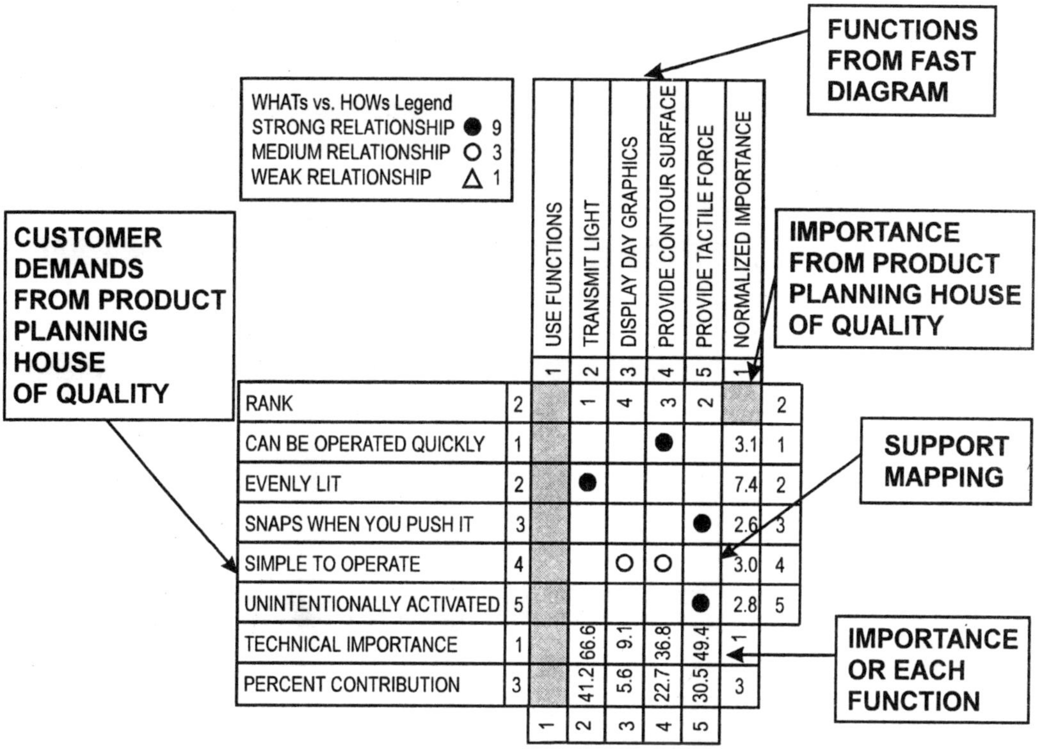

Fig. 11.11: Example of a Function Matrix

For the automotive controls case, the complete function matrix is illustrated in Fig. 11.12. Examining the function matrix, the top five functions are temperature resilience, antiwear, provide removal force, sealing, and strength. Only "provide removal force" requires further examination. Since the scope of the project includes maintenance, the removal force mapped to two maintenance demands, "cheap to replace" and "easy to replace." "Cheap to replace" is the most important customer demand, and "provide removal force" directly relates to labor, the most significant cost component of replacement cost. This should be considered as one of the most important requirements.

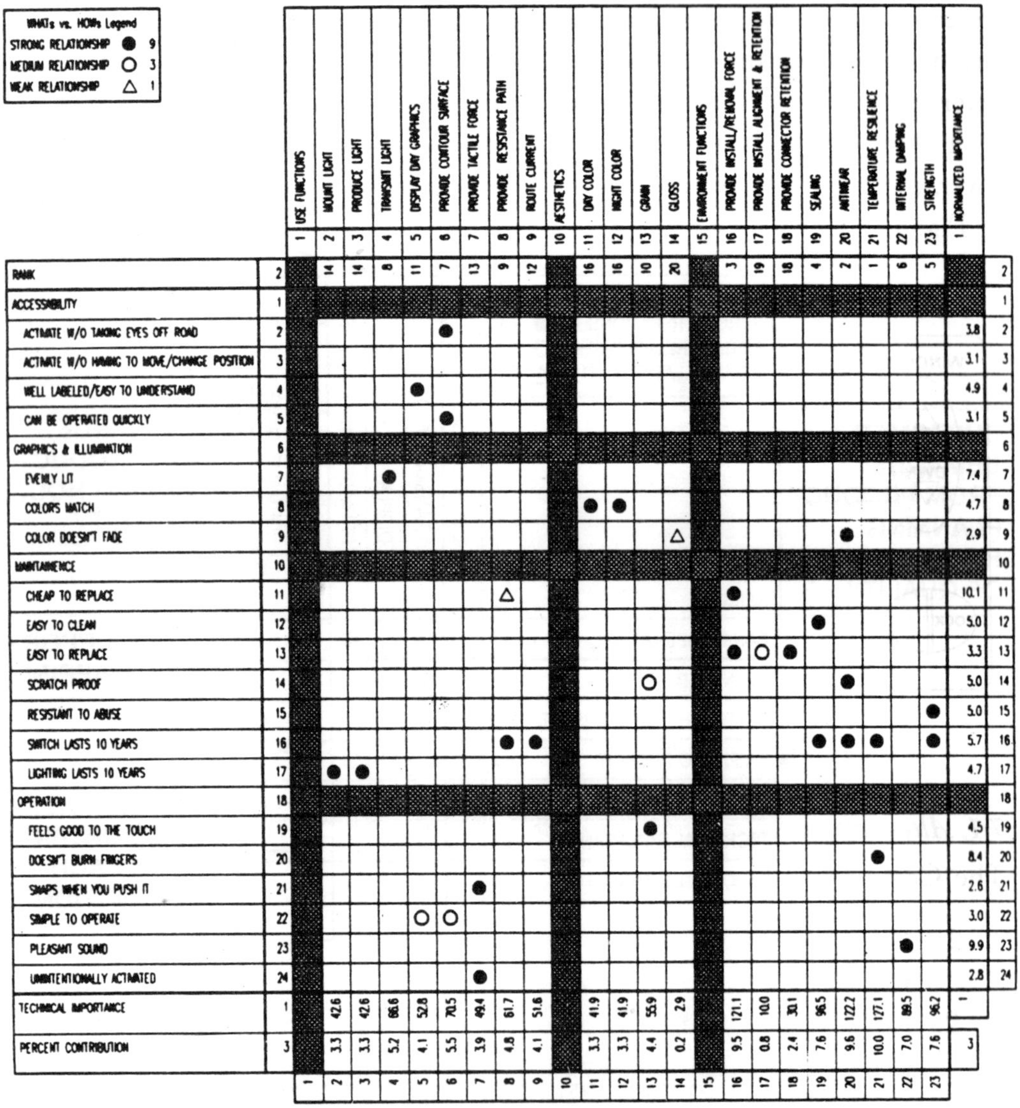

Fig. 11.12: Automotive Controls Function Matrix

No functions were mapped to "activate w/o having to move/change position." This customer demand is met by the packaging of the controls within the driver's reach, and is not a function of the controls mechanism.

7. Alternative Concepts Functional Evaluation — Step (8)

The concurrent engineering team next engages in generating alternative design concepts by brainstorming while examining competitive designs. Generated alternatives must meet customer, organizational, and government requirements as determined in the preceding step by the QFD function matrix.

For the controls case, three alternative were proposed with variations of the top cover, and variations in the internal current control mechanism. These are illustrated in Fig. 11.13.

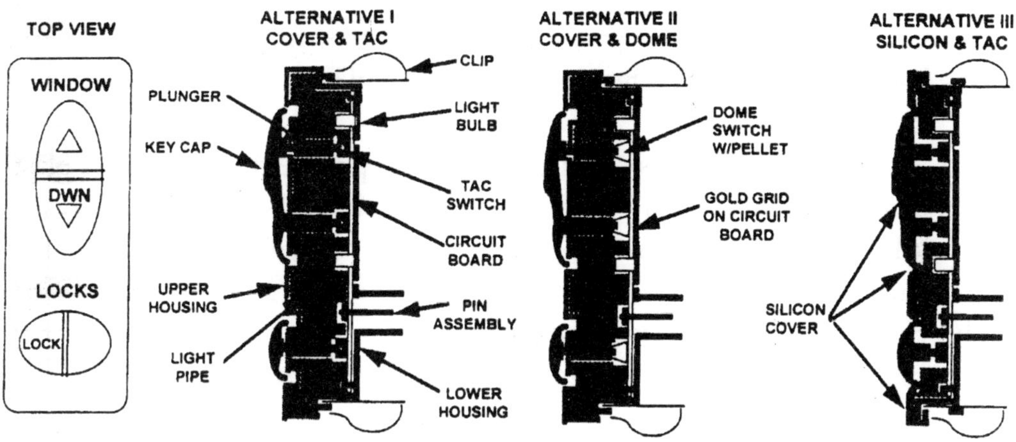

Fig. 11.13: Generated Altemative Design Concepts for Automotive Controls

7.1. Alternative design concept I

The Cover and Tac consist of the following components:

1. Plunger: A plastic extension of the key cap that activates the tac switch when the key cap is depressed by the operator.
2. Key Cap: A soft-touch painted cover that the operator pushes to activate a switch function. The key cap is painted with a white base coat and a soft-touch black top coat. Graphics are laser etched by burning off the black paint to reveal the white graphics underneath.
3. Upper Housing: A clear plastic part painted white as a base coat and black as a top coat. Graphics are laser etched by burning off the black paint to reveal white graphics underneath. The housing provides sealing, water management troughs, and a mounting surface for the key caps.
4. Light Pipe: A clear acrylic part that disperses light evenly from the bulbs to the upper housing and key cap graphics.
5. Clip: A metal formed part that retains the control into the door trim to mount the part and provides a removal force to prevent rattles.

6. Light Bulb: An incandescent source of light to back light the graphic during night-time driving. The light bulb is mounted to the circuit board and twisted during assembly to be locked into place.
7. Tac Switch: A tactile switch that turns current on and off to the window and lock motors for operation. The switch provides driver feedback that is closed by initially resisting the finger push and "snapping" away from the finger after peak travel force is obtained.
8. Circuit Board: A fiber part that routes current from the vehicle' wiring harness to the tac switches and light bulbs and back out to the window and lock motors.
9. Pin Assembly: A series of tin-plated copper pins held in a row by a plastic base. The pin assembly is soldered to the circuit board and engages the vehicles wiring harness connector to conduct current into and out of the circuit board.
10. Lower Housing: A plastic part that provides sealing and mounting of the switch's internal parts to form a control. The housing provides mounting for the clips.

7.2. Alternative design concept II

The Cover and Dome are identical to Alternative I, except that the tac switches are replaced by elastomeric dome switches, and the circuit board has a gold-plated contact grid. The variant component descriptions are as follows:

1. Dome Switch: An elastomeric dome switch made of nonconductive silicon. The dome is formed in a conical shape to provide a spring force when depressed. Current is conducted through a carbon-doped silicon pellet that is glued to the bottom surface of the dome. When the dome is depressed, the pellet shorts two gold grids on the circuit board together.
2. Circuit Board: A fiber material board identical to Alternative I, except two gold-plated grids are added under each dome switch.

7.3. Alternative design concept III

Alternative III, Silicon and Tac, is similar to Alternative I, except that the upper housing, key caps, and plungers have been combined into one component, a silicon cover. The variant component description is:

1. Silicon Cover: A single-piece silicon pad that varies in section thickness. The thick section acts to seal out the environment like the upper housing, and a thin section provides flexibility to actuate the tac switch like the key caps and plungers. The silicon is clear and transmits light to the extreme ends of the control, allowing shorter light pipe and a reduction in the overall height of the control.

7.4. Efficiency of alternative design concepts

The efficiency of each proposed design is calculated by taking the number of components minus one, and dividing by the number of functions. The more components in a design, the more internal interfaces that must be managed to ensure a good design. Eliminating components increases the inherent reliability of

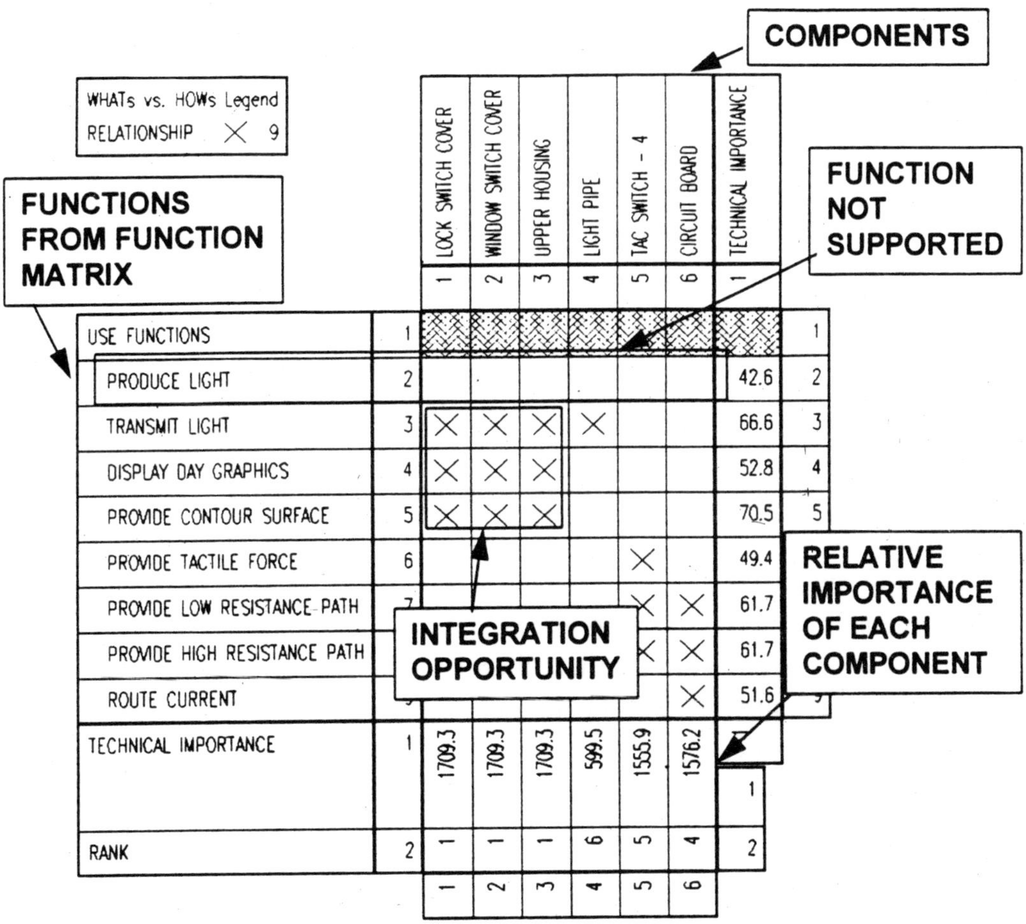

Fig. 11.14: Part to Function Matrix

a design, since components and complex interfaces that can malfunction are eliminated. To check for design functionality, each alternative is plotted on a part to function matrix. All functions should be mapped to a component; otherwise, the design would be incomplete. single functions when mapped to many components indicate an area for potential improvement by integrating components together into "chunks" to eliminate interfaces. An example of part to function matrix is shown in Fig. 11.14.

In our automotive controls case, each alternative's components are mapped to the required functions, and efficiency of each alternative was calculated to be:

Alternative I:
1 - (11-1) components/23 functions) = 56.5%

Alternative II:
1 - (11-1) components/23 functions) = 56.5%

Alternative III:
1 - (8-1) components/23 functions) = 69.6%

8. Concept Selection Matrix — Step (9)

The Pugh concept selection technique [10] computes an overall score for each alternative in order to select the best design. Each alternative is mapped to the evaluation criteria and compared to a baseline design. If in the judgment of the product engineering team, a criterion in an alternative is deemed better than that of the baseline design, it receives a preferred "+" score. If it is judged to be worse, it receives a less preferred "-" score, or an "S" score if equivalent. The resulting scores quickly provide a visual comparison indicating areas for potential improvements and possibly suggesting a new and better hybrid design, which we believe is the primary benefit of using this technique.

However, the above assumes that all criteria (functions) are weighted equally, which is not generally the case. Therefore, we have assigned the pluses, minuses, and "S" scores the values of +1, -1 and zero, respectively, and weighted them by the relative importance values for each function from the function matrix. Thus, weighted scores for each alternative were developed, and the alternatives were accordingly ranked. The technique is illustrated in Fig. 11.15.

In our automotive controls case, the baseline Silicon and Tac design was found to be better in satisfying the majority of the required functions. The other two

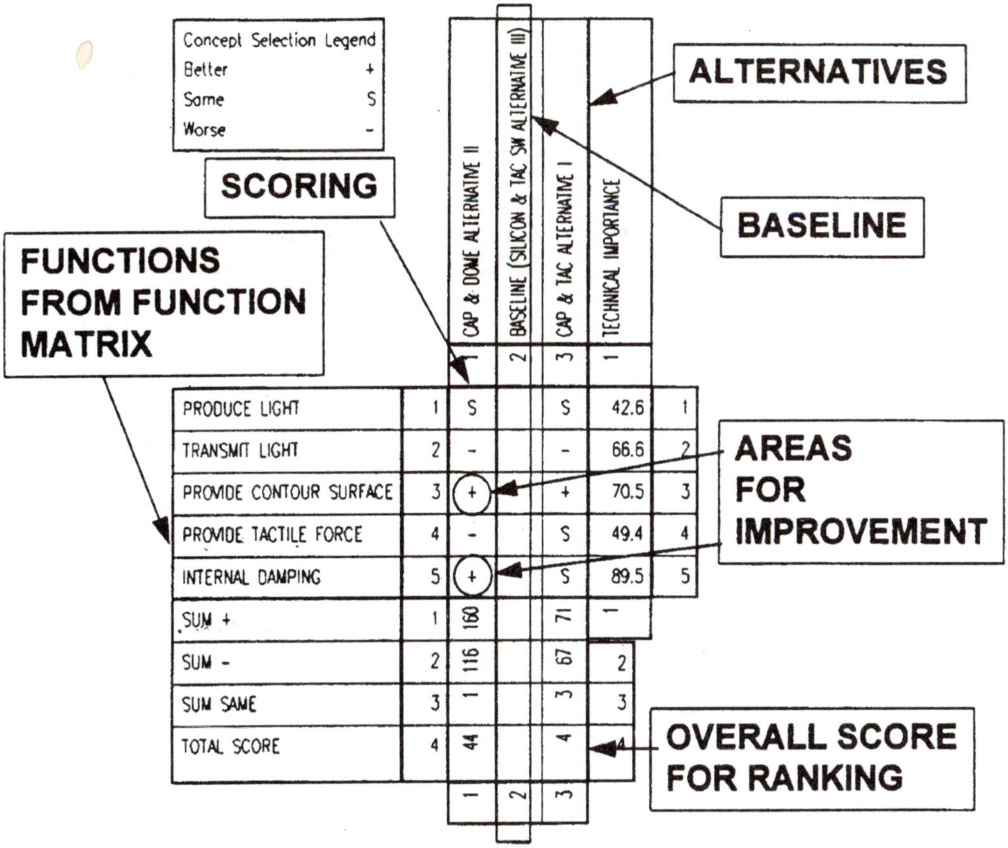

Fig. 11.15: Alternative Concept Selection Matrix

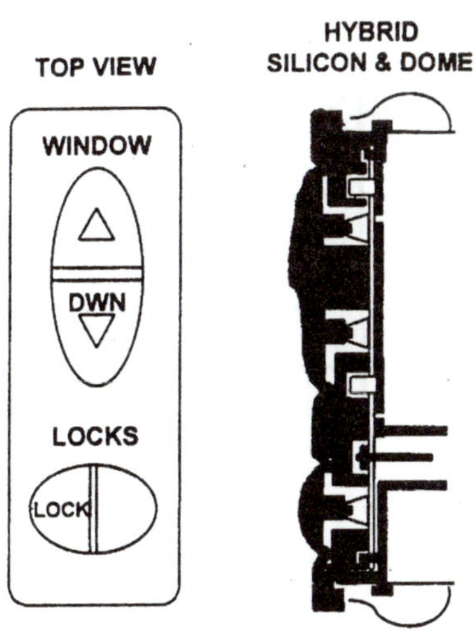

Fig. 11.16: New Hybrid Design Alternative

WHATs vs. HOWs Legend	
RELATIONSHIP	X 9

		1 SILICON COVER	2 LIGHT PIPE	3 DOME SWITCH - 4	4 CIRCUIT BOARD	5 HOUSING	6 BULB - 2	7 CLIPS - 2	8 PIN ASSEMBLY	1 TECHNICAL IMPORTANCE	
USE FUNCTIONS	1										1
MOUNT LIGHT	2				X					42.6	2
PRODUCE LIGHT	3						X			42.6	3
TRANSMIT LIGHT	4	X	X							66.6	4
DISPLAY DAY GRAPHICS	5	X								52.8	5
PROVIDE CONTOUR SURFACE	6	X								70.5	6
PROVIDE TACTILE FORCE	7			X						49.4	7
PROVIDE RESISTANCE PATH	8			X	X					61.7	8
ROUTE CURRENT	9				X				X	51.6	9
AESTHETICS	10										10
DAY COLOR	11	X								41.9	11
NIGHT COLOR	12	X	X				X			41.9	12
GRAIN & GLOSS	13	X								55.9	13
ENVIRONMENT FUNCTIONS	14										14
PROVIDE INSTALL & REMOVAL FORCE	15					X		X		121.1	15
PROVIDE INSTALL ALIGNMENT & RETENTION	16					X				10.0	16
PROVIDE CONNECTOR RETENTION FORCE	17					X				5.7	17
SEALING	18	X			X	X				96.5	18
ANTIWEAR	19	X								122.2	19
TEMPERATURE RESILIENCE	20	X		X	X	X				127.1	20
INTERNAL DAMPING	21		X							89.5	21
STRENGTH	22				X	X				96.2	22
TECHNICAL IMPORTANCE	1	6080.7	1782.8	2144.4	4283.4	4110.8	761.2	1089.7	464.7	1	1
RANK	2	1	5	4	2	3	7	6	8		2
		1	2	3	4	5	6	7	8		

Fig. 11.17: Hybrid Design Part to Function Mapping Matrix

alternatives received lower scores for the sealing, antiwear, and temperature resilience functions. However, it was determined that the baseline could still be improved by replacing the noisy tac switch with a dome switch. Thus, a new alternative hybrid design was proposed, as illustrated in Fig. 11.16.

Next, the function matrix for this selected new hybrid design was constructed in order to ensure its effectiveness. This is illustrated in Fig. 11.17.

9. Design Feasibility and Risk Analysis — Step (10)

Barriers to the realization of a selected alternative are defined as risk. Risk must be managed as an integral part of project management. According to Kepner and Tregoe [8], managing risk consists of identifying risks, quantifying the risk items, establishing a risk watch list, and developing a risk mitigation plan for each risk item.

Risks are identified by examining an alternative's components for new technology, complexity, and high levels of system interdependency. Quantifying risk is accomplished by assigning a numerical value between 0 and 1 for the probability of success or failure and the ensuing consequences for each alternative. A risk watch list consists of a set of milestones based on program execution timing that must be met for successful product delivery, *e.g.* completion of three times life switch durability testing. The risk mitigation plan defines risk reduction options, for concept alternatives, which could be implemented if planned milestones were not achieved.

9.1. Methodology for quantifying risk

The probability of success of each component is determined by rating the components in three areas: technical maturity, complexity, and system interdependence. The consequences of success are determined by examining the impact to component cost, delivery schedule impact, and the technical performance of each component. Often it might be easier to assign ratings when working with the consequences of failure, as opposed to success, and its impact on the component's cost, delays in scheduled delivery, and reduced technical performance. This is the approach that we have followed in this case.

The rating for an individual design was derived by averaging the ratings of its individual components. The mathematical representation are:

Probability of success (P)

$P_s = (P_{sm} + P_{sc} + P_{sd})/3$

where

sm = success maturity factor

sc = success complexity factor

sd = success dependency factor

Consequences of success (C)

$C_s = (C_{sc} + C_{ss} + C_{st})/3$

where

sc = success cost factor

ss = success schedule factor

st = success technical factor

and the Risk (R)

$R_f = (P_f + C_f) - (P_f \times C_f)$

were

$P_f = 1 - P_s$

$C_f = 1 - C_f$

The magnitude for assessing each success factor is determined by examining each risk item as listed the Tables 11.2 and 11.3.

Table 11.2: Probability of Success (Ps) Attributes

MAGNITUDE	MATURITY FACTOR (P_{SM})	COMPLEXITY FACTOR (P_{sc})	DEPENDENCY FACTOR (P_{sd})
.10 (Low)	State of the art Some research completed	Extremely complex	Performance dependent on new system schedule, facility, or associated vendor
.30 (Minor)	Technology available	Significant increase from baseline	Schedule dependent on system performance, facility, or associated vendor
.50 (Moderate)	Major change feasible	Moderate increase	Performance dependent on existing system performance, facility, or associated vendor
.70 (Significant)	Minor redesign	Minor increase in complexity	Schedule dependent on existing system, facility, or associated vendor
.90 (High)	Existing	Simple design	Independent of existing system, facility, or associated vendor

Table 11.3: Consequence of Success (Cs) Guideline

MAGNITUDE	TECHNOLOGY FACTOR (C_{st})	COST FACTOR (C_{sc})	SCHEDULE factor (C_{ss})
.10 (Low)	Technical goals/requirements cannot be achieved	Cost estimates increased in excess of 50%	Large schedule slip that affects subsystem/ component milestones or has possible affect on system's milestones
.30 (Minor)	Significant degradation in technical performance	Cost estimates increased by 20 to 50%	Development schedule slip in excess of three months
.50 (Moderate)	Some reduction in technical performance	Cost estimates increased by 5 to 20%	Small slip in schedule
.70 (Significant)	Small reduction in technical performance	Cost estimates increased by 1 to 5%	Minor slip in schedule (less than one month), requires some adjustments in milestones
.90 (High)	Minimal impact or no consequences	Budget estimates not exceeded, some transfer of money	Negligible impact on program, slight development schedule change compensated by available schedule slack

9.2. Risk assessment results for the automotive controls case

The automotive controls alternatives were examined for risks and it was found that the silicon cover, the dome switches, and the circuit board should be risk monitored. The silicon cover is a very large piece compared to other components in production. The largest automotive application of a silicon cover, a remote control key entry key fob, is less than one-half the size of the proposed automotive control. The dome

Table 11.4: Risk Alternatives

ALTERNATIVE	COMPONENT	RISK	STATUS
Hybrid silicon and Dome	Silicon Cover Dome Switches Circuit Board	.89 .68 .46	High Medium Low
Hard Kay Cap and Tac Switch	Kep Cap Tac Switch Circuit Board	.23 .25 .19	Low Low Low

switches had only been used in other applications to 40,000 cycles, and are now being applied to 60,000 cycles. the circuit board has a gold-plated grid system that forms the switch contact with the dome switch. The extended cycle target of an additional 20,000 cycles may wear the gold contact off the circuit board; thus the circuit board should be risk monitored.

ID	Task Name	Duration	Start
1	CONCEPT SELECTION	4w	4/22/96
2	DESIGN CONCEPT PART	2w	5/20/96
3	CONSTRUCT PROOF OF CONCEPT PA	4w	6/3/96
4	RISK TESTS	10d	7/1/96
5	HIGH RISK DURABILITY TESTS	2w	7/1/96
6	HIGH RISK SEALING TEST	1d	7/1/96
7	CONCEPT EVALUATION	1d	7/15/96
8	PROTO DESIGN	10w	7/16/96
9	PROTO TOOL CONSTRUCTION	40d	9/24/96
10	PAD TOOL	8w	9/24/96
11	CIRCUIT BOARD	4w	9/24/96
12	DOME PAD	6w	9/24/96
13	HOUSING	8w	9/24/96
14	CONTSTRUCT PROTO CONTROL	2w	11/19/96
15	TEST PROTO CONTROL	6w	12/3/96
16	PROTOTYE DELIVERY	0d	4/14/97
17	PROTO REDESIGN RISK RECOVERY	4w	7/16/96
18	RISK RECOVERY PROTO TOOLING	60d	8/13/96
19	KEY CAPS	12w	8/13/96
20	PLUNGERS	6w	8/13/96
21	TAC SWITCH	1w	8/13/96
22	CIRCUIT BOARD	4w	8/13/96
23	UPPER & LOWER HOUSINGS	12w	8/13/96
24	CONSTRUCT RISK RECOVER PART	2w	11/5/96
25	TEST RISK REVOVERY	4w	4/14/97

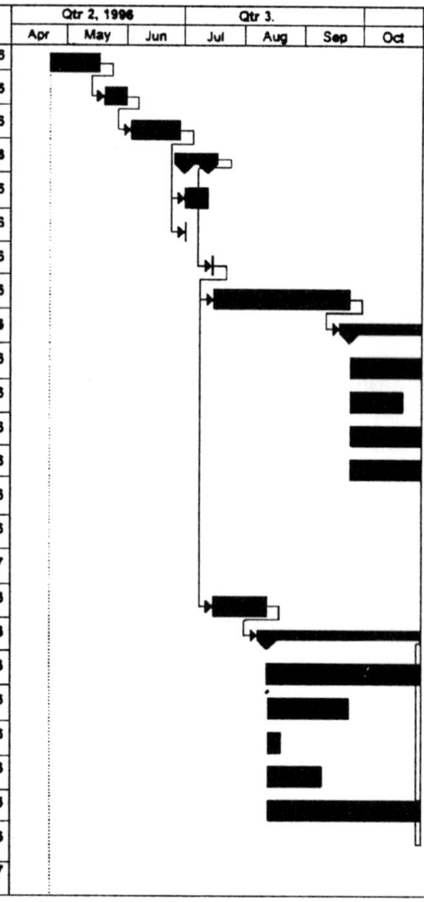

Project:
Date: 4/22/96

Task
Progress
Milestone
Summary
Rolled Up Task
Rolled Up Milestone
Rolled Up Progress

Fig. 11.18: Automotive Controls Risk Management Schedule

The risk and recovery plan alternatives are summarized in Table 11.4.

Consequently, a risk watch list of schedule milestones was generated to monitor the progress of the development program. If a risk milestone is passed without successful completion, the design must be changed to the mitigation alternative in order to keep the program on schedule. The project schedule is illustrated in Fig. 11.18.

10. Design for Assembly Analysis — Step (11)

Design for Assembly (DFA) is a methodology that enables a design team to analyze components of an assembly in order to reduce life cycle costs and increase customer satisfaction. A design team may apply DFA to develop new products or improve upon existing products. A product's life cycle cost consists of the costs to manufacture, assemble and service the product. Simplifying a product's components reduces manufacturing costs. Reducing the assembly time of a product through ease of handling, insertion, and fastening reduces assembly costs. Providing simple components increases inherent product reliability and reduces services costs.

Design for assembly/design for manufacturability (DFA/DFM) consists of three phases. The first phase is determining the assembly order and initial assembly time. The second phase identifies and eliminates unnecessary parts. The third phase makes the remaining parts easy to assemble. A helpful DFA methodology is suggested by Boothroyd and Dewhurst [5]. The (B&D) DFA methodology provides the engineer with guidelines for part number reductions. The guidelines are specified in manual look up tables and with the assistance of a computer software methodology that is used to help redesign the control assembly.

The manual B&D method was used, and the following assumptions were made prior to performing the analysis. The first assumption was that our product will be manually assembled. All components were assumed to come in a box and randomly oriented. In reality, many parts might be oriented during packaging to make them easier to handle. For our purposes, consistency in the analysis was more important than the unidentified packaging process.

10.1. DFA — phase I

Phase I starts with specifying the assembly order and the identification of assembly cost. The initial assembly order is determined from past experience. The hybrid control's pre-DFA assembly sequence is illustrated in Fig. 11.19. The directional

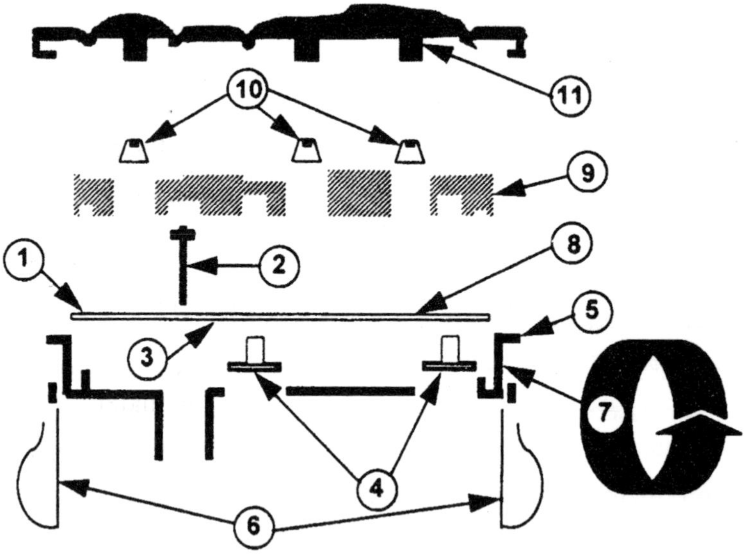

Fig. 11.19: Hybrid silicon and Dome Pre-DFA assembly

circled arrow indicates that a flip is necessary to perform assembly. The assembly process is then detailed step by step to determine the amount of time necessary to select an individual component from a supply box (handling) and to add or attach to the assembly (insertion).

For handling, the B&D method utilizes metrics to determine the amount of time necessary to select a part from a supply box, called alpha (α) symmetry and beta (β) symmetry. Alpha symmetry is determined by the degrees of rotation about an axis perpendicular to the axis of load before a part repeats its orientation. Beta symmetry is determined by the degrees of rotation about an axis parallel to the axis of load before a part repeats its orientation. A sphere has α and β values of 0 degrees, while a cone has an α = 360 degrees and β = 0 degrees, when loading point-down into a hole. Additionally, a penalty time is assessed for the number of hands required, the use of grasping aids, the large size, and in the event that the parts might tangle or stick together.

For an insertion operation, the B&D method characterizes the amount of time required to add or attach the part to the assembly. The length of time is dependent as to whether the part is added but not immediately secured, immediately secured, the amount of deformation required to secure, and if a secondary operation is required to secure.

The analysis for the hybrid controls design yielded the values of 117.6 seconds of assembly time, which at a labor rate of $30 per hour results in a cost of $0.98.

10.2. DFA — phase II

Phase II consists of eliminating unnecessary parts. The B&D method specifies an efficiency metric to rate each design as calculated by the equation:

Efficiency = (Minimum parts * 3 seconds/part//Total assembly time in seconds
In order to decide if a part is theoretically necessary, three questions are posed:

(1) Does the part move relative to other parts?
(2) Does the part have to be made of a different material?
(3) Does the part have to be disassembled in order to allow the addition of other parts?

If the answer to any one of these questions is a "yes," then the part is considered theoretically to be a necessary part. The hybrid controls components were found to be necessary (minimum) parts. The efficiency of the hybrid design was calculated to be 18 per cent.

Parts that were candidates for elimination are the clips and the process of integrating the dome switches into a dome pad. The DFA clip-elimination analysis indicated that the annual savings were $16,330, with a payback period of 0.67 years. The integration of the dome switches into a dome pad assembly resulted in an annual savings of $1,980, with a payback of 1.01 years. Both proposals had a payback period that is sufficiently close to a mandated 1 year time, and were accordingly accepted. The DFA analysis is illustrated in Fig. 20, which indicates that the proposed hybrid controls design has a total assembly cost of $ 0.52 with an efficiency of 34 per cent. This is a 47 per cent reduction in assembly cost and a 16 per cent increase in part efficiency.

10.3. DFA — phase III

Phase III consists of making the parts easier to assemble. This phase was actually conducted simultaneously with Phase I. The insertion times were evaluated for each part and any penalties noted for the removal operation. Redesign of the component details was performed to achieve the minimum insertion penalties. Components were modified as follows:

1. Tapered guide pins were added to the housing to ease alignment of the circuit board, dome pad, and light pipes.

DATE: **MAR 29, 1996** EVALUATOR: **D. J. GONZALES**

DFA WORKSHEET FOR HYBRID SWITCH (AFTER DFA)

ASSEMBLY RATE/HOUR	$30

NO	PART DESCRIPTION	QTY	DIMENSION W	DIMENSION L	DIMENSION T	APPHA	BETA	HANDLING REASON	HANDLING CODE		HANDLING TIME (SEC)	INSERTION REASON	INSERTION CODE		INSERTION TIME (SEC)	TOTALS OPERATION TIME	TOTALS COST	MIN PARTS	OPERATION DESCRIPTION
1	CIRCUIT BOARD	1	25	100	1.5	360	360	EASY TO GRAB	3	3	2.51	PLACE IN NEST	0	0	1.5	4.01	$0.03	1	PLACE
2	PIN ASSEMBLY	1	20	25	10	360	180	PINS NEST	8	3	5.6	SNAP TO BOARD	3	0	2	7.6	$0.06	1	ADD
3	SOLDER	1										SEPARATE OPERATION	9	5	8	8	$0.07		SOLDER
4	BULBS	2		6	2	360	0	DIFFICULT TO PICK UP	2	9	3.38	SCREW IN BULBS	3	8	6	18.76	$0.16	1	ADD & TURN
5	HOUSING	1	35	110	25	360	360	EASY TO GRAB	3	0	1.95	PLACE IN PRESS	0	0	1.5	3.45	$0.03	1	PLACE
6	BOARD ASSEMBLY	1	25	100	25	360	360	EASY TO GRAB	3	0	1.95	DROP INTO HOUSING GUIDES	0	0	1.5	3.45	$0.03		ADD
7	DOME PAD	1	25	100	10	360	360	DIFFICULT TO PICK UP	3	5	2.73	DROP OVER HOUSING PINS	0	2	2.5	5.23	$0.04	1	ADD
8	LIGHT PIPE	1	20	100	15	360	360	ESY TO PICK UP	3	0	1.95	DROP INTO HOUSING & SNAP	3	0	2	3.95	$0.03	1	ADD & SNAP
9	SILICON COVER	1	40	115	10	360	360	DIFFICULT TO PICK UP	3	5	2.73	PUSH OVER HOUSING LIP	3	1	5	7.73	$0.06	1	ADD
																0	$0.00		
																0	$0.00		
																0	$0.00		
																0	$0.00		
																0	$0.00		
																0	$0.00		
																0	$0.00		
																0	$0.00		
																0	$0.00		

TOTAL PARTS	7
TOTAL TIME	62.18
TOTAL COST	$0.52
EFFICIENCY	34%

ALPHA SYMMETRY = THE DEGREES OF ROTATION ABOUT AN AXIS PERPENDICULAR TO THE AXIS OF LOAD BEFORE A PART REPEATS ITS ORIENTATION

BETA SYMMETRY = THE DEGREES OF ROTATION ABOUT AN AXIS PARALLEL TO THE AXIS OF LOAD BEFORE A PART REPEATS ITS ORIENTATION

MINIMUM PARTS = 1 IF YOU CAN ANSWER YES TO ANY ONE QUESTION BELOW:
1. PARTS MOVE RELATIVE TO OTHER PARTS ALREADY ASSEMBLED.
2. MUST BE OF A DIFFERENT MATERIAL (INSULATION, ELECTRICAL INSULATION, VIBRATION DAMPING etc.)
3. PART MUST BE SEPARATE FROM ALL OTHER PARTS ASSEMBLED, OTHERWISE THE ASSEMBLY OF PARTS MEETING ONE OF THE ABOVE CRITERIA COULD BE PREVENTED.

EFFICIENCY = (MIN PARTS X 3 SECONDS PER PART)/TOTAL TIME IN SECONDS

Fig. 11.20: DFA analysis for Hybrid Silicon and Dome Assembly

2. The light pipe was tapered and alignment guide rails were added to the housing to improve loading of the light pipe.
3. The housing was revised to add chamfers to the pin assembly holes to ease pin assembly installation.

The writers disagree with the conventional approach of making the parts easier to assemble a separate and last phase. This repeats work already completed to assess the assembly time. Both phases should be combined into phase one to shorten the design time. The final post-DFA design is illustrated in Fig. 11.21. Note the elimination of the clips, elimination of the flip operation, and integration of the dome switches into a dome pad.

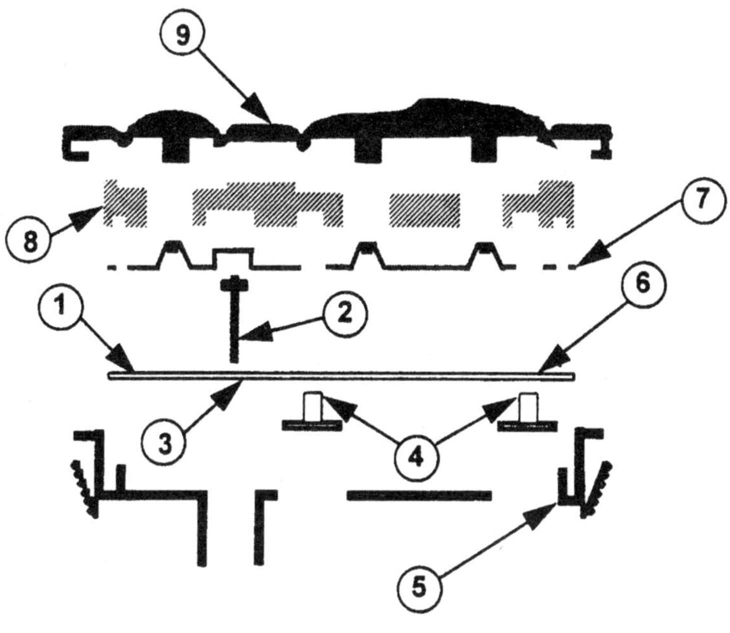

Fig. 11.21: Hybrid Silicon and Dome Post-DFA assembly

10.4. The risk alternative design

The risk plan in step (10) required that the alternative Silicon and Tac Control design be considered as a parallel standby alternative. Consequently, a similar DFA analysis was performed for the risk alternative design, yielding a total assembly cost of \$0.67 and a design efficiency of 26 per cent. Although these values are worse than the those selected for the hybrid design, they represent improvements of 31.6

per cent in cost and 8 per cent in efficiency over the old design. The assembly process for the reduced risk design is illustrated in Fig. 11.22.

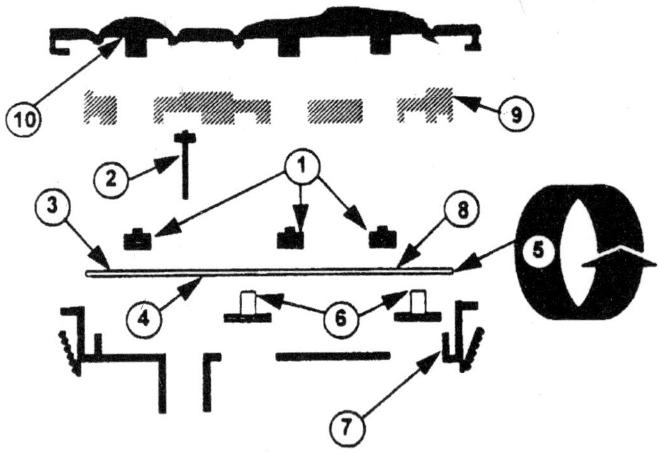

Fig. 11.22: Reduced Risk Hybrid Silicon and Dome design, Post-DFA assembly

11. The Production Assembly Process — Step (13)

The production assembly process is drawn up after the completion of the DFA study in the previous step (11), and is illustrated in Fig. 11.23 below. Standard symbols for storage, operation, and inspection are used to represent various operations. The flowchart constitutes a subset of the total assembly operations, since testing of subassemblies and that of the final product are not represented. The assembly process may be improved upon after the completion of the process fault tree analysis in step (14), which is not discussed in this paper.

12. The Parts Planning Matrix — Step (15)

Now the design requirements from the previous steps are to be entered into the QFD parts planning matrix as the "Hows." The QCs from the product planning matrix with their respective relative importance values are mapped into the parts (components) design characteristics in a manner that is similar to the method used in the product planning house of quality phase in step (4), and the relative importance of each characteristic is computed. These are partially illustrated in Fig. 11.24.

Target values for each design characteristic were developed. Values for the characteristics that should be tracked and inspected, as determined from the fault tree analysis in step (14), were added to the "How Much" section of the matrix.

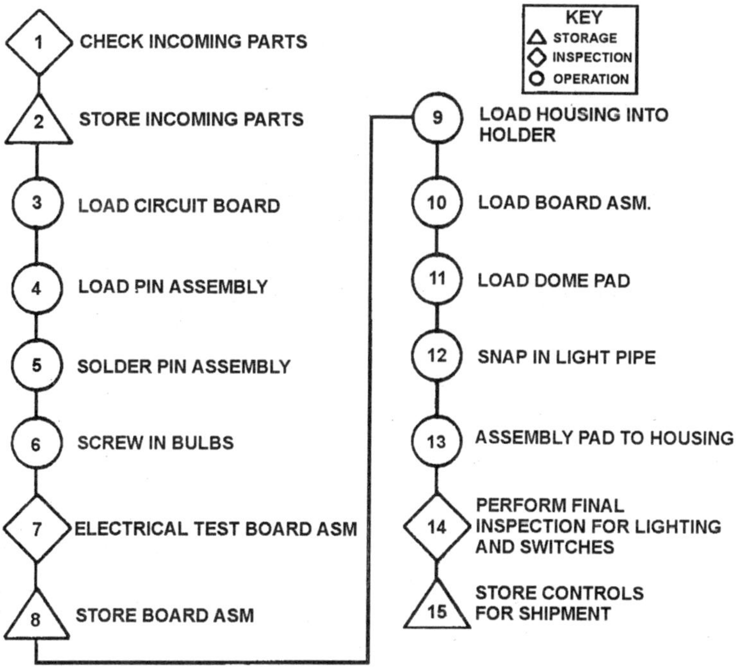

Fig. 11.23: Automotive Controls production assembly process

These characteristics were separated into two groups: the first pertaining to part characteristics and the second to the assembly process. These were thus displayed in the next step (16), as separate parts process planning and assembly process planning matrices, respectively.

13. The Process Planning Matrix — Step (16)

The conventional QFD methodology is followed from this point forward. However, the parts planning matrix was partitioned into two parts: one for processing parts and another for controlling the assembly processes.

13.1. Process planning matrix for parts

The parts planning matrix for parts was generated by rolling down from the preceding step each component's design characteristics and relative importance values into the "Whats" columns. The corresponding matrix for the silicon pad was generated in partnership with the second tier supplier. The equipment and process specifications for each required process were entered in the respective "How Much" cell of the matrix. Component attributes that are key to the successful processing

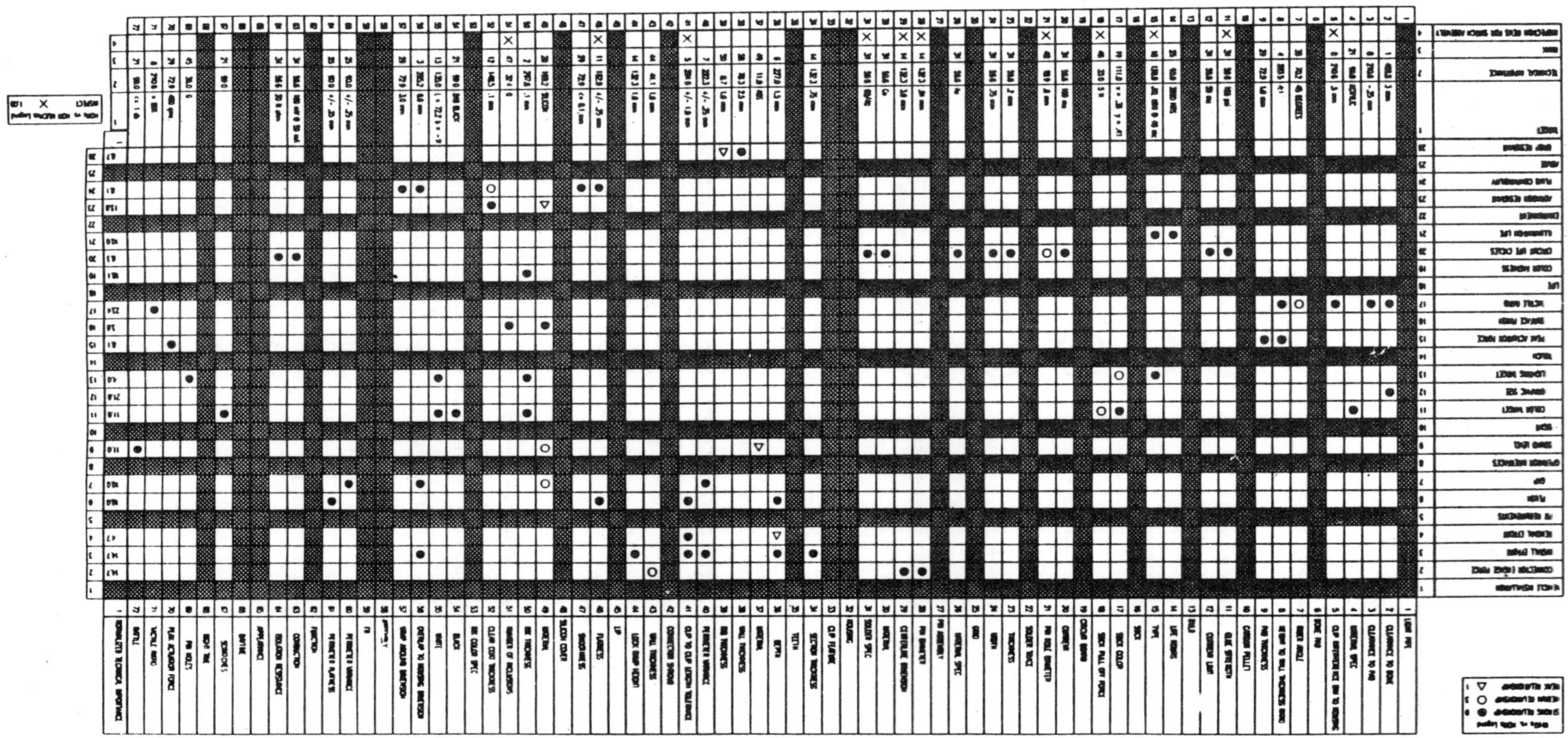

Fig. 11.24: The QFD Parts Planning Matrix for Automotive Controls

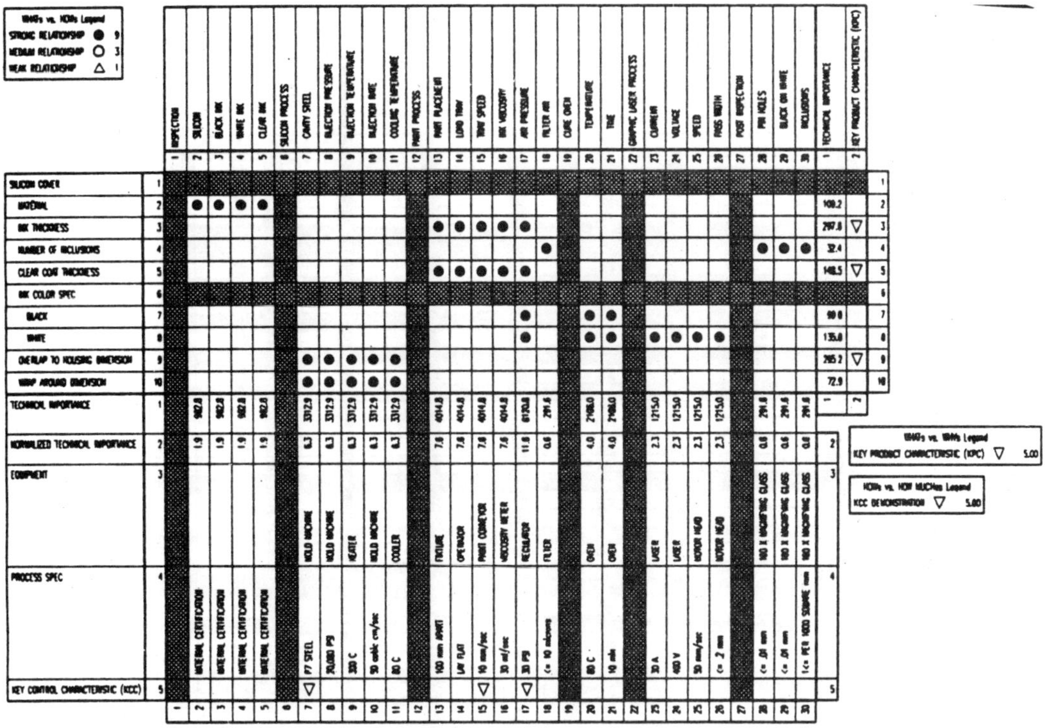

Fig. 11.25: Silicon Pad Tier II Supplier Process Planning Matrix

of the component must be inspected and controlled. These were identified from the fault tree analyses in the previous step (14). At General Motors Corporation, these inspection attributes are designated as key product characteristics (KPCs). The KPCs are to be monitored during part processing by controlling key critical control (KCC) variables in order to keep the process under control and thus consistently produce good quality components. Fig. 11.25 partially depicts the process planning matrix for the silicon pad, which was jointly developed with the parts supplier.

13.2. Process planning matrix for assembly

The parts planning matrix for the controls assembly was generated by rolling down the assembly characteristics and their relative importance values into the "Whats" columns of the matrix. The outputs from the assembly process in step (13), and the information from the process fault tree analysis, were utilized to determine the "Hows" columns. The controls assembly key process characteristics (KPCs) and key critical control (KCC) variables for equipment and the assembly process were

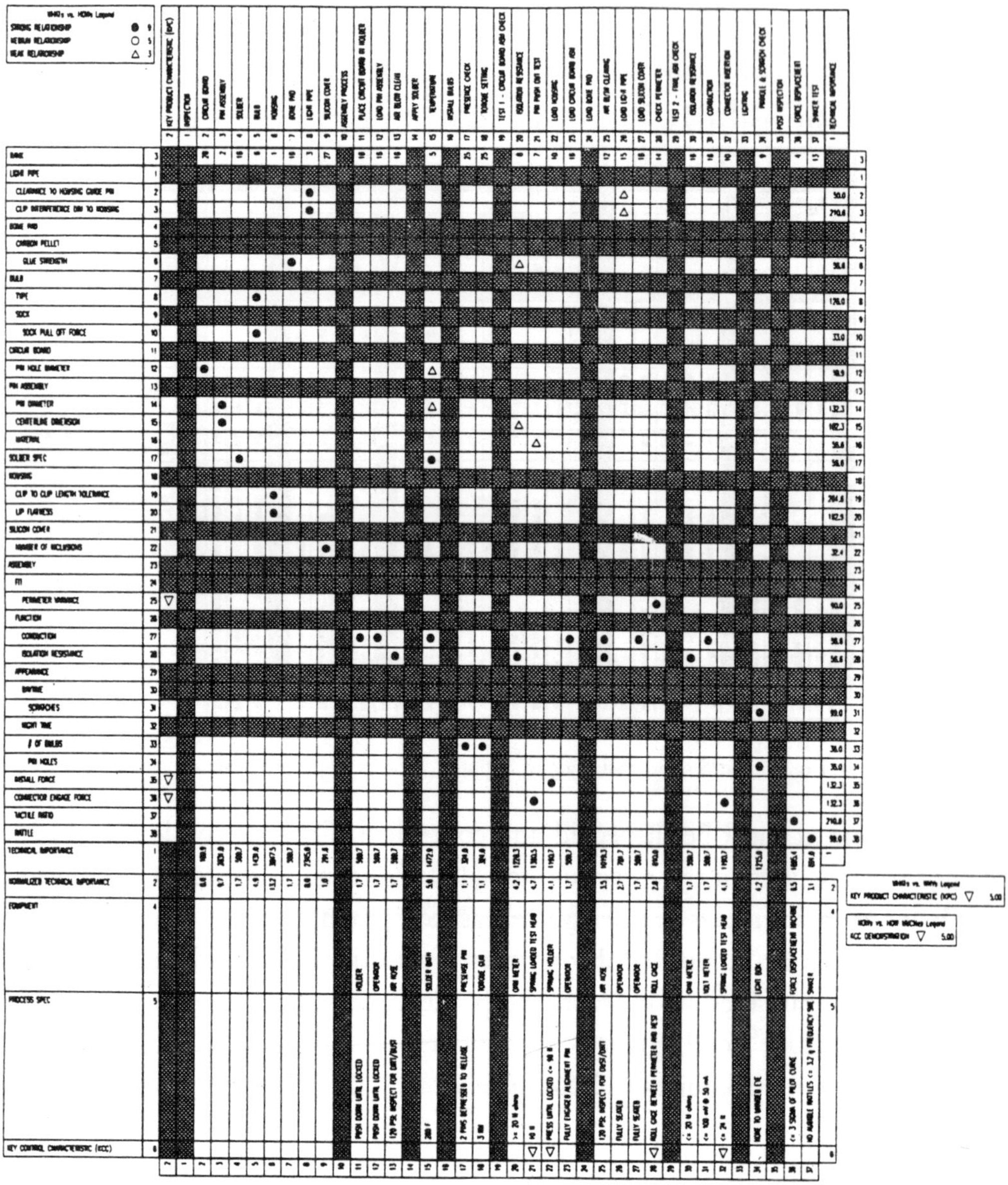

Fig. 11.26: Automotive Controls Assembly Process Planning Matrix

specified in a similar manner to that of the components described in the above section. Fig. 11.26 partially depicts the assembly process planning matrix for the automotive controls case.

14. The Manufacturing Planning Matrix — Step (17)

The manufacturing planning matrix is constructed by rolling down from the preceding step the process requirements and specifications, while appropriately noting the key critical characteristics (KCC)s, to form the rows of the matrix. The "Hows" columns are specified by teams from various production departments, utilizing existing planning tools in order to assure the readiness of the manufacturing organization and to monitor the performance of the plant itself in order to keep the KCCs in control.

For example, the team checks that the tooling department designs for error proofing, maintenance instructions, and gauge design are made ready. The manufacturing department readiness is gauged by the completion of station process sheets and machine qualification. The quality assurance department readiness is gauged by the planned training activities of operators; the completion of the documentation for gauge requirements, including repeatability and reproducibility (R&R) analyses; and the planning of the X-bar and R quality control charts for each work processing station. Conferences with suppliers are to be held now in order to jointly agree on shipping and quality requirements and the availability of test and inspection master gauges for in-process tests.

Fig. 11.27 illustrates a typical manufacturing planning matrix for the controls assembly. The matrix could be enhanced by the addition of manpower schedules, and the recording of the percentage of completed planned activities, and could thus be utilized as a readiness tracking document.

15. Conclusion

We have tailored the general QFD methodology for the concurrent development of a parts assembly of medium complexity, namely that for an automotive controls assembly. The proposed systematic process tied together many systems engineering techniques which are not traditionally utilized in product design and development. The QFD methodology is a powerful planning and communication vehicle within a development team, and across development teams.

The use of the Kano and the affinity (KJ) techniques enabled us to categorize and prioritize the voices of the customer and the producer, and the regulatory requirements, within the usage context of the product. We believe that this is a beneficial and important step for development teams to follow, in order not to translate the customers' voices erroneously out of context.

Additionally, we believe that it is crucial for development teams to translate the prioritized requirements, in order to realize them, into functions and not

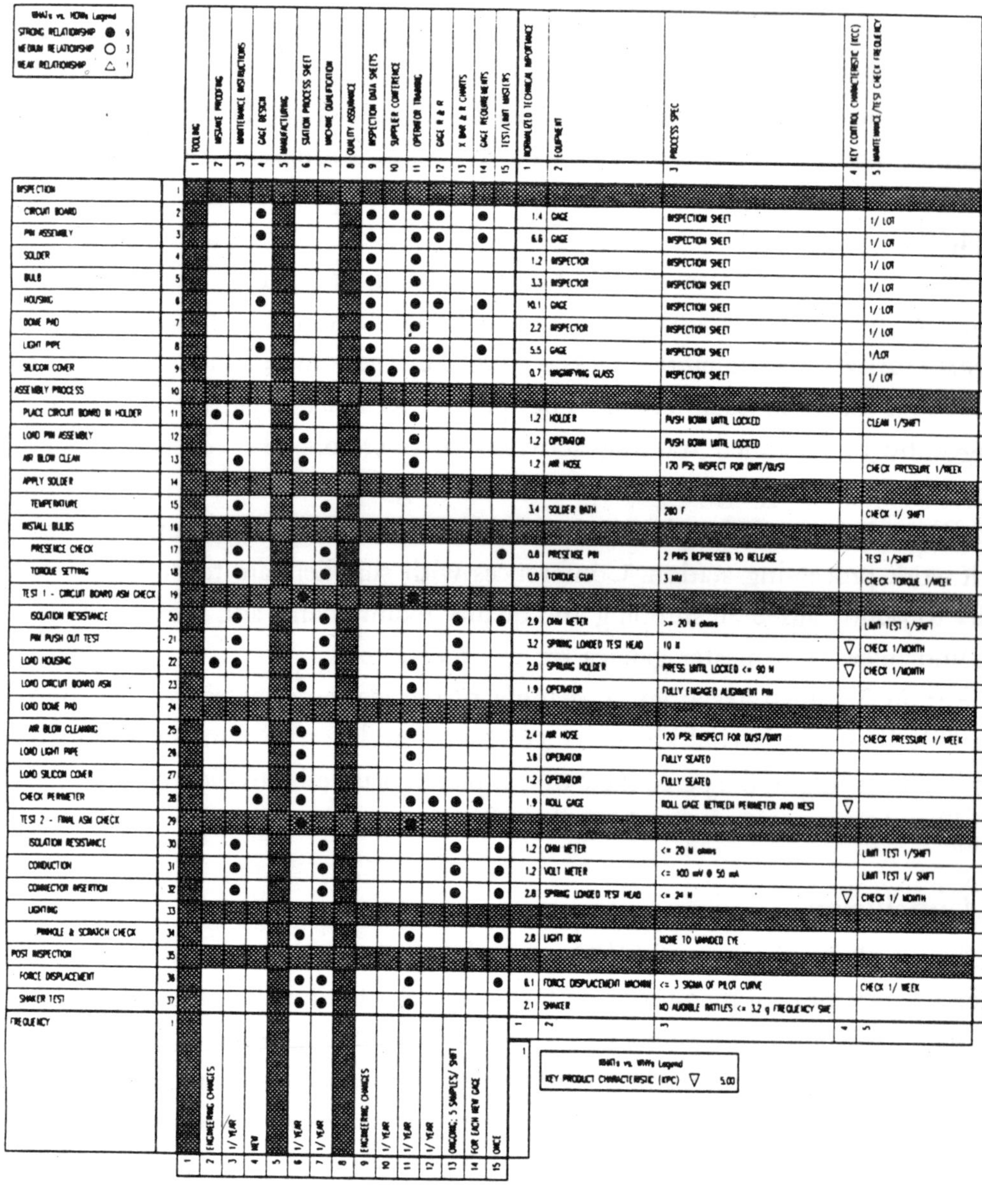

Fig. 11.27: Automotive Controls Manufacturing Planning Matrix

directly into physical parts. This allowed our team to search for creative design alternatives and not be limited to preconceived concepts. Also, the incorporation of risk analysis methodology simultaneously enabled us to realistically select the feasible alternatives. The utilization of DFM/DFA techniques served further to translate the cooperative efforts of design and manufacturing engineers into produceable designs at an optimum cost.

The systems approach, which we have proposed and followed in this case study, allows the incorporation of reliability and cost justification analyses. The final controls design is a preferred and defensible solution. Because if was generated through a structured process that facilitates the collaborative efforts of market planners, product design engineers, manufacturing engineers, managers, and suppliers.

The power of QFD as a tool for implementing concurrent engineering is limited only by the willingness of development teams to adapt this systematic methodology to fit their needs, in order to satisfy demanded requirements at an acceptable cost and in a short cycle time.

References

1. Y. Akao (ed.), *Quality Function Deployment: Integrating Customer Requirements into Product Design,* Productivity Press 1990.
2. K. Akiyama, *Function Analysis,* Productivity Press, 1991.
3. A. Aswad, "Quality Function Deployment: A Tool or a Philosophy," Society of Automotive Engineers, Paper No. 890163, 1989.
4. A. Aswad, "QFD in Theory and Practice," *Proceedings of the 3rd Symposium on QFD, American Society for Quality Control*, *G.O.A.L and ASI,* June 1991.
5. G. Boothroyd, P. Dewhurst, W. Knight, *Product Design for Manufacture and Assembly,* Marcel Dekker, 1994.
6. General Motors Corporation, *Market Research Study, Section 6.9* (confidential), 1995.
7. N. Kano, *"Attractive Quality and Must-Be Quality," Quality JSQC,* Vol. 14, No. 2, 1984.
8. C. H. Kepner, B. Trego, *The Rational Manager: A Systematic Approach to Problem Solving,* McGraw-Hill, 1965.
9. S. Mizuno (ed.), *Management for Productivity Improvement: The 7 New Q.C. Tools,* Productivity Press, 1988.
10. S. Pugh, *Total Design,* Addison Wesley, 1991.
11. S. Shiba, *et al., A New American TQM, Productivity Center for Quality Management,* Productivity Press, 1993.

SECTION TWO
Short Papers

12

Design Frameworks and Tool Interoperability in Modern EDA Systems

Imad Sahbouni
Scientific Studies and Research Centre, Damascus - Syria

Abstract

The increasing complexity of electronic designs (circuits and systems) forces design teams to become larger and more geographically-dispersed. This new situation is imposing a challenge on EDA tool developers to provide innovative solutions in a Concurrent Engineering Environment. This paper summarizes the new trends in EDA tool development related to design framework and toll interoperability. Both existing standard solutions and the need of new standards in the area of user interface, workflow management and tool management are highlighted, and their impact on design strategies analyzed.

1. Introduction

As Moore's law states, semiconductor technology process is doubling its capability, in terms of performance and circuit density, approximately every 18 months. The capability of Integrated Circuit Computer-Aided Design (IC-CAD) tools has always been behind the capability of silicon technology, thus creating a well-known gap between what the technology process is capable of and what IC-CAD tools can support.

Since technology now moves on rapidly to deep submicron processes, one important question facing circuit designers is: how several million gate equivalent chips should be processed? It is obvious that designers do not only need the best CAD tools, especially Electronic Design Automation (EDA) tools, available on the market, but more importantly, they tend to incorporate those heterogeneous tools into their development environment, with minimum effort. One should not have to invest additional resources in writing translators for data; instead standards aiming to facilitate the incorporation of new tools into customer environments are required.

Furthermore, as the complexity of chips (and electronic systems in general) increases, the size of design teams required to develop them increases. Consequently, the complexity of managing design workflows will increase dramatically, making traditional design methods incapable of maintaining an acceptable level of productivity. There is an urgent need to define and implement new design methodologies enabling the design team to manage the state of the design process in a Concurrent Engineering Environment. Standards to support multiple design managers and multiple design processes are also required.

This paper summarizes the new trends in EDA (and IC-CAD) tool development related to design framework and tool interoperability. Current environment and requirements in the areas of user interface, workflow management, tool communication and tool management are briefly presented, and their consequences on the design process analyzed.

2. Platform and User Interface

Two major platforms are encountered today for EDA applications:

(i) Workstations running variants of UNIX operating system (*e.g.*, SUN Solaris, HP-UX, IBM AIX, Digital UNIX, ...); and
(ii) PC-type machines running Microsoft Windows.

The second platform is more and more adopted in PCB designs, FPGA/CPLD applications and some low-end ASIC designs, while the first one is usually reserved for integrated CAD environments.

Due to the manufacturers' continuous efforts to offer competitive price/performance ratio, UNIX running on desktop workstations is expected to remain a leading platform. As almost all major vendors are now members of the Common

Open System Environment (COSE) alliance, they will be compliant with the COSE Desktop Environment (CDE) standard [3] for graphical user interface and window management environment. This standard will logically be the dominant standard over the next decade.

In the PC world, Microsoft's Windows (Windows NT, Windows'95) is a clear leader. Also, OLE 2 [4] and Microsoft-endorsed CAD standards will be logically adopted by future EDA applications on the PC platform.

Apple OS 7.5 running on the Macintosh PowerPC platform is the biggest concurrent to Microsoft in the PC market, with IBM OS/2 Wrap coming in the next position. However, there are virtually no major EDA applications running on these platforms today. Apple is actively preparing the migration towards Copland operating environment. Even if this new platform is not expected to be a major player in the EDA world, it should be monitored.

In order to maximize the level of productivity of design teams, the operating environment and user interface of the design system and its tools play an important role. In many ways, the UNIX and Windows environments have migrated to the point that they are similar enough to each other that a user of one environment can quickly move to the other. The important point is that the environment, as seen by the user, must provide move to the other. The important point is that the environment, as seen by the user, must provide the same capabilities and "look-and-feel", independent of the underlying hardware and software.

3. Workflow Management

Workflow management (also called design management) denotes the automated support to a prescribed design methodology across a set of design objects, design steps, and design tools. Workflow management support include:

- formal definition of the design methodology:
- completeness checking of design steps and assistance (or control) in determining the next allowed design steps;
- association of design tools for each design step;
- using a notification system for coordinating the tasks of the design team members;
- library distribution management;
- design status monitoring; and
- version control and release management.

Design teams involved in projects with a large number of design steps and tools are finding an increasing necessity to incorporate workflow management automation to guarantee consistency in the overall design process. There is a growing interest in formal definition of the design methodology due to (i) the increased complexities of semiconductor design, (ii) the number of designers involved with a design entity, and (iii) the necessary interaction across multiple design domains and geographic locations.

Workflow management tools are commercially available from EDA suppliers and other commercial companies. Each has particular functional strength and capabilities in terms of system platforms supported, ease of use, ease of integration of tools, checking, reporting, etc... Examples of the most popular workflow managers include Cadence's Team Design manager [5] and View Logic's View Flow [8].

In the current state of the art for workflow management systems, it is clear that

- the formal definition of a complete design methodology is a complex task. Design methodologies are often design-specific and cannot therefore be standardized.
- customers desire the ability to use multiple design managers and to goggle between them with minimum impact. They also require the ability to move design information from one design manager to another as the design progresses. It is therefore imperative to adopt a standard enabling design methodology to be portable across compliant design managers.
- potential customers of workflow management systems require the ability to encapsulate specific design tools into the chosen design manager without the need of modifying the tools (cf.*4). Therefore, a standard interface between the workflow management tools and the CAD tools should be developed to support tool activation/deactivation.

4. Design Tool Management

Electronic design tools and systems have evolved rapidly over the last decade. Yet new requirements will drive the development of new tools that are not even envisioned today. Such tools should be inserted into the design process as soon as they are available. This changing environment places a challenge on tool developers to provide tools that are easily installed and encapsulated into the environments chosen by the designers and CAD integrators.

Using EDA design tools today is problematic in that each tool has its own requirements for proper execution. Having to remember the installed tool location (= directory path), executable name, command syntax, and required and optional arguments necessary to invoke a tool often leads to errors. In addition, a given tool may require execution from different environments (*e.g.*, from the graphical desktop or from a workflow manager). Today, encapsulation and integration of tools differs from one tool to another in every development environment. This may be costly and error-prone, and can lead to a longer time-to-market. Some IC-CAD and EDA system providers, however, offer "open" environments consisting of an infrastructure of software and interfaces that enable the integration and interoperability of design tools and subsystems. Such an environment is commonly called a Framework [1]. Examples of the most popular frameworks include Cadence's Design Framework II [6], Digital Equipment's PowerFrame (7) and ViewLogic's OpenFrame [9].

Two major aspects of tool management must be considered:

- The first aspect is that individual EDA tools have historically been limited to providing a set of services to the individual design engineer. These services include the launching and stopping of tools, encapsulating the required inputs and outputs for a given tool, and grouping several interdependent and/or interworking tools together. Many of the EDA frameworks available today provide these capabilities. Furthermore, managing an EDA tool has often been viewed from the perspective of a single user. However, in today's environments, tool management must be viewed from a more global perspective. Larger design teams are working with a greater number of tools, spread over a larger geographical area. Tool managers must be able to manage and track the status of tools on remote hosts and in heterogeneous environments.
- The second aspect is associated with the management of computer systems. The rise in complexity of the design problem has lead to an increase in the number of design tools used by most users. In large design environments, installing and managing these tools has become time-consuming. the methods for installing, licensing, and upgrading

tools differ with each vendor and are often inconsistent even between tools from a single vendor.

The following subsections address the most important issues related to design tool management.

4.1. Inter-tool communication

Electronic design systems are rapidly evolving to geographically-dispersed, network-based environments. Innovative approaches that enable tools to perform cooperative design processing are clearly needed. It must be possible for tools to interact in an intelligent way via inter-tool communication and messaging schemes across the network.

A tool manager must have the ability to start, stop and determine the current status of individual tools in order to manage them adequately. One way to accomplish this would be to build a "monolithic" environment containing all the tools the manager wishes to control. However, this solution does not provide the flexibility needed for today's multi-vendor environments. A more efficient alternative is to provide specific means of interaction between tools, via dynamic inter-tool communication schemes. Since users need to manage tools from a variety of vendors, a standard message passing mechanism is required.

In the UNIX environment, the ToolTalk [3] messaging facility is already defined as a powerful mechanism for inter-tool communication. Extensions to ToolTalk must be provided to meet the inter-tool communication requirements, namely between tools running in the Windows environment and those in the UNIX environment [2]. Such interoperability would best be provided by the operating environment suppliers (i.e., the UNIX or Windows providers).

4.2. Tool encapsulation

A tool encapsulation standard is required to capture the structural aspects of a tool. These include the tool's executable name and location information, tool class, operating environment requirements, and input and output requirements (along with their data types). It must be possible for this standard to enable highly-automated encapsulation of tools into multiple usage environments including:

- graphical user interface environment (*e.g.*, CDE);
- workflow management environment;

- vendor-specific environment (*e.g.*, a framework); and
- non-graphical environment (*e.g.*, tool execution via script files or command-line invocation).

For example, in a graphical environment, the encapsulation of the tool may result in the user being presented with a dialog box and asked to enter information such as the location of a design object. To enable encapsulating the structural aspects of tools (*e.g.*, inputs, outputs, launch mechanism), a common tool encapsulation method is required. This standard must support tools that operate in either graphical or non-graphical environments [2].

4.3. EDA system management guidelines

Another important aspect of tool management is from the system management perspective. The rise in complexity of the design problem has lead to a proliferation of EDA tools that are often aimed at specific problems. In many user environments, the number of tools (and multiple versions of these tools) has increased dramatically, and this is expected to continue. As a result, managing the installation and licensing of these tools has become a problem large enough to impact designer productivity.

Users need advice on the best methods for managing their EDA systems. A set of guidelines and best practices should be collected and shared with users. This document could recommend a common tool installation procedure be developed, such as the one used by tools in the Windows environment.

5. Conclusion

As it was stated in this paper, maintaining control of large-size designs requires innovative approaches and tools that support concurrent, hierarchical and incremental design manipulation. More powerful EDA tools are expected to emerge constantly, bringing about rapid evolution of design environment. IC-CAD and EDA systems must be designed in a way to allow easy integration of these innovations as soon as they become available.

In order to be competitive, an IC-CAD integrated system must be able to:

- exploit multiple operating environments and user interfaces;
- enforce design methodologies and process management; and
- use tools from multiple tool vendors.

Open EDA framework allowing the use of communicating design tools and multiple workflow managers tend to satisfy the above-mentioned needs. They can be considered as an important enabling technology which promotes Concurrent Engineering approaches.

References

1. Concurrent Engineering (Aspects Technologiques). *Patrick Jagou.* Collection Systèmes d'Information. Hermès. 1992.
2. EDA Industry Standards Roadmap. CAD Framework Initiative. 1995.
3. The UNIX Programming Environment. *Brian Kernighan & Rob Pike.* Prentice-Hall. 1992.
4. *Microsoft Windows: User Manual (Programming Environment).* Microsoft Corporation. 1995.
5. Cadence Team Design Manager. Data Sheet. Cadence Data Systems. 1995.
6. Cadence Design Framework II. Technical Reference. Cadence Data Systems 1993.
7. DEC PowerFrame. Data Sheet. Digital Equipment Corporation. 1993.
8. ViewLogic ViewFlow. Data Sheet. ViewLogic Systems Inc. 1994.
9. ViewLogic OpenFrame. Technical Reference. ViewLogic Systems Inc. 1994.

13

Computer Aided Design for Life-cycle

Mohammad Ammar Al-Salka
B.Sc, M.Sc, Ph.D.
Scientific Studies and Research Center, Damascus - Syria

Abstract

Total design demands that products should be designed taking into account all the phases of the product life-cycle. Proper consideration of the product life-cycle at the design phase can greatly reduce the ***time-to-market*** *of products and help in* getting it right first time. *This paper outlines a computer-based process for assisting designers in developing products that satisfy all the requirements of the product life-cycle. This process is part of an integrated conceptual design support and analysis system (called* CODSAS*) which has been developed by the Author in the context of a Ph.D. project at the University of Wales, Swansea. the system can capture knowledge from expert users of the system which can later be consulted by novice designers to help them identify and rank design objectives and subsequently evaluate design alternatives to reach an optimum design.*

1. Introduction

Since the introduction of digital computers to industry and academia they have been used in many engineering design applications, from simple design calculations, through computer-aided drawing and solid modelling, to finite element analysis and simulation. Yet, few computerised systems for supporting the total design of products exist today.

Recent developments in computer technology, artificial intelligence, and design science raised the possibility of applying computers to tall phases of the design process.

This paper describes a computerised process for evaluating alternative design solutions against the design objectives. This process is part of an integrated design support environment called CODSAS (Conceptual Design Support and Analysis System).

2. The Life-Cycle of Engineering Products

The life cycle of a product starts with the recognition of the need for this product and terminates with its liquidation or disposal. Between these two extremes the product goes through a number of phases as shown in Fig. 13.1. It can be seen that design is the first phase in this life-cycle. Subsequent phases greatly influence the design process. For example, the lack of a technology to weld aluminium in the production phase influences the choice of materials during the design phase. Similarly, if market considerations dictate that the final cost of the product should not exceed some value, then the freedom in selecting solution during design is restricted. These influences are shown by the feedback arrows in Fig. 13.1.

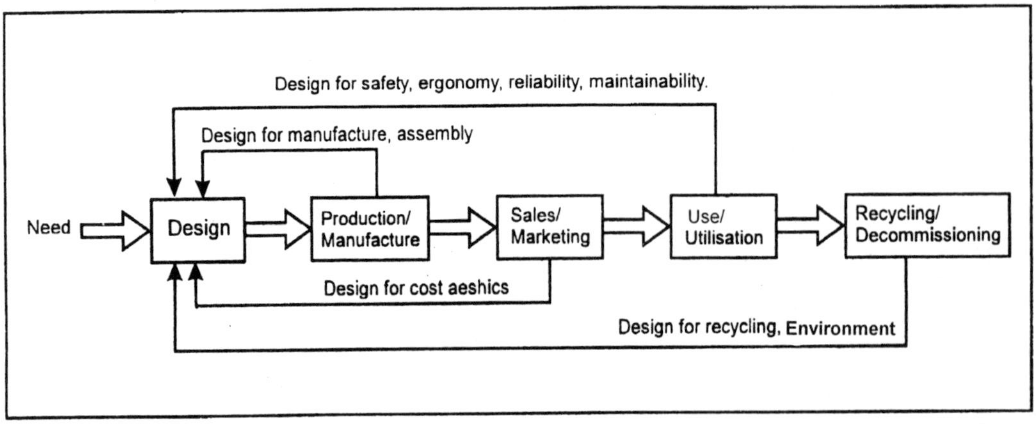

Fig. 13.1

Recently, there has been great awareness of the importance of taking the subsequent phases of the product life-cycle into consideration when designing new products. Examples of this awareness include Design for Manufacture [1], Design for Assembly, Design for Quality [2], Design for Safety, Design for

Maintainability, and Design for Ease of Recycling [3], Meerkamm [4] call these areas *Design-for-X.*

In *total design* [5], design for life-cycle is accounted for through the objective evaluation of **design alternatives** against the **technical and economic criteria** of the design problem at every stage in the design process.

2.1. Phases of the design process

It is generally agreed that engineering design can be divided into four recognisable phases:

- Clarification of the task.
- Conceptual Design.
- Embodiment Design.
- Detail Design.

The aim of the task clarification phase is to clarify the design task and to expand the initial *design brief* into full design specifications of the product.

The aim of the conceptual design phase is to devise the concept of the artifact. According to Hubka [6], this concept is "an abstract, incomplete anatomical structure, formless with the exception of action localities". The conceptual design phase is crucial, particularly when designing new innovative products, or when a completely new design for an existing product is required. It has been estimated that up to 85 per cent of the product cost is committed by the end of the conceptual design phase [7].

The aim of embodiment design is to determine the layout and forms, and to develop a product in accordance with technical and economic considerations [8].

Finally, the aim of detail design is to determine the final dimensions, tolerances, and surface properties, and to produce detailed component drawings, production documents, and bills of materials.

3. Systematic Design Methodologies

Historically the beginnings of design science can be traced back to the middle of the last century when scientists started to think of machines as assemblies of recognisable machine elements. However, it was not until the 1960's and 1970's that the subject of engineering design came under the focus of the scientific community as a research area in itself. During this initial period scientists were interested in *design methodologies*. Today the most respected text on systematic design methodologies is generally considered to be that of Pahl and Beitz [8].

The primary motive behind all design methodologies is the drive to rationalise, systematise and improve current design practice, which is still largely based on ad-

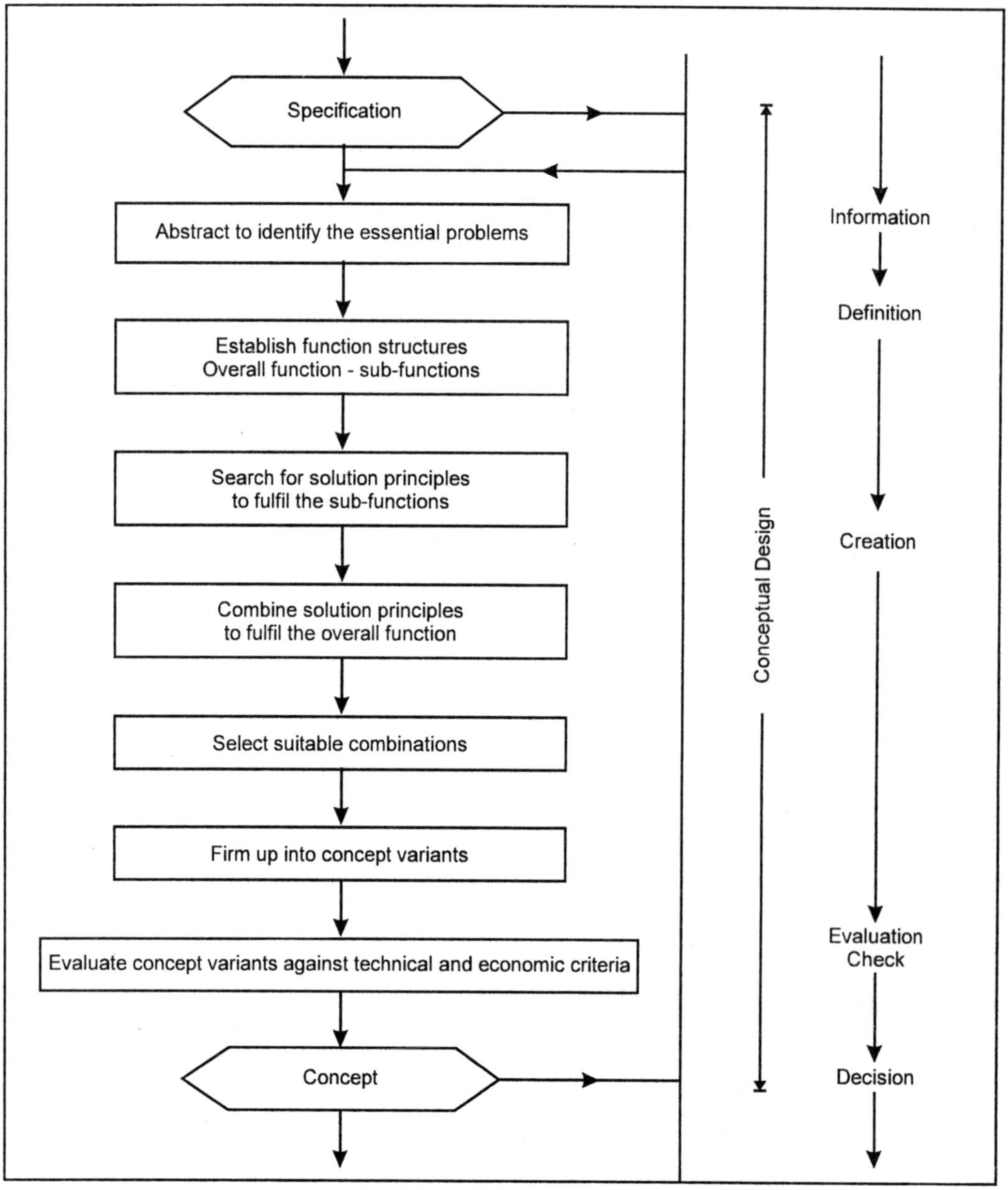

Fig. 13.2

hoc methods and intuition. Design methodologies recommend **prescriptions** of how the design process should be performed. For example, Fig. 13.2 shows the steps of the conceptual design process according to Pahl and Beitz [8].

3.1. Principles of methodological design

Regardless of their particular strategies, models, or methods, the aim of all design methodologies is to help designers generate optimum designs. By careful examination of existing design methodologies, it is possible to identify a number of principles which underlie all of these:

- Abstraction.
- Lateral, or divergent, thinking followed by
- Objective evaluation against the design objectives (Convergent thinking).
- Design for life-cycle.
- Solution-neutral modelling of the evolving artifact.

Design methodologies encourage the use of lateral (lateral (creative or divergent) thinking at every stage of the design process. Whenever a problem is identified, lateral thinking should be used to determine all possible solutions to this problem. Even those solutions which may seem trivial or absurd should not be eliminated at this stage.

When all possible solutions for a problem have been found, objective evaluation must be performed to select the best candidate. This process should be carried out throughout the design process. Thus the design process will be characterised by a series of cycles of divergent-convergent as shown in Fig. 13.3.

It can be seen that decision making is a fundamental and recurring activity in (engineering) design. In fact, decision making can be regarded as a characteristic of design rather than one of its techniques.

It is obvious that a rational design process should be based on rational decision making, i.e., rational selection of alternatives. **To enable rational selection, the alternatives must be evaluated with respect to a number of objectives which reflect the life cycle of the product.**

3.2. Systematic evaluation methods

Many methods of multiple criteria decision making have been developed [9]. Broadly speaking, all these methods rely on using some sort of a *decision matrix*

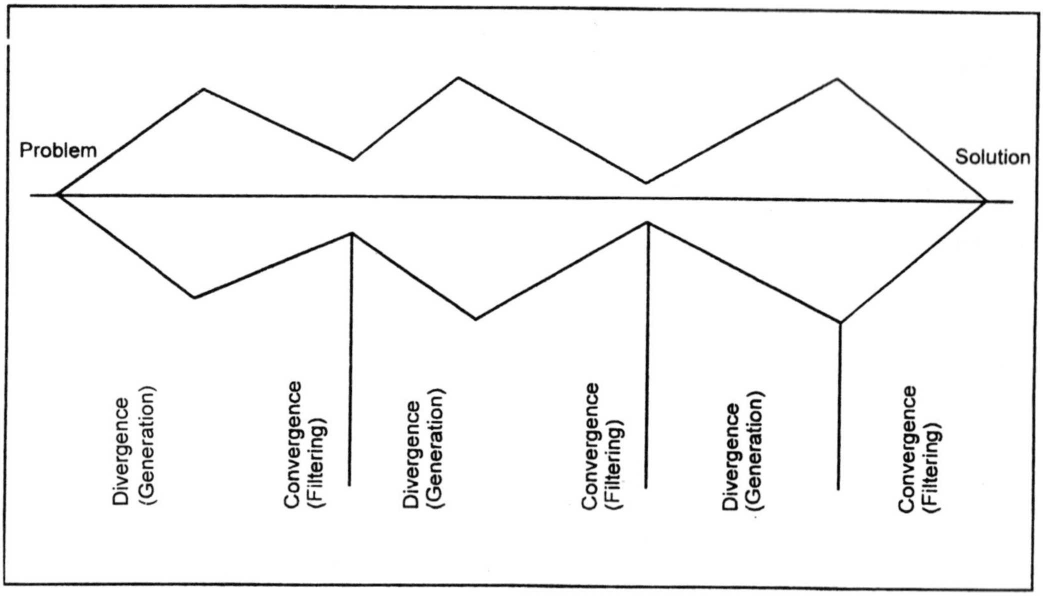

Fig. 13.3

[10] or *evaluation chart* [8, 11]. The main steps of any evaluation exercise can be summarised as follows:

- Identifying the design objectives, from which the evaluation criteria can be derived.
- These criteria may then be ranked or weighted according to their relative importance.
- Identifying the attributes, or parameters, (if any) of the evaluated systems which correspond to the evaluation criteria. For example, the "number of components" of a product can be used to assess the value of a product with respect to the low complexity objective (criteria).
- Assessing (rating) the value (score) of each alternative, with respect to every criteria. These values may be directly assigned, or they may be calculated from the value functions corresponding to the criteria.
- Applying some evaluation method to the resulting matrix (or evaluation chart) in order to select the most promising alternative(s).

In the light of the above discussion, the crucial role of evaluation in design cannot be under-estimated, and the need for appropriate tools to support rational evaluation methods can be clearly realised. In the next section, a computerised environment for total design is briefly described.

4. *CODSAS:* A Computer Based Conceptual Design Support and Analysis System

This section describes a prototype design support system called *CODSAS* that provides an integrated, consistent framework for carrying out engineering design. *CODSAS* can be customised by means of a novel programming language called the ***Design Procedures Programming Language (DPPL)*** to provide support for entirely different design processes. Further information about DPPL can be found in [12]. The system reflects the *wholistic* approach towards design which is adopted in this work. Hence, it provides support for all the activities of conceptual engineering design, from problem formulation to finalising the concept.

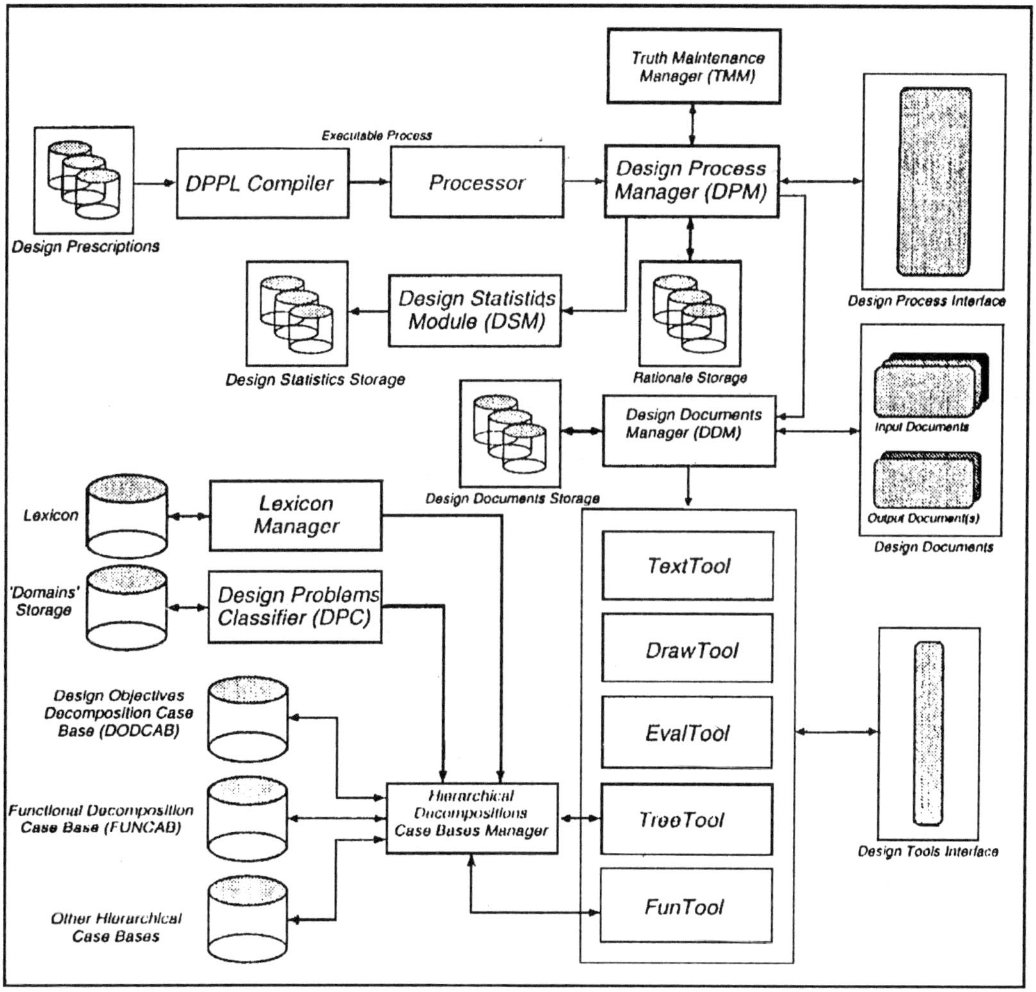

Fig. 13.4

The overall structure of CODSAS is shown in Fig. 13.4. The functionality of each module is briefly explained below. The reader can refer to [12] for detailed description of these modules.

The compiler module translates the high level description of a design process, *i.e.*, a DPPL program, into executable code the can be executed by the processor module. This is a virtual processor implemented in software. The processor drives the rest of the system.

The Design Process Manager (DPM) creates, initiates and terminates the design tasks, records the design history and manages user interactions through the design process interface.

The Design Documents Manager (DDM) is responsible for creating design documents, opening and closing input and output documents and starting the appropriate *tool* which corresponds to the *language* of the output document. These tools include *TextTool, DrawTool, TreeTool, EvalTool,* and *FunToll* for creating textual, graphical, hierarchical, tabular, and structural language documents respectively.

The Truth Maintenance manager (TMM) initiates a truth maintenance cycle every time the designer revises an old document. The TMM scans the design history and re-activates design tasks which rely on the revised document for input. This in turn may generate more revised documents, which should be considered when scanning the rest of the design history.

The Design Problems Classifier (DPC) helps the designer classify the design problem according to various attributes, maintain a record of all classifications created in this way and subsequently help in retrieving the most relevant case from design case bases.

The Hierarchical Decompositions Case Bases Manager is responsible for managing hierarchical case bases such as the Design Objectives Decompositions Case Base (DODCAB) and the Functional Decompositions Case Base (FUNCAB).

The lexicon is a simple electronic dictionary and thesaurus, which is used to assist in the approximate matching of natural language phrases.

Finally the Design Statistics Module (DSM) is used for the purposes of design research whereby it can be used to record the frequency (how many) and duration (how long) of different design tasks.

4.1. Evaltool: Systematic evaluation of design alternatives

The aim of *EvalTool* in *CODSAS* is to provide the designer with a framework for evaluating alternatives, that minimises the effort needed to carry out an evaluation, reduces the possibility of errors, and allows the designer to use different evaluation strategies.

The general form of a weighted assessments evaluation chart in *EvalTool* is shown in Fig. 13.5. This chart follows the norm defined by Pahl and Beitz [8].

	Alternative Number (Index)			0		1		2	
No.	Evaluation Criteria	w%	Parameter	M	V	M	V	M	V
1	low susceptibility to vibrations	14.0	natural frequency	410.0	17.3	2370.0	100.0	300.0	12.7
2	high mechanical safety	26.0	expected mech safety	0.0	40.0	0.0	70.0	0.0	0.0
3	small number of somponents	10.0	number of parts	30.0	66.3	45.0	49.4	89.0	0.0
4	many standard parts	20.0	ratio of standard parts	0.3	60.0	0.2	40.0	0.5	1000.0
5	easy maintenance	20.0	time and cost of maint	20.0	33.3	10.0	66.7	30.0	0.0
6	quick exchange of connection	10.0	time to exch connect	1.0	75.0	4.0	0.0	3.0	25.0
	Total value (WRAM method)				0.78		1.00		0.42

CODSAS version 0.1 Date: Thy May 11 17 59 23 1995, Project name : Rig, Document name: Evaluation Chart

Fig. 13.5

In such a chart, the evaluation objectives (or criteria) are listed down the rows of the chart while the alternative are listed across the columns. Each objective can be assigned a weighting (w), between 0 and 100, which reflects its importance to the evaluation. The use value of each alternative should be entered into the V (Value) field of that alternative. In *EvalTool,* this value should be in the range [0, 100] (percentage score).

Some of the evaluation objectives could be associated with a certain parameter or attribute of the evaluated alternatives (solutions). The magnitude of these parameters should be entered into the 'M' (Magnitude) field of each alternative. The use values can then be computed from the parameter magnitudes by means of an appropriate *value function* [8].

Once the individual values of all alternatives have been assigned, the total value of each alternative can be calculated. Various methods of assessing the total value, such as various forms of the arithmetic mean or the geometric mean, can be used [13].

4.2. Treetool: Identifying design objectives

As mentioned above, in order to evaluate different design alternatives, a number of evaluation criteria must be identified and ranked (weighted). An effective method of identifying design objectives is the *objectives tree method* [8]. An objectives tree is a hierarchy of objectives and their sub-objectives. **The sub-objectives are arranged vertically into levels of decreasing complexity, and horizontally into objectives areas which correspond to the phases of the product life-cycle,** such as manufacturing, marketing, and operational objectives. The evaluation criteria are derived form the lowest level sub-objectives, *i.e.*, the leaves of the tree.

This hierarchical order helps the designer to determine whether or not all decision relevant sub-objectives have been covered. Furthermore, it simplifies the assessment of the relative importance (weight) of an objective in comparison with the others. In use value analysis, weightings are based on factors ranging from 0 to 1 (or from 0 to 100). The sum of the relative weighting factors (RWF) of the sub-objectives at any level in the tree must be equal to 1 (or 100) so that percentage weights can be assigned to the criteria. The absolute weighting factor of a sub-objective is calculated by multiplying the RWF of this sub-objective by the AWF of its parent objective. To calculate the AWFs of the leaves of the tree (which correspond to the weights of the criteria), one must start from the root of the tree and works his way down the tree, calculating the AWFs for each level before moving down to the next lower level.

TreeTool allows the designer to identify and decompose design objectives easily and efficiently, provides range checking, and automatically calculates the values of the absolute weighting factors. Fig. 13.6 shows an example of an objective tree created by *TreeTool.*

Novice designers may encounter some difficulty in decomposing a design objective, such as production cost, into lower level sub-objectives. Furthermore, they may fail to assign appropriate values to the relative weighting factors of these sub-objectives. One way of supporting (novice) designers in decomposing and ranking design objectives is to enable them to re-use previous decompositions, which have been generated by expert designers, in a similar design problem.

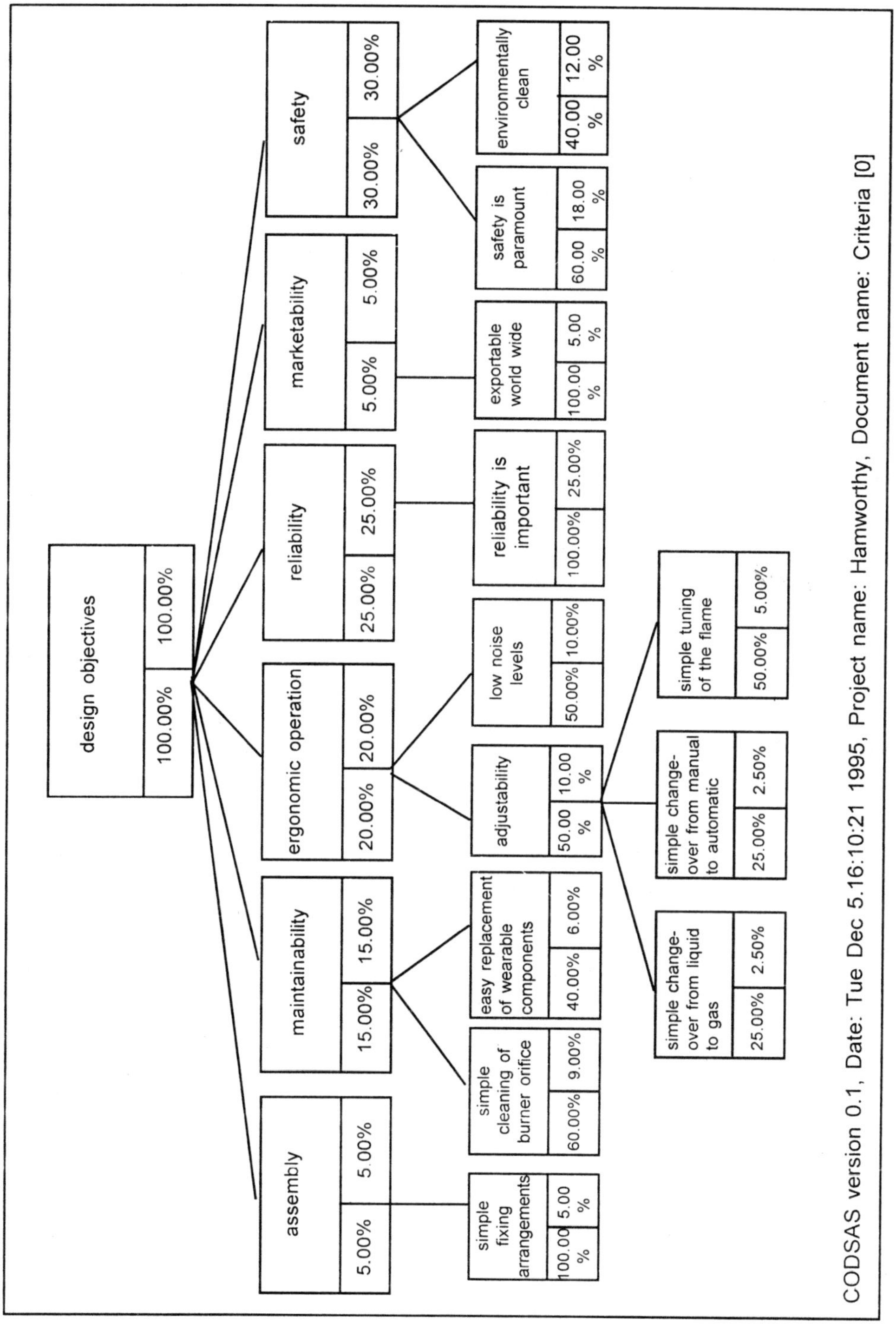
design objectives
100.00%
100.00%
assembly
5.00%
5.00%
maintainability
15.00%
15.00%
ergonomic operation
20.00%
20.00%
reliability
25.00%
25.00%
marketability
5.00%
5.00%
safety
30.00%
30.00%
simple fixing arrangements
100.00 %
5.00 %
simple cleaning of burner orifice
60.00%
9.00%
easy replacement of wearable components
40.00%
6.00%
adjustability
50.00 %
10.00 %
low noise levels
50.00%
10.00%
reliability is important
100.00%
25.00%
exportable world wide
100.00 %
5.00 %
safety is paramount
60.00 %
18.00 %
environmentally clean
40.00 %
12.00 %
simple change-over from liquid to gas
25.00%
2.50%
simple change-over from manual to automatic
25.00%
2.50%
simple tuning of the flame
50.00%
5.00%
CODSAS version 0.1, Date: Tue Dec 5.16:10:21 1995, Project name: Hamworthy, Document name: Criteria [0]

Fig. 13.6

To this end the Design Objectives Decomposition Case Base (*DODCAB*), which can capture and store objectives decompositions for later use by other (novice) designers, has been developed. In the next section, the theoretical foundations, structure, and functionality of *DODCAB* will be described.

4.3. Design Objectives Decomposition Case Base (DODCAB)

4.3.1. Case-based reasoning: The main idea of case-based reasoning (CBR) is to re-use the solutions to old problems to solve new similar problems. Case-based reasoning [14, 15] involves two main steps:

1. Looking in memory for solutions to previous problems which are similar to the current problem, and
2. Adapting these solutions to fit the current problem, taking into account differences between the current and previous problems.

Case based reasoning is a more practical alternative to expert systems particularly in a domain independent environment such as *CODSAS.*

The idea of the Design Objectives Decompositions Case Base (*DODCAB*) is as follows. Experienced designers using the system (*CODSAS*) can add their decompositions (objectives trees) to *DODCAB* which is then updated to account for the new information. *DODCAB* can capture, and subsequently provide, two types of information about the design objectives:

1. *Qualitative:* What are the sub-objectives of a design objective.
2. *Quantitative:* What are the appropriate values of the relative weighting factors of these sub-objectives.

In order for DODCAB to provide fairly accurate information it must be stable. Two questions of stability arise here, corresponding to the qualitative and quantitative aspects of *DODCAB.*

Qualitative Stability

Qualitative stability in this context means that after a sufficiently large number of cases (decompositions), all of which belong to the same *domain,* have been added to the case base (i.e. *DODCAB*), adding further cases will not lead to the addition of new objectives to the case base. For this to be true, more or less the same set of design objectives must always be identified.

In today's competitive markets, the issues of cost, safety, ergonomy, maintainability, reliability, manufacturability, marketability, recyclability, and so on are almost always regarded as targets in virtually all design problems. The difference between different types of design problems, however, is in the emphasis or relative importance given to these objectives. In designing for the domestic market, for example, cost is more important than reliability while designing for the military market is the opposite extreme where cost is of little importance compared to reliability.

Hence, it is reasonable to assume that the first level of design objectives is stable for all types of design problems. The same is true for lower level sub-objectives. For example, maximum use of standard parts is almost always a sub-objective of manufacturability. The same could be true for lower level sub-objectives. For *example, maximum use of standard parts* is almost always a sub-objective of *manufacturability.*

Quantitative Stability

Quantitative stability means that after a sufficiently large number of cases, all of which belong to the same domain, have been added to the case base, the addition of new cases should not dramatically disturb the average values of the relative weighting factors. In order for this to be true, it is assumed that the different experts who will add their decompositions to *DODCAB* will more or less agree on the values of the relative weighting factors (FWFs). Empirical evidence support this assumption. Eckenrode [16] conducted a study in which he collected the judgements of a number of experts about the relative value (weight) of a set of criteria (objectives). As a result, Eckenrode found high concordance between the judges (experts) which indicated that *"a group of experts with relatively similar experience in the areas of interest can agree on the value of the criteria to be applied to that area..."*. Eckenrode also found out that the concordance between experts decreases as one moves from a relatively specific system to a more general one. This concordance also holds for experts from different backgrounds. Hurst [17] used questionnaires to obtain the ranking of a set of design criteria from 13 individuals (judges) coming from different disciplines. He found that the majority of weightings by the separate disciplines were similar.

4.3.2. The structure of DODCAB: DODCAB is a network data-base [18]. A network data-base consists of a collection of records which are connected to one another through links. A link is an association between precisely two records. A hierarchical network, or a forest, is a network in which the records are organised into a collection of trees.

In *DODCAB,* each objective is represented by a node in the network and is linked to its sub-objectives by a *has-sub-objective* relationship (link), Fig. 13.7. Each node contains the following information:

1. The objective itself, *e.g.* low production cost.
2. The problem type, or domain (D), to which this objective belongs.
3. The number of sub-objectives (Ns) which descend from this objective.
4. The number of decomposition cases of this objective (Nc), i.e. how many cases contributed to the decomposition of this objective.
5. A pointer (link) to each of the sub-objectives.
6. Each link between this objective and a sub-objective is tagged with the sum of the relative weighting factors (Wt) for this sub-objective across all cases.

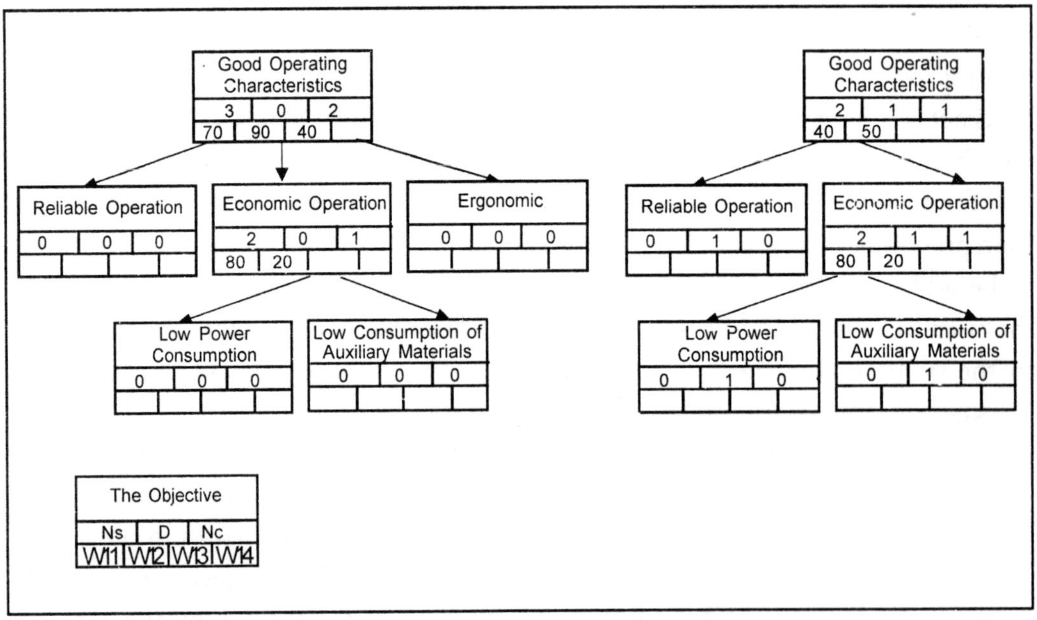

Fig. 13.7

The average RWF of a sub-objective across all cases, can be calculated by dividing the sum of the RWFs (Wt) by the number of cases (Nc).

4.3.3. Adding decompositions to DODCAB: Fig. 13.8 shows a simple example of the incremental evolution of *DODCAB*. In this example, three cases of objectives trees (decompositions) are added to *DODCAB*. Initially *DODCAB* is empty. When the first tree, Fig. 13.8(a), is added to *DODCAB*, a new node (in *DODCAB*) will be created for each of the objectives of the tree, and the appropriate links created between these nodes. Furthermore, each link is tagged with the value of the Wt corresponding to this link. In the second stage, the tree in Fig. 13.8(b) is added to the case base. Since the two objectives "Reliable Operation" and "Economic Operation" already exist in the case base, no new nodes are created for these objectives. The objective "Ergonomic" is a new one and there fore a new node is created and a link from "Ideal product" to "Ergonomic" is created. The sum of the relative weighting factors (Wt) is incremented by the value of the RWF of the corresponding tree node. In the third stage, the tree in Fig. 13.8(c) is added. No new nodes or links are created in this case, however the appropriate Wt values are incremented.

4.3.4. Retrieving previous decompositions: To obtain advice about the possible decompositions of an objective during the development of an objectives tree, the designer selects (clicks on) the objective that he wishes to decompose. The program will then search the appropriate domain in *DODCAB* for this objective and if found will follow the links from this objective to find all its sub-objectives. The program then presents the user with a list of these sub-objectives who can select any of them to be added as a sub-objective to the objective being decomposed. In this sense the user can retrieve a subset of the sub-objectives of an objective as appropriate to the problem at hand.

Since design statements are expressed by statements in natural language, the same objective may be expressed by entirely different phrases. For example, the two phrases "Small production cost" and "Low cost of Manufacture" represent the same objective, although they have quite different lexical and syntactic structures. Therefore, when searching for objectives in *DODCAB*, it is essential that the search procedure is able to recognise the similarity of objectives that have different syntactic structures. Failure to do that can cause two problems:

1. *Duplication:* When adding new cases to *DODCAB,* the same objective, in a different lexical and/or syntactic form, may be added twice. For example,

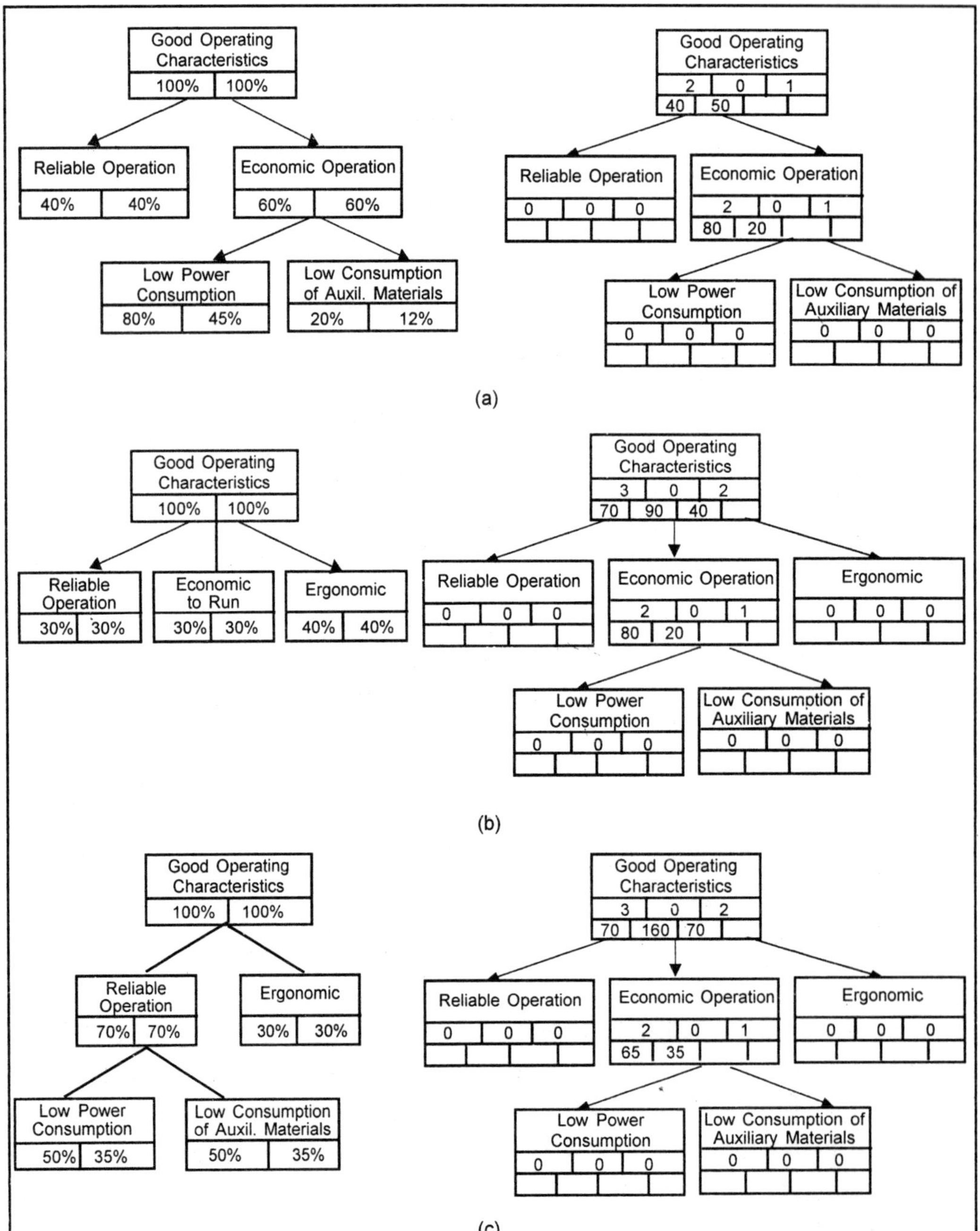

Fig. 13.8

in Fig. 13.8, if the program was not able to recognise that the two statements "Economic Operation" and "Economic to Run" represent the same objective, then the objective "Good Operating Characteristics" would have had two different sub-objectives corresponding to "Economic Operation" and "Economic to Run" respectively, which is obviously an undesired situation.

2. *Failure to Retrieve Objectives:* When trying to retrieve objectives from *DODCAB,* the program may fail to find an objective if it is expressed in a (slightly) different form.

To find an objective in *DODCAB,* the program scans all the objectives in *DODCAB* and calculates the similarity of each of these objectives to this one using an approximate matching procedure. Further information about this procedure can be found in [12]. Those objectives which have a non-zero score are added to a hit-list in order of similarity, i.e., the most similar objective at the top of the list, and least similar at the bottom. In the absence of an exact match, the user is presented with the hit list and prompted to select the matching phrase (if any).

4.3.5. ***Retrieving relative weighting factors:*** As mentioned earlier one of the aims of *DODCAB* is to help the designer in finding the appropriate values of the RWFs of the nodes of an objectives tree. In *TreeTool,* the RWFs can either be entered by the user, or retrieved from *DODCAB.*

The procedure for retrieving the RWFs from DODCAB can be explained with the help of the simple example shown in Fig. 13.9. To retrieve the RWFs of the sub-objectives of "Good Operating Characteristics", the user must click on the node of this objective. The program will then search for the "Good Operating Characteristics" objective in *DODCAB,* and if found will look for those sub-objectives (of this objective) whose RWFs have not been entered by the user, i.e. "Ergonomic" and "Economic Operation". In order to facilitate this operation each node in the objective tree is tagged with a flag that tells whether or not the RWF for the node has been entered by the user. RWFs entered by the user will not be changed by the program.

If all the sub-objectives are found[1], the RWFs of these sub-objectives are then retrieved from *DODCAB.* Retrieving the RWFs from *DODCAB* is not

1. Which will always be the case when an objective has been decomposed with the help of *DODCAB.*

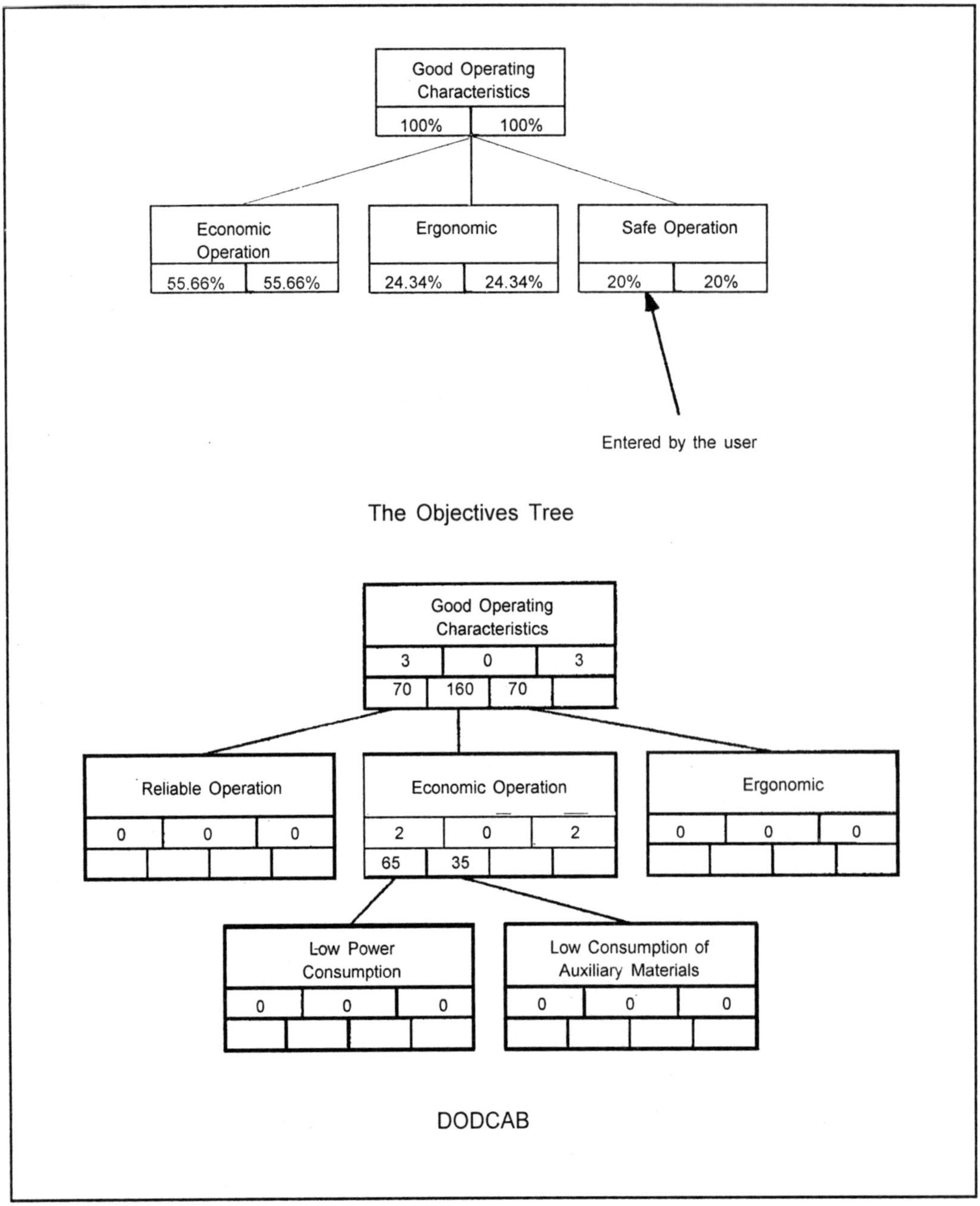

Fig. 13.9

straightforward, however, because some of the sub-objectives in *DODCAB* may have no matching sub-objectives in the objectives tree, and because the value of the RWFs of some of the sub-objectives may have already been entered by the user. To take the above factors into account, the *raw* RWFs should be adjusted as explained below.

The unadjusted average value of the RWF of sub-objective j (Wru(j) is calculated by dividing the total of the RWFs (Wt) corresponding to this objective (see Fig. 13. 7) by the number of decomposition cases (Nc) of the parent objective.

$$W_{ru}(j) = {W_t}/{N_c} \tag{1}$$

In this example, the unadjusted average RWFs for the "Ergonomic" and "Economic Operation" sub-objectives are 70/3 = 23.33 per cent and 160/3 = 53.33 per cent respectively.

Since "Reliable Operation" is one of the decompositions of "Good Operating Characteristics" in *DODCAB,* but is not among the sub-objectives of "Good Operating Characteristics" in the objectives trees, the retrieved RWFs should be adjusted to preserve their relative importance. The adjusted value of the RWF of sub-objective j (Wra(j) can be obtained from the equation:

$$W_{ra}(j) = \frac{W_{ru}(j)}{\sum_i W_{ru}(i)} \times 100 \tag{2}$$

In this example, the adjusted RWFs for the "Ergonomic" and "Economic Operation" sub-objectives are:

$$W_{ra}\ (Ergonomic) = \frac{23.33}{23.33 + 53.33} \times 100 = 30.43\% \tag{3}$$

and

$$W_{ra}\ (Economic\ Operation) = \frac{53.33}{23.33 + 53.33} \times 100 = 69.57\% \tag{4}$$

Since the RWF of "Safe Operation" has already been specified by the user as 20 per cent, the above values (which are based on a total of 100) should be re-adjusted to take this into account. the final value of the RWF of sub-objective (j) (Wr(j) is calculated from the equation:

$$W_r(j) = W_{ra}(j) \times \frac{T_r}{100} \tag{5}$$

Where Tr is the remaining available total of the retrieved RWFs:

$$T_r = 100 - \sum_i W_{rs}(i) \tag{6}$$

where $W_{rs}(i)$ is the value of the RWF of sub-objective (i) which has been specified by the user. In this example, the value of the remaining total is 80 per cent, and the final RWFs for the "Ergonomic", "Economic Operation" and "Safe Operation" sub-objectives are 24.34 per cent, 55.66 per cent, and 20 per cent respectively.

Alternatively, by combining Equations 2, 5, and 6, the final value of an RWF can be directly evaluated from the equation:

$$W_r = W_{ru} \times \frac{100 - \sum W_{rs}}{\sum W_{ru}} \tag{7}$$

6. Summary

The ever increasing pressures of competition is forcing producers to aim for reducing the time-to-market of their products and minimising the possibility of re-designing imperfect products. To this end, their is a growing need for computer based systems that can help in achieving this goal. In this paper, a computer-based environment for supporting designers to generate optimum designs that satisfy the design objectives of the product life cycle is outlined. Full details of this system can be found in [12].

A novel approach for capturing and re-using design objectives decompositions and their relative weightings has been described. It has been shown that the resulting case base can be both qualitatively and quantitatively stable. The procedures for adding and retrieving information from such a case base have been discussed. It should be noted that the idea behind *DODCAB* is generalisable to other types of hierarchies such as functional decompositions [8, 12].

References

1. Pighini U. *et al.*, *Methodological Design for Manufacture,* International Conference on Engineering Design (ICED'89), The Hague 1989, pp. 399-414.
2. Hubka V., *Design for Quality,* International Conference on Engineering Design (ICED'89), The Hague 1989, p. 1321.
3. Beitz W., "Design for Ease of Recycling", *Journal of Engineering Design*, Vol. 4, No. 1, 1993, pp. 11-23.
4. Meerkamm H., "Design for X- A Core Area of Design Methodology", *Journal of Engineering Design*, Vol.5, No. 2, 1994.
5. Pugh S., *Total Design,* Addison-Wisely, 1991.
6. Hubka V., *Principles of Engineering Design,* Butterworth Scientific, 1982.
7. Oh V., Langdon P., and Sharpe J., *Schemebuilder: An Integrated Computer Environment for Product Design,* Lancaster Int'l Workshop on Engineering Design, CACD'94, Lancaster University, Lancaster, England, 1994.
8. Pahl G. and Beitz W., *Engineering Design: A Systematic Approach,* The Design Council, London, 1988.
9. Hwang C. L. and Yoon K., *Multiple Attribute Decision Making: Methods and Applications,* Springer- Verlag, 1981.
10. Sen P. and Yang J., *A Multiple Criteria Decision Support Environment for Engineering Design,* ICED'93, The Hague, 1993, pp. 465-472.
11. Starkey C.V., *Engineering Design Decisions,* Edward Arnold (a division of Hodder and Stoughton), 1992.
12. Al-Salka M. A., *Models and Computer Based Support Tools for Conceptual Design in Mechanical Engineering,* Ph.D Thesis, Department of Mechanical Engineering, University of Wales, Swansea, 1996.
13. Hubka V. and Eder W. E., *Theory of Technical Systems,* Springer- Veralg, Berlin, 1988.
14. Riesbeck C. K. and Schank R. C., *Inside Case Based Reasoning,* Lawrence Erlbaum, 1989.
15. Kolodner J.L., *Case-Based Reasoning,* Morgan Kaufman, 1993.
16. Eckenrode R.T., "Weighting Multiple Criteria", *Management Science*, Vol. 12, No. 3, November 1965, pp. 180-192.
17. Hurst K. S., *Experiences with an Expert System for Concept Selection,* ICED'93, The Hague 1993, pp. 473-480.
18. Korth H.F. and Silberschatz A., *Database System Concepts,* second edition, McGraw Hill, 1991.

14

Concept Evaluation Methods Associated with Virtual Prototyping Techniques as Means for Reducing Lead Time in Product Development

Carlos Cziulik
Department of Mechanical Engineering
University of Surrey, Guildford - Surrey, UK

Abstract

This paper describes an approach to reduce the time spent for product development, at the design stage. The approach is fully integrated into concurrent engineering context, since issues related to its fundamental tripod -shortening the lead time, quality improvement and costs reduction-are being addressed, concerning the early phases of the design process. It is based on improving the quality of alternatives evaluation, at the conceptual design stage, and using ***virtual reality*** *principles, in order to avoid any kind of physical prototyping. The central idea is to assure that the design, when concluded, encompasses the highest possible level of quality and, thus, the actual production (manufacturing and assembly) can be developed smoothly. The realisation of this idea requires a more precise understanding of evaluation and selection methods, used at the early stages of design, and virtual engineering technologies.*

Keywords: *Design Process, The Conceptual Design Stage, Concept Evaluation, Solid Modelling, Virtual Prototyping.*

1. Introduction

Industry is always looking for ways of improving the quality of its products, reducing the costs and shortening the lead time involved in all stages of product development. This pressure is occurring, mainly, because the global economy is replacing local markets, and communication and transportation are facing an enormous progress. On the other hand, price and high quality are no longer the bases of competitive advantage. In order to keep their effectiveness, companies are being asked for continuing, rapid and innovative responses to multiple and most of the time, conflicting performance measures, assigned by changes in customer expectations and market opportunities.

In order to develop products effectively and efficiently, different approaches have been proposed. Concurrent Engineering, Lindberg [8], Design for Assembly, Boothroyd [2], and Life Cycle Analysis, Lee [6], are some examples.

However, in industry, most of the time and attention have been spent on the **"production-side"** of product development (machining technologies, materials flow, organisation). The **"design-side"** has been considered a secondary activity, that cannot be improved, even though design researchers have been providing methods and approaches, showing the advantages of their use, **Blessing [1]**. Nowadays, using advanced management techniques, associated with different manufacturing strategies (Just in Time, Flexible Layouts), the **"production side"** able to process an order with low levels of waste (time, material, energy). Nevertheless, the **"design side"** is still does not have tools to assess, rapidly and with confidence, the quality of a design, and frequently, the design team have to use prototypes to validate a product configuration. Yet, conventional prototyping is time consuming, expensive (tooling and machining) and requires qualified labour. Additionally, trendy rapid prototyping techniques are also expensive (machine-wise, skilled people involved) and time consuming (for preparation and actual fabrication). To overcome these limitations, some engineering areas, realising the potentialities of **virtual reality** advances, are envisaging ways of applying its developments to **virtual prototyping.**

The main intention of this paper is to present an effective approach for shortening the lead time for product development. This can be achieved by applying reliable methods for alternatives evaluation, during the conceptual design stage, and use of **virtual prototyping** techniques, in parallel with the embodiment and detailing phases.

The structure of the paper is as follows: Section 2 presents an overview of the design process, paying special attention to conceptual design, Section 3 emphasises the importance of the evaluation process during the conceptual design stage. Section 4 describes basic ideas about **virtual engineering** and shows, through an example, the potentialities of this technology. Conclusions are drawn in section 5.

2. The Design Process

During recent years, a lot of research has been carried out trying to understand how the design process occurs, with the benefits of a more systematic and methodical approach to the design activity being mentioned in several sources, like Pahl &

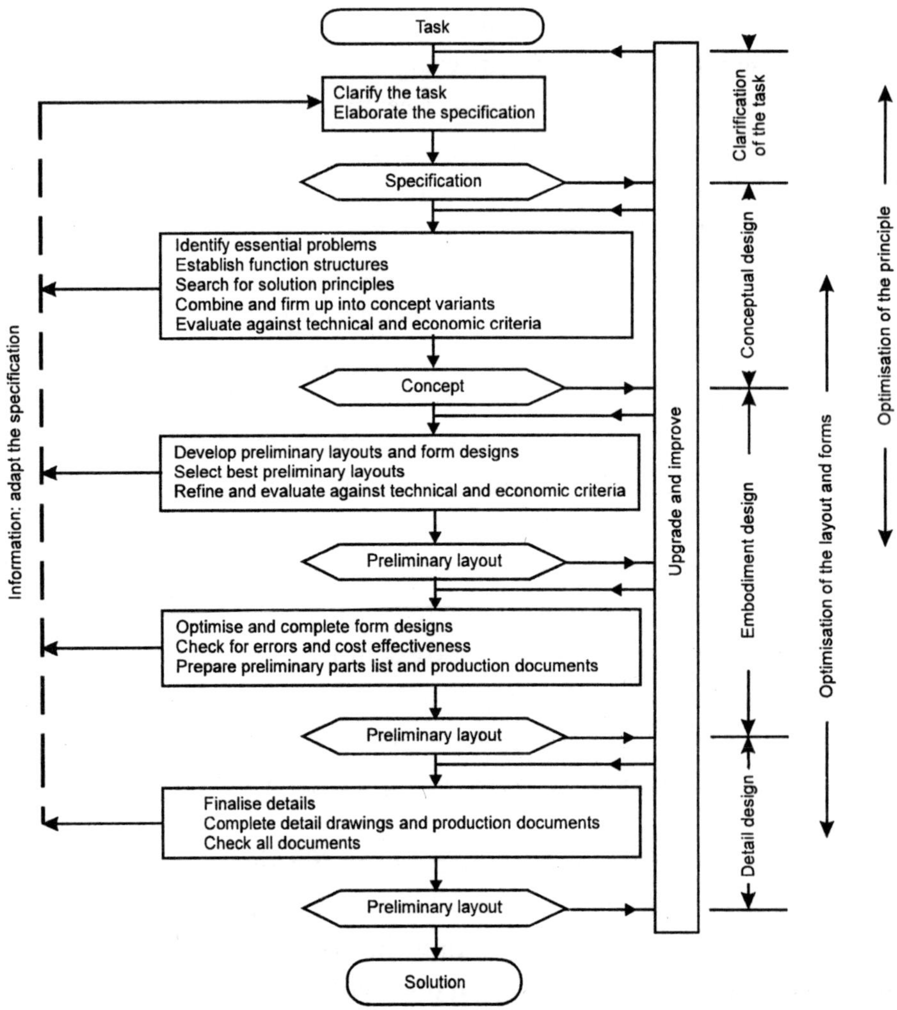

Fig. 14.1: Stages of design process according to Pahl & Beitz [9].

Beitz [9], Pugh [10] and Ullman [11]. One of the most successful methodologies in both, academic and industrial arenas, is the prescriptive model developed by Pahl & Beitz [9], see Fig. 14.1.

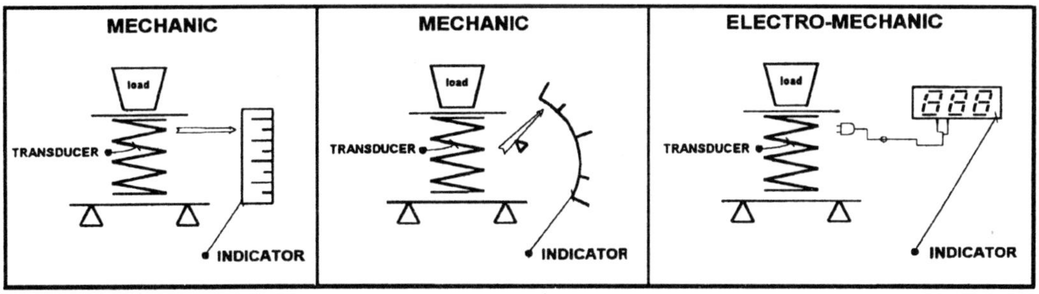

Fig. 14.2: Three different concepts for a measurement instrument

It is composed of a sequence of phases, starting from task definition to solution documentation. Conceptual design, one of the phases mentioned in this and other approaches, is considered here, as being all the activities that are accomplished in order to find one or more concepts that fulfil the requirements of the problem stated. The activities involved are: task definition, requirements specification, principle solution generation and conceptual model realisation. Possible ideas or combinations, partial or global, are, in general, represented as diagrams and sketches that translate the designer's intents (see Fig. 14.2) and which include all the information needed for the development of the next design phases.

The process starts with the needs' identification, aiming to explore all aspects involved with them. A set of design requirements is defined, trying to describe the problem in a qualitative, quantitative, functional and non-functional way. These requirements work like a control mechanism, comparing alternatives with customers' needs. The main functions that the systems should perform are defined and arranged, identifying the relationship between them and determining sufficient details for specifying the principles that will satisfy them.

The generation of alternatives can be performed in different ways and using several techniques, that will characterise the use of creativity during the design process. Next, using synthesis procedures, parts will be put together, generating a set of configured alternatives. Concluding this stage, evaluation procedures check how close the characteristics of concepts generated are to the design requirements. One or more alternatives will pass to the following development phases. The previous descriptions give an introduction to the early stages of the design process and are included by most authors who have studies the subject.

3. The Evaluation Process During the Conceptual Design Stage

According to Ishii [7], there is a consensus amongst researchers that decisions made during the early stages of design define more than 80 percent of the life-cycle cost. Additionally, Ullman [11] states that 75 percent of the manufacturing costs are already defined by the end of the conceptual design stage. Therefore, decisions at this stage must be made accurately in order to reduce the number of redesign activities at both, embodiment and detailing levels.

On the other hand, most of the time, cost and quality are being seen as pre-requisites and no longer represent a competitive advantage. In this way, companies are challenged to develop their products as soon as possible, if they want to keep their position on the market. Thus, the key issue that arises in this scenario is **time** with all its derivations.

The opportunity for saving time, during product development, at the design phase, seems to appear at the conceptual design stage. This occurs because of the following reasons:

1. Embodiment and detail design have well-established methods and technologies for speeding product development, at these respective stages. Tools for analysis (Finite Element Method, kinematics Analysis, for example) are becoming cheaper and easy to use. In the same way, several CAD packages incorporate auxiliary detailing techniques (Genius 13, Optegra), allowing a consistent way of manipulating information (tolerances, standard components and representations).
2. The embodiment design stage encompasses a large amount of analysis, that in some cases, is costly and time consuming. Consequently, examining a wrong alternative will input additional costs to the design activity and will increase the time for presenting the ideal combination of material, shape and features.
3. The detail design phase, that supplies the information needed for defining the process for machining the part, the precision of the machines, the availability of them, among others, is also an activity that requires expertise and time to be accomplished. Thus, the more precise and consistent the

evaluation at the early stages of design is, the less time is spent for detailing.

Several authors have been investigating evaluation methods applied to the early stages of design. Binary Evaluation, Evaluation Chart and rating Diagram are examined by Pahl & Beitz [9] and the Method of Controlled Convergence was devised by Pugh [10], just to mention some of them. Most of researchers have been concerned with means for comparing the solutions achieved with the requirements specified. However, this approach has been proved weak, since it does not consider further implications of a chosen alternative.

On the other hand, it is reasonable to think that a more precise evaluation of the design solutions can only be performed when the embodiment and detail design are finished. This conflict, between lack of information at the early stages and reliability of alternatives evaluation has been investigated by Cziulik [3]. This research intends to develop a computer software for supporting alternatives evaluation, during the conceptual design stage. The model being elaborated aims to enhance designers confidence in the solution chosen as well as to reduce. hence saving time. The procedure explored is composed, basically, of two stages. The first is a *"pass-fail"* assessment, where possible solutions are checked against the initial specifications. Only those matching the requirements will proceed to the next step, which intends to rank the alternatives, in order to define the one that has the best potential to become a successful product. To perform that, some implicit information (manufacturing processes, materials to be used), that usually arises only at the embodiment and detailing stages, will be brought to the conceptual phase, using an extensive computer database and the expertise gathered by the design team. Therefore, the decisions can be made more confidently and errors can be minimised, early in the design process, which can reduce the lead time for product development, as mentioned previously.

4. Virtual Engineering

In the past, **virtual reality** techniques were basically exploited by the defence sector. However, with the recent developments in computer technologies (performance and cost reduction, for instance) some engineering areas have found their way in the **virtual reality** world. As its main aim is to reproduce, as close as possible, some aspects of a real environment, it is possible to foresee that in the near future, engineering will be able to substitute physical prototype techniques by virtual models, which has already originated a new expression, that is **virtual engineering (ve)**. According to Kim *et al.* [5], **virtual engineering** is a computer controlled environment that responds to user interactions, allowing visualisation and manipulation of virtual models. Basically, the **ve** system is composed of a reality engine (computer system, external hardware), input/output devices, software and geometry.

Therefore, instead of producing a three dimensional (**3D**) model of a part, using a **CAD** package, and either:- **a**/ generating drawings and fabricating the actual prototype, with conventional manufacturing technologies; or **b**/ translating this **3D** information into another model that will be read by the rapid prototyping system, for the prototype development; - the designer could use the original **3D** model for performing product evaluation, using a virtual environment. In this way, the design team can achieve a high level of visualisation and understanding of an element, which is important in areas like ergonomics, machining and assembly, among others. Parameters like colours, commands positions, sizes of symbols (for visualisation, for example) can be assessed by customers (how can give a prompt feed-back) and suggested changes can be implemented easily, since they will imply modifications in a file, instead of accomplishing physical alternations, which are, most of the time, expensive and time consuming. Another advantage is that, regarding the size of the files, different alternatives can be electronically produced, stored and compared more easily than, sometimes, cumbersome physical devices.

Figures 14.3, 14.4, 14.5, and 14.7 show different aspects of a full solid model of a mechanic system for generating chaotic movements, Cziulik [4]. In this work, some analyses were performed such as centre of gravity definition for positioning the handle; physical interference verification between the components, total weight calculation, layout study for transportation (space optimisation), just to mention some of them, without building the prototype. Others could be conducted like vibration and thermal analysis (heat generated by the motor) but they did not belong to the scope of the mentioned work. It is important to notice that in this case the designer still could not interact with the model (turn the buttons, "sense" the weight, verify ease of assembly since the work was carried out using a conventional **CAD** system, although some subjective aspects were considered (colour's combination, symbol's position). Virtual prototyping can offer different ways for the design team to interact

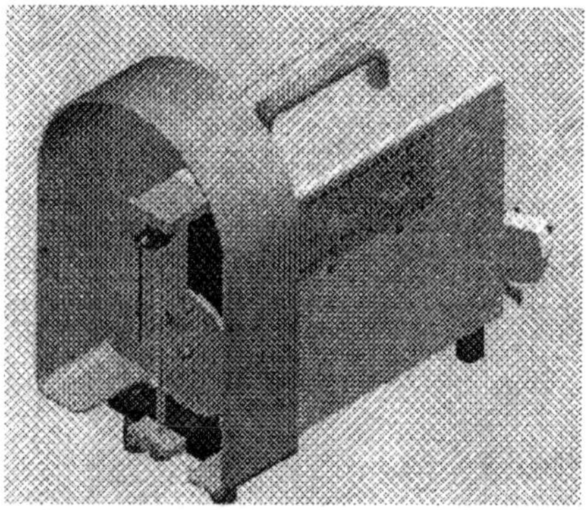

Fig. 14.3: Vertical Oscillating Pendulum (VOP)- Main View

Fig. 14.4: VOP - Back View

Fig. 14.5: VOP - Layout for Transport

Fig. 14.6: VOP - Subassembly "Indicator System"

Fig. 14.7: VOP - Subassembly "Protection Cover"

with the model, as if its members, from different specialities, were manipulating a real feature of the device. This interaction did not happen in the mentioned case-study, because the model visualisation occurred in a flat screen (2D), despite the fact that the solid model was actually generated.

Quite simple interfaces, such as stereoscopic glasses (a device which combines two small cameras, allowing stereo visualisation) and data gloves (which transfer information to and from a model, via hand), offer the opportunity of "seeing" and "feeling" the concept being designed, which is very important since a co-operative environment can be created amongst designers, who can share opinions and present contributions from their past experiences. Viewing, either a part of the whole assembly, from different angles can bring some ingenious insights. Additionally, with a virtual prototype, not only the design aspects can be enhanced, but also maintenance procedures checked (ease of access, time spent) and operation routines practised.

Considering all the above points, they lead to the conclusion that, instead of spending money and time with physical prototyping (either, conventional or rapid prototyping), the same solid model used for embodiment and detailing, could be transferred immediately to a **ve** environment, for what could be called, the final judgement by the end user. With the fast developments taking place in computer technologies (software and hardware) and a better understanding of the whole design process, physical prototyping tends to become an unnecessary step in the product development cycle. In the near future, concept analysis and several kinds of verifications will be performed in real time, allowing to develop a product, from designing to manufacturing, faster, better and cheaper.

5. Conclusions

This paper describes an approach towards saving time at the design stage, based on improvement of alternatives evaluation, at conceptual design stage, and avoiding any kind of physical prototyping.

Associating reliable methods for concepts evaluation with **virtual prototyping** techniques can lead to saving time during product development, at the design level. The first one, will allow only the most promising concept to go the following stages (embodiment and detailing) while the second, can verify the consistency of the solution generated, without to physical models.

Further studies should be conducted to develop mechanisms to integrate the concept generation phase with **ve** technologies, in order to allow only the best possible design alternative to be analysed and detailed, and so, reducing even more the time to put the product on the market.

References

1. Blessing, L.T.M., (1994). *A Process-Based Approach to Computer-Supported Engineering Design*. Cambridge: Lucienne T.M. Blessing.
2. Boothroyd, G., & Dewhurst, P., (1989). *Product Design for Assembly*. Wakerfield: Boothroyd and Dewhurst, Inc.
3. Cziulik, C., (995). *Development of a Computer Based Model for Conceptual Design Evaluation of Mechanical Systems*. Transfer Report From MPhil to Phd. Department of Mechanical Engineering. Guildford: University of Surrey.
4. Cziulik, C., (1995). *Vertical Oscillating Pendulum. Design for Manufacture Perspective* Design for Manufacture - Module D-4, AMMT Course. Guildford: University of Surrey.
5. Kim, B., Kim, S.; Sonthi, R. & Gadh, R., (1994). "Virtual Engineering Environment Applications: An Overview". In: Mason, Jim, *Design for Manufacturability*. Proceedings of the 1994 Design for Manufacturability Conference, Chicago, IL, USA, Mar 14-17. Vol. 67. New York: ASME. pp. 1-11.
6. Lee, D.E., & Melkanoff, M.A., (1993). "Issues in Product Life Cycle Engineering Analysis". In: Gilmore, Brian, *Advances in Design Automation*. Proceedings of the 19th Annual ASME Design Automation Conference, Part 1 (of 2), Albuquerque, NM, USA, Sep 19-22. Vol. 65 (1). New York: ASME. pp. 75-86.
7. Ishii, K., (1995). *Life-cycle Engineering Design*. In: BEHUN, J. Richard, *Design for Manufacturability*. Proceedings of the 1995 National Design Engineering Show and Conference, Chicago, IL, USA, Mar 13-17. Vol. 81. New York: ASME. pp. 39-45.
8. Lindberg, L., (1993). *Notes on Concurrent Engineering. Annals of the CIRP*. Vol. 42 (1), pp. 159-162.
9. Pahl, G., & Beitz, W., (1988). *Engineering Design. A Systematic Approach*. London: The Design Council.
10. Pugh, S., (1991). *Total Design*. Workingham: Addison-Wesley Publishers.
11. Ullman, D.G., (1992). *The Mechanical Design Process*. New York: McGraw-Hill.

15

A New Concept for Manipulating Machine Tools Through a CNC System

T.El-Midany[1]*, A.El Mallah*[2]*, N.El Chazly*[3] *and M.El-Bayoumy*[4]

[1]*Prof. Production Engg. Dept., Egypt* [2,3]*Prof. Mech. Engg. Dept., Egypt*
[4]*Research Asst., Mech. Engg. Dept., Egypt*

Abstract

The local industry suffers from the unmatched inaccurate products due to the variance in labor skills and mentality, so it was beneficial to use NC and CNC machines in production lines, in spite of the big fixed cost, high maintenance cost and the high cost of idle time. The present work aims at investigating the ability of accomplishing the design of electrical and mechanical parts of the control system, and to overcome its problems and the computer programming ones, taking into consideration the compromising between the simplicity of both the controlling circuits and the computer program. A computerized numerical angular motion control system; based on a stepper motor, has been built. the control system is used to control a light duty lathe through a special personal and user friendly computer program. The aim is to achieve a low cost, easy to construct and easy to maintain, computerized control system guiding the carriage and cross-slide of the lathe. the system is found to be matching the desired accuracy, taking into consideration the cost reduction compared to similar systems.

Keywords: *CNC, ICs,series and parallel ports,stepper motor,buffering, latching, clock.*

1. Introduction

Recently as a trend developing country's economy is getting biased towards liberal policies such as reduction of importing taxes, the local market and local limited industries started to suffer from the low prices of the high quality imported products.

Advanced countries products showed a great potential to beat similar developing countries products, surprisingly not only in both quality and price but also in technical features, as a direct result for the main difference between developing countries industries and other ones which are found to be in the level of manipulating and mastering M/C tools.

The industrial problems in developing countries arise from lack of serious machine tool design and production plans. Since importing the machine tools is a costly operation for the developing countries [1]. So the usually imported machine is from the universal purpose type. bulky machines to satisfy the different factory needs with minimum number of machine tools. This leads us to face industrial tragedies like seeing a general purpose 3 m. length CNC lathe dedicated for producing a 10 mm length product, resulting in low productivity and huge over cost.

The local industry in the developing countries is incapable of designing and constructing bulky and highly specialized M/C tools, which necessitate importing them when needed. Since real production policies rely on mastering machine tool's technology and cost, a great consideration is given to M/C tools developing policies.

Developing M/C tools by using the computer to control its mechanical motion [2,3,4,5] is not a hard task to accomplish [6,7], even without sacrificing the accuracy or speed [1], since modern control ICs have been developed to handle this task with fewer parts and better performance [8,9].

So the aim of the present work is to investigate a CNC actuator design and the construction case and difficulties, as an attempt to prove that developing and using a CNC mechanism is not as difficult to adopt [6.7] as it is said to be in local industry. A two step motor and electronic circuits specially designed and built for this purpose, both controlled by an IBM compatible PC, were employed to decide and control the proper required velocity and acceleration of the desired motion of both steppers. A Computer program has been developed to facilitate and familiarize the interaction between the system user and the

CNC system in order to encourage the small industries to adopt this newly developed system.

2. The Developed System

The system is basically constructed to manipulate a light duty lathe by controlling its carriage and cross-slide travel throughout the processing task, using a computerized electromechanical system. The system first thought of design was to leave the intersection line between the computer and the electronic circuits, floating, to give it the flexibility for reducing both system repair and maintenance cost, and system overall cost. The system principal design consisted of a computerized, electromechanical component, and stepper motor (SM) connected to a light duty lathe machine in Fig. 15.1.

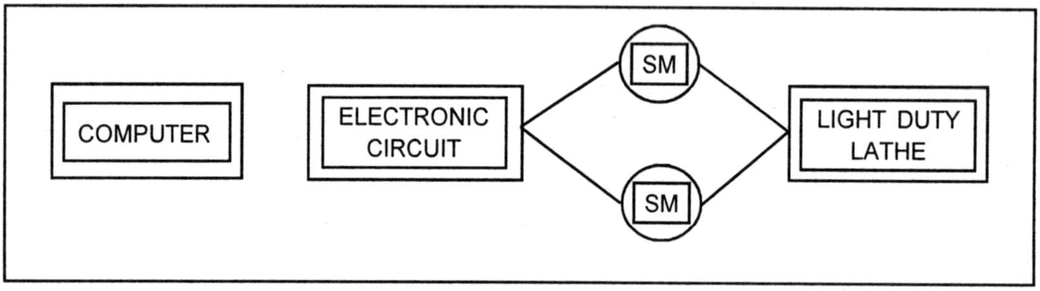

Fig. 15.1: The developed system layout

The new technique for stepper driving using the computer generated logic pattern relying on external timing circuit. is a developed approach to minimize the overall complications, specially the need for sophisticated inefficient timing algorithm, taking the most benefit all system of the available high processing and communicating speeds featured in the new generations of computers.

The system consists of both software and hardware designed to accomplish the controlling task with maximum flexibility in modification and upgrading. The system has been designed relying on the specially developed software to decrease the overall system cost complications, through shifting the majority of the system duties to be handled by programming.

3. Software Description

In order to facilitate and make familiar the system to the ordinary user, a special user-friendly program is developed. this program is capable of dealing with the required part data through different treatings, till coming out with the controlling signals and delivering them to the control circuit. The program is internally divided into 5 subprograms each of which accomplishes a specific function, Fig. 15.2 represents the program layout.

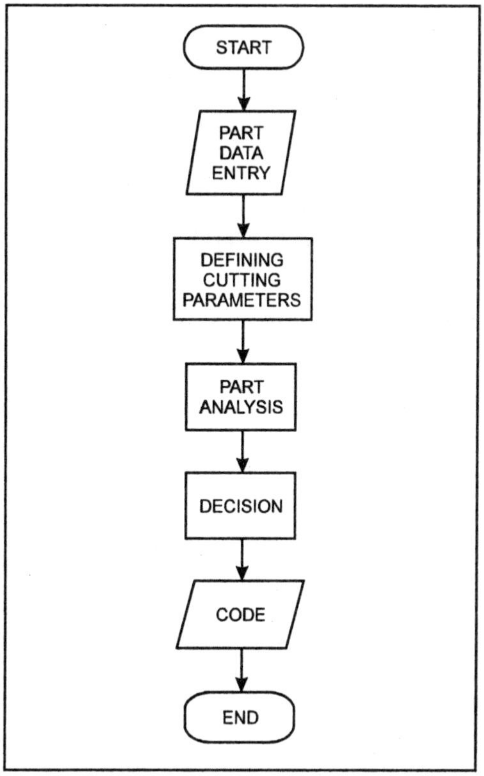

Fig. 15.2: Program block diagram

3.1. Part data entry

Through this subprogram, the user is allowed to enter the part data with a special technique developed to simplify it. The proposed technique depends on dividing the required workpiece to smaller parts with easy to describe shapes. Each part is described by its two ends diameters and its length Fig. 15.3. The entered data is treated to describe the outer contour of the workpiece. The subprogram has the flexibility to keep entering the data required for the workpiece and finally, to start the assembly stage Fig 15.4 allowing for tight control on the workpiece data entry.

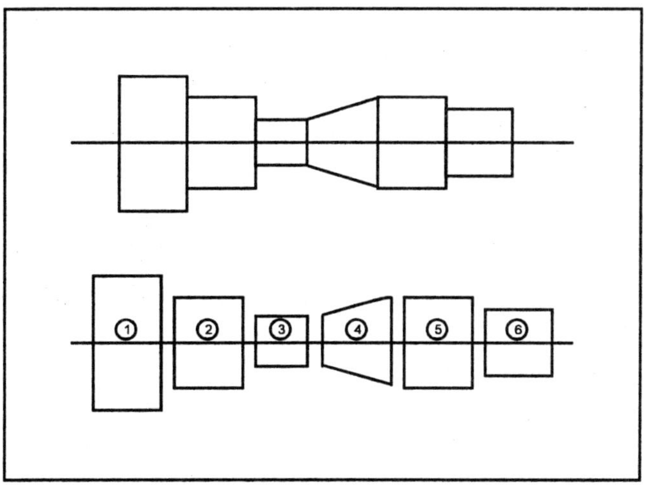

Fig. 15.3: Workpiece geometry data

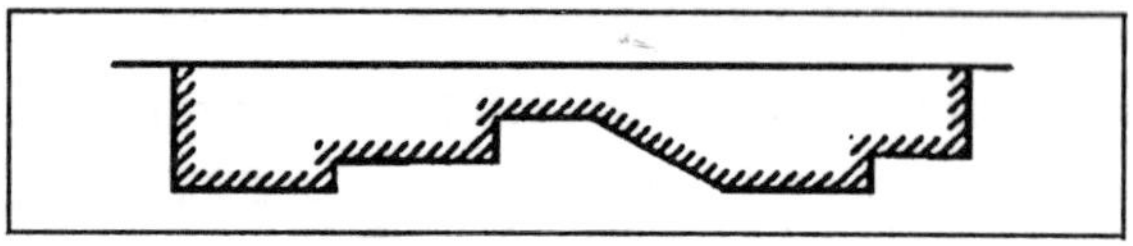

Fig. 15.4: Workpiece final shape

3.2. Defining cutting parameters

This subprogram selects the most suitable cutting conditions for the workpiece machining using a special data base designed for different materials.

3.3. Part analysis

The subprogram determines the rough cutting surface contour taking into consideration the finishing depth of cut according to stored data base Fig. 15.5.

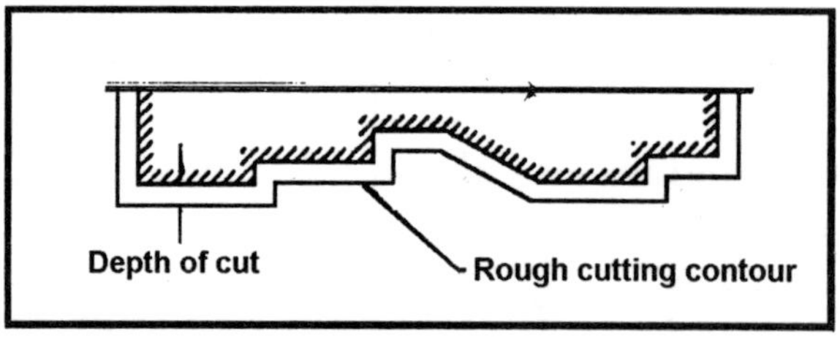

Fig. 15.5: Determining the rough cutting surface.

3.4. Decision

This subprogram decides the sequence of cutting surfaces and then deduces the shortest and best cutting tool path through the whole operation Fig. 15.6.

3.5. Code

This subprogram converts the previously deduced cutting tool path into a special controlling code capable of driving the developed electromechanical interface between the computer and the lathe, to accomplish the required carriage and cross slide motions, and so carrying out the required machining task.

4. Hardware Description

The computer as the most powerful computation tool with its enormous, still increasing speeds, has to communicate with different systems in order to transform

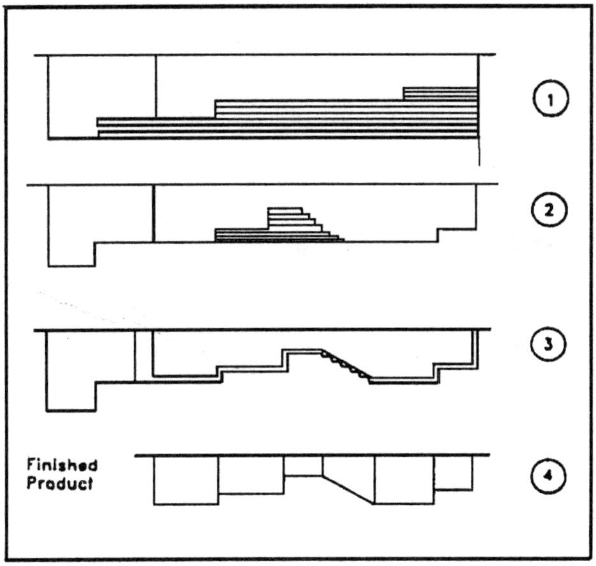

Fig. 15.6: Decision making for the required sequence of operations

this huge computational capabilities to a real world beneficial activities, such as controlling electrical and electromechanical devices etc.

The computer exchanges data mainly through standard input/output (I/O) devices which passed through a lot of developing data exchange history. These standard (I/O) devices are divided into three groups: Input devices. Output devices, and Input/Output devices, which are the computer standard devices capable of both collecting data from the computer and sending data to the computer, for example:

(a) **Serial Port.** The least common denominator of computer communication, since it deals basically with sending data through two wires, a data signal line, and a ground to extended distances, resulting in a real reduction in overall communication cost.

(b) **Parallel Port.** Well defined, convenient, fast and probably the most trouble-free connection with the computer as long as the used cables are not longer than 3 m. to avoid the crosstalking problem. Parallel refer to the fact that this port conducts signal through eight separate wires, one for each bit of the data byte, so the bits signal runs in parallel from and to the computer [10]. The computer parallel port is designed according to the Transistor Transistor Logic (TTL) family specification as an inhibited standard for the IBM and compatible, levels of signal voltage and current are so well defined.

The Proposed Circuit. The main concept taken in the circuit design is to cut down the circuit cost and to keep it as simple as possible without sacrificing its performance, simplicity is often said to be the ultimate sophistication. The circuit communicates with the computer through the parallel port to transform a specially treated data into a physical controlling signals capable of achieving the controlling operation. the circuit duty could be divided into 5 sub-duties each of which accomplishes a specific function, Fig. 15.7 illustrates the complete circuit.

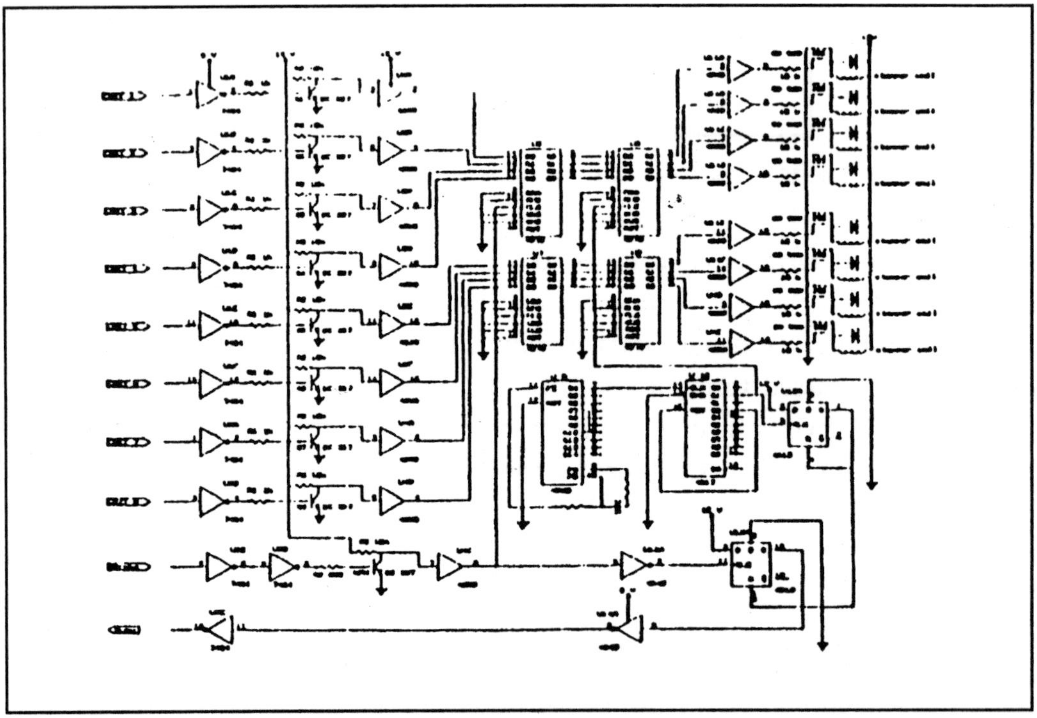

Fig. 15.7: The Designed Circuit

4.1. Buffering and level shifting

This portion of the circuit is designed to buffer the computer parallel port output to achieve a higher safety for the computer port against any circuit break-down, and to shift the computer (TTI.) signals level to (CMOS) recommended operating voltage level to increase the circuit noise-immunity.

4.2. Latching the port data

After the computer port data is buffered and level shifted, the data is latched using a pair of 4076 ICs each contains a 4 D type Register, the data is latched as soon as it is available from the port, then the circuit declares that it is busy and incapable of receiving another signal temporarily.

4.3. Clock

It is responsible for the harmony of circuit operation, a 4060 Timer/Divider is used to generate the required clock pulses, getting different frequencies through the divider featured in this timer. The 4060 output is fed to 4017 decade counter connected as a divider to allow much flexibility in achieving required frequencies Fig. 15.8.

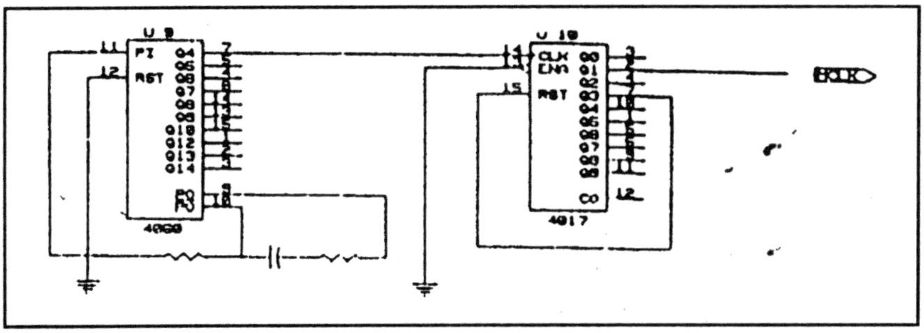

Fig. 15.8: Master clock circuit.

4.4. Precise timing latching

The latched port data is available but with out real timing since the computer is responsible for data sending with out timing obligations. So a pair of 4076 ICs is used to load the previously latched port data in precise timing, synchronized with the circuit declaration of the need for the next data byte as soon as the port can send it, Fig. 15.9.

4.5. Power switching

Since the signals are originally designed to be the logic level pattern of the power signals required to drive the stepper motors, they are used to switch the power using a set of V-MOS-c FETs. A logic level reduction is carried out using 4050 non inverting buffers to match the V-MOS-C FETs driving requirements in Fig. 15.10.

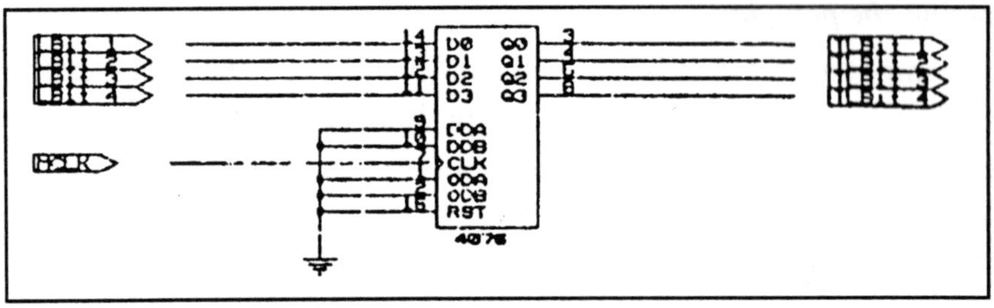

Fig. 15.9: Precise timing latching circuit

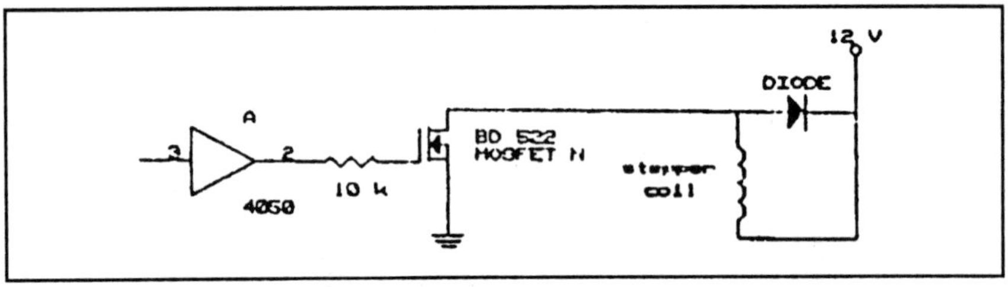

Fig. 15.10: Power switching circuit

Conclusions

1. The developed system configuration is capable of driving mechanical systems through modifications in power switching and stepper motors. It is a new concept for manipulating machine tools through a CNC system to overcome the suffering of the local industry from the unmatched inaccurate products due to the variance of labour skills and mentality.
2. Further modifications through the developed system could be accepted, to enhance the system capabilities and to extend its range of application.
3. The system in hand has been designed to overcome many of other systems complications such as the need for timing algorithm. The developed hardware and software cut down the overall system cost, and complications.
4. The developed computer control system guides the carriage and cross-slide of the lathe machine. Desired accuracy and reduction compared with similar systems have been maintained.

References

1. Werneck, M.M.," Development of a Microcomputer Based x-y Plotter: A Preliminary Report", *International Journal of Computer Applications in Technology*. Vol. 6. No. 2. pt 3. 1993, pp. 141-146.
2. Balkovoj, A.P. Kozachenko, V.F., Kudryashov, A.L.," A Small-sized System for Controlling Stepping Motors by Using Personal Computers", Elektrotekhnika in 7. July 1994, pp. 53.
3. Knight, Terence, Zilouchian, A., Szabo, B., "Design and Implementation of Position Feedback Controllers for an x-y Table", *Proceeding of the IEEE SOUTHEASTCON*. 1994.
4. Fadul, Faisal, Arnold, Louis, "Modular CNC System for Multi Axis Motion Devices", *Computer in Industry*. V. 20. N. 2, Aug 1992, pp. 203-208.
5. Innes, Richard," Industrial Applications of Stepper Motor Systems", IEE Colloquium on stepper motors and their control, London, UK, IEE Colloquium, No. 17, Jan 25, 1994.
6. Kim, Jeong-Du, Kim, Myung-Hwan, "Study on Design of CNC Lathe for Education and Application", *International Journal of Production Economics*, Vol. .25, No. 1-3, Dec. 1991, pp. 169-180.
7. Inage, Toshiyuki, Hashimoto, Hideyuki, Tsushima, Kazunori, "Circular Path Control of Horizontal Two Link Robot Driven by Stepping Motor", Transaction of the Japan Society of Mechanical Engineers. Part C. C. 60. No. 570. Feb 1994, pp. 612-617.
8. Oberwallner, Christian, Sturzer, Manfred, "IC Driver for two-phase Stepper Motors: Better Performance, Fewer Parts", *Siemens Components*, Vol. 27, No. 1, Jan-Feb 1992, pp. 25-28.
9. Amaratunga, Gehan, Kwan, Kin-wah, Tso, M.; Crawley, Engl, "Single-Chip CMOS IC for Closed Loop Control of Step Motors", *IEEE transaction on Industrial Electronics*, Vol. 36, No. 4, Nov 1989. pp. 539-544.
10. Winn L. Rosch, *Hardware Bible*, First printing, 1992.
11. Paul Horowitz, Winfield Hill, *The Art of Electronics*, Second ed. 1989.
12. Murry Sargent, Richard L. Shoemaker, "*The IBM Personal Computer from the Inside Out*". Adison-Wesley. Revised ed. 1989.
13. Say, M.G., Taylor, E.O., *Direct Current Machines*, ELPS & PITMAN. Second ed. 1982.
14. Allen L. Watt, *Using Assembly Language*, Que Corporation, 1987.

16

The Concurrent Engineering Development of the Electric Motors and Drives Industry in Egypt

Aziz I. Said

Faculty of Engineering, Ain Shams University, Cairo, Egypt

Abstract

It is noted that technology plays an important role to save raw materials and to protect our environment. In fact, market economy affects quality and production and is strongly related to environmental protection, cost-effectiveness, and energy saving. The concurrent engineering to develop electric motors for electormechanical and electronic industry in Egypt has taken timely measures to cope with anticipated international developments. Some technological adoptions are proposed to increase efficiency, to improve energy conservation, saving and environment.

This paper intends to assist industrial plant and building engineers in making intelligent choices from an energy efficiency standpoint when they are selecting electric drives. Further, it is hoped that information presented in this document will aid those engineers in establishing the proper procedures for electric drive operation, production and maintenance. It is concluded that how can business respond to standardization, shortening product life cycles, innovation and other solutions including consulting, financing, hardware, software, and service.

Key Words: *Concurrent engineering, Electrotechnical industry, Proper specification, Maintenance, Energy saving, Process development, Standardisation.*

1. Introduction

In concurrent product, process design and development, the cost, energy saving, and efficiency represent very important factors to decide whether a certain operation will be carried out or not, although political and other considerations may intervene sometimes. The engineer has to adopt the cheapest and most convenient schemes after having study of the relative costs of the possible schemes considering quality, market requirements and co-operative agreements. The concurrent development of electric drives industry in Egypt has taken some steps to obtain high productivity ensuring at the same time high quality [1, 2]. This is achieved by using reengineering and automatically continuous process improvement [3, 4, 5].

Electric drives are becoming more and more popular and common for their simplicity, cleanliness, reliability, long life, easy starting, low cost, facility for remote control, etc. Basically, an electric drive system is defined as a form of machine equipment designed to convert electric energy into mechanical energy and provide control of this process [6, 7]. The main elements of an automatic electric drive system are illustrated by the block diagram in Fig. 16.1. The power conditioner

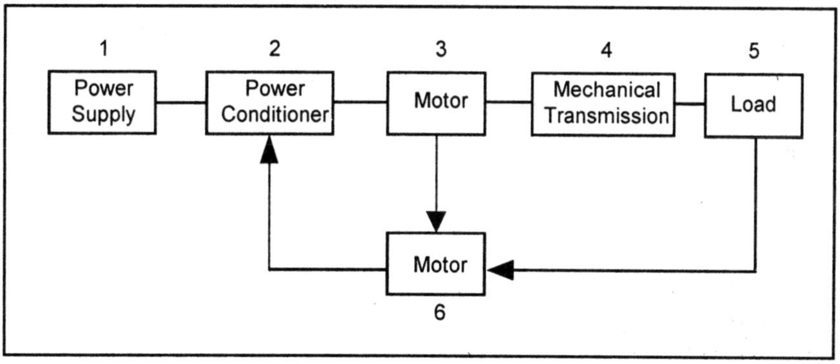

Fig. 16.1: Elements of an Automatic Electric Drive System

controls the electric power to the motor to achieve a specified characteristic, where it is a suitable type of electronic converters as shown in Fig. 16.2.

The controller receives two feed back signals: The load (speed or position) and the motor (current or voltage). A logic unit receives these two signals, together with the command signal, and produces the proper signals that control the power conditioner. Micro-processor based controllers are often used to incorporate complex logic functions into only a few components and hence result in increased reliability and reduced cost [8].

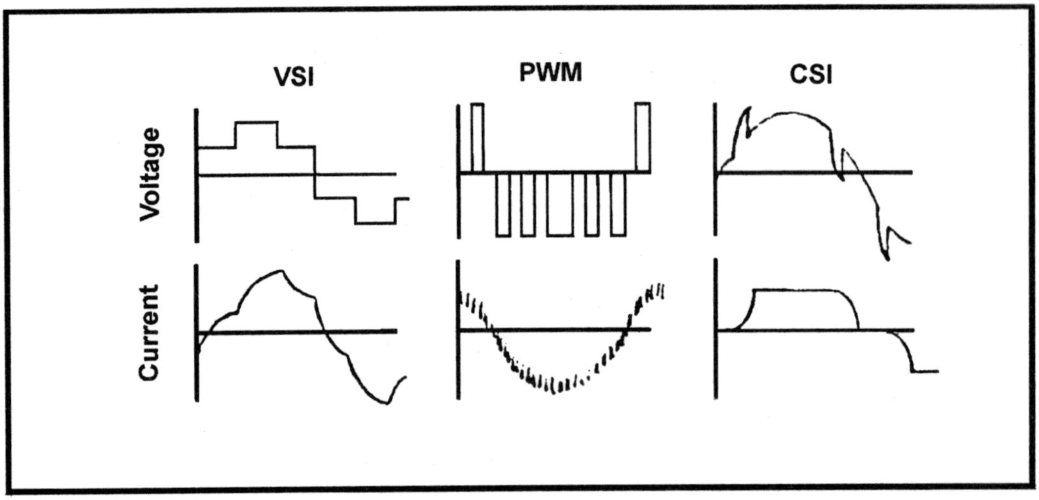

Fig. 16.2: Characteristics Waveforms of Step-Wave Forming VSI & CSI and PWM

The use of electric drives is continuously expanding in all fields of industrial, commercial and other services activities such as electrified transport, agriculture, building construction, and office and home appliances. The rapid development in all these fields is accompanied by the use of automatic control systems for individual drive units as well as for complete plants. Modern electric drives and production processes, combined with modern means of automatic control including automatic operation, regulation, and monitoring, present the following outstanding advantages:

- productivity increase and hence a radical decrease in the production cost per unit.
- consistent and high quality products,
- minimum electrical energy consumption, and
- improved working conditions in industry.

It is economically feasible to fully automate some sections of a manufacturing department, and even an entire production plant using new types of electronic devices for control, computers, nueral networks and expert systems. The predominant trend in the development of electric drives is precisely in this direction, as it will ensure the mass production of a large amount of consistent and high quality products at the least possible cost and time.

2. Proper Specification of Electric Motors and Drives

In this section, it is intended to assist industrial plant and building engineers in making intelligent choices and proper procedures for selecting the suitable electric drive, its operation and maintenance. Electric motors can be purchased as unitary devices for particular applications, or often as an integral part of devices such as compressors, blowers, air conditioners, lifts or moving stairs, conveyer systems, domestic appliances, or pieces of process equipment. They are relatively efficient in their conversion of energy to useful work, especially when compared to other types of prime movers and they also have the advantages of being relatively inexpensive, easy to service and replace. However, their energy efficiencies can degrade over time, particularly when they are used in harch environments and/or are not properly operated or maintained. In most industrial, commercial plants, electric motors account for more than half of the plant's total electricity consumption. Therefore, there is still a tremendous opportunity for energy savings by the proper specification, selection, operation, and maintenances of electric motors and drives.

The best method to evaluate torque requirements is to superimpose the speed against torque of the drive equipment on the speed against torque diagram of the motor, which are generally available from their manufacturers. Beside horse-power and speed, the most important specification is the voltages to be applied. There are limits to the combinations of power and voltage available. Because of the mechanical and operating difficulties involved with current and voltage requirements, organizations, have developed standards for motor sizes according to voltage as shown in Fig. 16.3.

As this section has shown, the proper specification of the motor involves much more than specifying voltage and number of phases, desired motor speed, shaft direction and power output. A number of factors have to be considered, which are summarized as:

1. ensuring that the motor will produce sufficient torque to start and drive the load,
2. choosing a motor enclosure appropriate for its environment,

Voltage	Motor Size (hp/kW)
230 or 4601	up 100/up to 75
460 or 575	100 to 600/75 to 450
2300	200 to 4000/150 to 3000
4000	400 to 7000/300 to 5250
6600	1000 to 12000/750 to 9000
13200	3500 to 2625 to 18750

Fig. 16.3: Recommended Motor Sizes for Different Voltages

3. ensuring that the motor's insultation is appropriate for its operating conditions,
4. including ambient temperature and altitude in the specification,
5. choosing motor bearings appropriate to the application,
6. making a choice between standard-efficiency and high-efficiency motors,
7. comparing between different types from the points of view of costs, size, and power supply, and
8. choosing an appropriate starter to ensure long motor life.

Again, the decision for concurrent development assesses the effects of the choosen motor upon the process, which is normally initiated by the acquiring information scale sensing-intuition and then moved to the decision making scale thinking-feeling as shown in Fig. 16.4 [9].

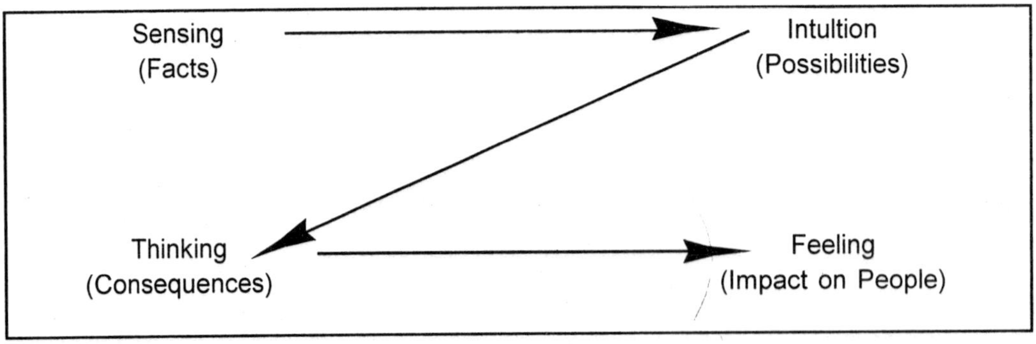

Fig. 16.4: The Decision Process

3. Operation and Maintenance of Energy Efficient Motors

The efficiency of an electric motor and its service life can be negatively affected by improper operation and poor motor maintenance and inspection practices. Further, if a motor is to be rewound, poor quality materials and workmanship can reduce the "repaired" motor's efficiency and power factor. Also different types of electrical insulation may be used on the windings, resulting in the capability to operate at different temperature levels. While smaller motors may be line-started, large motors are usualy connected to a starter to reduce the applied voltage and consequently limit the initial starting current. The guidelines for inspection and maintenance that lead to the proper operation of an energy efficient electric motor are:

1. The input voltage should be measured periodically to ensure against out-of-range voltage and in the case of multi-phase motors, voltage imbalance, which can caused failure because of excess temperature rise. A 3.5 per cent voltage imbalance can result in an approximate 25 per cent temperature rise in some motors.
2. On a regular basis, measure the ambient temperature near each unit and compare that figure to the motor's specification, a replacement at the unit is necessary for other environment.
3. For similar conditions, inspect each motor and its surroundings regularly to ensure that it si not subjected to excessive environmental dust, or other contaminants. If necessary, replace with a more appropriate enclosure type.
4. Check the temperature of the motor causing excessive temperatures can indicate insufficient ventilation, motor overloaded, or bearing failure. Determine the cause and either correct it or replace the motor.
5. Check that all equipment in the power supply and distribution system associated with maintaining the proper voltage level at the motor's terminals are installed properly and in good working order.
6. Inspect the connections at the motor's terminals to ensure that they are tight and properly insulated.
7. In case of air-cooled and water-cooled motors, frequently inspect motor passage and flow is present to maintain the desired temperature.
8. Lubricate motor bearings and all mechanical-drive components properly and at the specified intervals to ensure against bearing damage and to avoid problems caused by lubricants being thrown into the windings.

9. Store spare units in a warm, dry place to preserve insulation quality and avoid corrosion. Protect especially against the presence of moisture in any form.
10. Ensure that all mounting fixtures and fasteners, and pulleys, belts, and couplings are tight and secure. Frequently check operating motor for excessive vibration and alignment.
11. If motor failure does occur, a thorough analysis should be performed to determine the cause and to ascertain whether the preventive maintenance procedures should be modified.

It is noted that integral horsepower motors have a design life of operation which is approximately double that of fractional horsepower motors. When one motor experiences a failure, it is usually discarded, unless it is of special design and/or a spare is not readily available. Larger motors can be repaired or rebuilt a number of times before they are ultimately scrapped. Seal failure, bearing problems and electrical short circuit in a winding represent the most common types of failure of an electric drive. Rotor or stator coils that experience a failure can be rewound, but this task is usually performed by a contractor who specializes in this types of work.

Studies in idustrialized developed countries have shown that poor rewinding can reduce the motor efficiency by as much as 1 per cent. Low labor and material costs in Egypt may make motor rewinding less expensive than replacement with a new motor. A number of industrial plants maintain their own rewinding shops, while the remainder of the motors are rewound by small workshops. The quality of workmanship of rewinding can be rather poor. The loss of efficiency in the rewinding process depending upon the rewinding techniques. Heating the motor above 350°C to facilitate insulation removal can destroy the interlamination resistance and thus increase the magnetic (core) losses. In fact, all the losses can be adversely affected during rewinding. For example, using a smaller diameter or lower quality wire for the rewind increases the stator I^2R losses; reducing the stator turns can reduce the motor power factor; damaging the stator or rotor can affect the air gap geometry and affect the stator losses. Windage and friction losses can be affected by a change in bearing or grease, by fan substitution, or by assembly procedure.

The fact that rewinding costs are generally low make it incorrect to recommend that electric motors no longer be rewound. What is required is a knowledge of the negative impact or rewound motor performance of the use of poor quality materials and rewinding practices. Studies in the United States and European countries indicate that proper rewinding can restore the motors to their original efficiencies, but high labor costs often make the repair efforts on small motors uneconomical. the much lower labor costs in Egypt should make even careful rewinding economically attractive. For continuously operating or high-use motors, it may be advisable to replace the motors instead of rewinding them, since even a 1 per cent drop in efficiency could significantly increase energy costs. Rewound motors could be kept as spares or for applications on equipment in occasional use. This additional operating cost must be weighed against the difference between the cost of a new motor and the cost of the rewinding. If this payback period is relatively short, consideration should be given to the purchase of the new, higher-efficiency motor.

4. Electric Motors and Drives in Egypt

Practically, electric motors can be purchased as unitary devices or as an integral part of an equipment such as pumps, compressors, blowers, workshops, machines, lifts, conveyor system, domestic appliances, etc. A field study, carried out by the Academy of Science and Technology, estimates the annual requirements of all sizes of electric motors in Egypt to be around 1.2 million units, having a total rated power of about 8 million hp and a total cost price (in the year 1990) in the order of 100 million pounds [10]. A rather conventional classification of electric motors, which is useful in describing their application fields and consturction features, is given in Fig. 16.4 together with an estimation of the annual demand of the Egyptian market for each group. Small (including fractional hp) and medium motors amount, in number, to over 95 per cent of the total annual demand. In power, they constitute only about 50 per cent, and in price about 80 per cent of the total.

The field of application of Fractional hp motors embraces appliances for homes and offices (fans, washing machines, office machines, etc.) Small motors are commonly constructed for operation on single-phase 220V or 3-phase 380/220V mains. They are employed for large number of industrial applications such as machine tools, small pumps and compressors, textile machines, refrigeration and air conditioning, blowers, etc., and small industrial drive systems. Medium sized motors are predominantly of the 3-phase type with squirrel-cage or slip-ring rotors and operating voltage in the range 380-1000 V. This group is needed for most traction systems (cranes, lifts, conveyors, elevators, etc.), pumps, compressors and industrial drive systems. Large motors are always in three-phase construction with slip-ring or squirrel-cage rotors for operating voltage up to 11 KV. Synchronous motors are also used for large drive systems such as large compressors, blowers, centrifugal pumps, grinding and rolling mills in the paper, Cement and metal industries. Very frequently, starting and continuous speed control of these motors are achieved through electronic frequency and voltage control.

Mainly, the manufacture of electric motors in Egypt is concentrated on fractional hp and small motors and a very limited range of medium-size motors. Fig. 16.5 shows an estimation of the local production and import of electric motors in Egypt in the year 1990. The imported motors have wide-varying qualities and prices, and are built according to different standards and specifications. This fact makes the task of selecting a suitable motor for a certain application from the local market more difficulty since it necessitates a careful consideration of the detailed specifications of motors of different origins.

Range	Size	Power hp	Annual Demand
A	Fractional hp	<1	800,000
B	Small	1-10	250,000
C	Medium	10-100	100,000
D	Large	>100	40,000

Fig. 16.5: Annual Demand of Electric Motors (1990)

The important environment conditions in Egypt, which can adversely affect electric motors, are the ambient temperature, dust, humidity and salt deposits. Most electric motors are designed for temperature conditions compatible with class B insulation, i.e. a temperature rise for 90°C above an ambient temperature of 40°C (maximum operating temperature 130°C). As ambient temperatures reach 50°C in Upper Egypt in summer, it is reccommended to specify the motor for an ambient temperature of 50°C with class F or class H insulation (maximum operating temperature 155°C). High dust content in the air is frequently encountered in

Egypt, particularly in spring (March to May) due to the Khamassin Wind. Humidity does not normaly present a particular problem except near sea costs where also salt deposits may damage the windings. Using proper standard motor enclosures to ensure a higher degree of protection depending on the ambient conditions of the motor as regards dust, penetrating water and any other contaminants.

Size Origin	Fractional hp <1hP	Small & Medium 1-100 hp	Large 100 hp	Total
Import	620	300	40	960
Local Manufacture	175	25	–	200
Total	795	325	40	1160

(Thousands of units)

Fig. 16.6: Local Manufacture and Imports of Electric Motors

A considerable portion of the public power supply must be set aside for the operation of electrical household appliance, and small industrial plants. This is supplied by 220 or 380V through a tap changing transformer station to step-down the supply voltage to the proper value. It is noted that energy savings gained from electrical household appliances make a considerable contribution to reduce the demand for the primary energy sources needed to generate electricity and, therefore, represent a saving for the general economy. Using new sensors, or sensors with narrower tolerance ranges and improved insulation will also increase energy saving.

Naturally, studies regarding feasibility must be carried out on spot by the Egyptian manufacturers concerned in close cooperation with manufacturers of other countries, to provide the technical know-how for training, consultation and start-up on site. A further increase in local production is obtained with a subsequent decrease in imports and in order to keep up with worldwide technical development, Egyptian manufacturers have to cooperate with reputed manufacturers.

Finally, international standards are prerequisites for the development of international worldwide market. Standardization refers to the methodical work carried out jointly by the parties connected to unify the design of equipment and production of goods for the benefit of all. It promotes rationalization and quality assurance in industry, science, technology and public administration to serve the safety of both persons and objects and to provide order and information for the production process. It is noted that standardization for electrically operated household appliances is performed by the IEC (International Electrotechnical Commission). ISO (International Standard Organisation) and IEC have established a formal agreement, starting the relations between them to complement each other and to form a system for international standardization as a whole. There are three important factors: safety, operating characteristics and/or performance and selection of materials or components, it is found that safety represents top priority in standardization of household appliances.

5. Conclusion and Remarks

The concurrent engineering and technology is always the way which is considered in this paper for industrial development in order to satisfy the customer needs. It is a socio-economically integrated which covers all the impacts. The proper specification, operation and maintenance of energy efficient motors and drives is introduced. Then, the situation and the demand of the electric motors and drives industry in Egypt is given. Finally, the effective application of standardization on the electric motors and drives industry which depends upon the conscious effort of companies is indicated. It is found that concurrent engineering is very important for manufacturing, production and quality.

1. The trend towards ever shortening product life cycles in electrotechnical industry, major technological advances must be incorporated into new products to save energy.
2. Companies have to access, plan and to apply concurrent engineering with cost-effective best management practices.
3. For proper specification and better choice of suitable drive or equipment, the ISO-CG must train all employees to adopt standards for accuracy, control and competitiveness.
4. Companies have to maintain an active, continuous, self monitoring program

to ensure compliance with government and process development requirements.

5. The demand of measurement of the impact of the concurrent engineering on industry and economy needs understanding and cooperative agreements remember "you can't control or develop what you can't measure".

6. Acknowledgements

The author is greatly indepted to Dr. A.H. Said, Secretary General of the Arab School of Science & Technology, Damascus, Syria, and to the Dean and Head of Electrical Department, Faculty of Engineering, Ain Shams University for encouragement and support. He would also like to thank his colleagues from the Academy of Science & Technology, Egyptian Organization of Industrialization, and Federation of Egyptian Industries for useful suggestions, valuable discussion and documentation.

References

1. C. Robert, Benchmarking, (1984), *The Search for Industry Best Practices that Lead to Superior Performance*, American Society for Quality Control, Milwaukee.
2. T.H. Darvenport, (1993), *Process Innovation: Reengineering Work through Information Technology*, Harvard Business School Press, Boston.
3. R.L. Manganelli, and M.M. Klein, (1994), *Reengineering Handbook*, American Management Association.
4. J.H. Harrington, (1991), *Business Process Improvement: The Breakthrough Strategy for Total Quality, Productivity, and Competitiveness*, Mc Graw-Hill, New York.
5. G.D. Robson, (1991), *Continuous Process Improvement: Simplifying Work flow Systems*, The Free Press, New York.
6. R.W. Smeaton. (1973), *Motor Applications and Maintenance Handbook*, Katson Publishing House.
7. P. Balbir Singh, (1975), *Electrical Utilisation*, Kaston Publishing House.
8. A.S. Awad, (1995), "Speed Control of a DC Drive Based on Optimal Performance", M.Sc. Thesis, Faculty of Engineering, Ain Shams University, Cairo, Egypt.
9. J. Adair, (1995), *Effective Teambuilding*, Pan Books, London.
10. STC Report, BS-004, (1991) *Annual Requirements of Electric Motors in Egypt*, Academy of Science and Technology. Cairo, Egypty.

17

A Novel Arabic Trainer: An Example of a Concurrent Continuous Design, Production and Development System

Dr. Mohamed A. El Hamalaway

Professor of Computer Engineering,

Departments of Systems and Computers Engineering,

Faculty of Engineering, Al Azhar University, Cairo, Egypt

Abstract

Through a working mechanism incorporating an industrial establishment and some university staff it was possible to design and produce an innovative trainer which takes into account the working environment in our underdeveloped societies. The training system is expandable to cover Electricity, Electronics, Logic and Physics. The system is modular in design so it could be used in many levels and specialties. The training system was designed and produced in Egypt. It is an example of a good working relationship between university and industry. That relationship started at the design phase and continued through both production and development phases.

The trainer consists of some fixed general purpose modules and some dedicated modules to perform specific experiments. Working instructions on the device is in Arabic to go with the Arabic experiments manuals to push Arabization a step forward. The system structure philosophy is presented. The system was built using advanced CNC machinery, showing that mechanical design factors must go parallel to electronic design factors and to usage convenience.

Design factors governing the trainer are covered showing that development is a part of the training system. Other design factors related to trainees and related to availability of system parts locally are also discussed.

The trainer is an open ended system which means that development must go parallel to design in the manufacturing process.

1. Introduction

Trainers and development systems are essential instruments in any electronic laboratory. Their need comes from having a large number of experiments to be performed, with almost similar elements. Thus a modular approach would lead to few modules dedicated to such different experiments; beside some other serving modules of a general purpose nature. Such approach instead of the experiment setup have resulted in saving equipment cost. At the same time this approach helps trainees perform their task easier than using the normal training setups as a lot of redundancy; hence a waist of effort; is eliminated. Embedded in the design of open ended trainers, there is a strong relationship between design, production and development phases of any industrial product [1].

2. University-Industry Interaction

Admiring all imported items and looking down to all locally manufactured items is a mental status pointing to a serious defeat status enough to convert human beings in our societies from producers to consumers. Such status is not only specific to non-educated people but surprisingly to university staff in our societies; who teach what is good and bad to others. Unfortunately such attitude colours all activities in our underdeveloped societies. We can see clearly such mental attitude if we calculate the percentage of Arabic products purchased compared to foreign items we purchase in our societies. The result of such calculation is almost nil even if it is calculated in our universities in spite of having some local products with acceptable quality internationally [2, 3].

Lifting up the industry is the responsibility of the university and specifically the engineering colleges. With great regret that is what we breach but not what we practice. We rarely hear about university-industry linking projects to build a specific product or even a prototype. But to say the truth we always hear about a project to study something. In almost all cases such study have at the end its place under small particles of dust normally found in our societies.

Universities must play its role in uplifting production quality and volume in different establishments in the society. Such role executed through scientific means must constitute the backbone of all educational establishments. This is needed not only to correct university path but also to correct the society system itself. University-industry interaction is a must in our societies. Such interaction would push the society forward and would raise the scientific standard of university staff themselves. One couldn't imagine that in engineering colleges most of the staff cann't practice what they teach! Is this the needed university staff attitude? Each speciality must have an application in the society whether that would be in the form of industrial product or another form. We always breach for a working relation between the university and the industry in the society for the benefit of both establishments and firstly for awakening our society to attain its previous role which it played for long periods in history.

Such relationship is not a momentary pulse but it is a continuous relationship constituting an essential part in production systems. Production in our phase of development needs a lot of feedback to push our societies. Production must not only produce specific products but it should support such products. We have to look to production as if we are delivering a long term service. Such approach would force us to consider seriously after-sales support, guarantee, service, development and quality [4].

2.1. Scientific instruments

Scientific instruments industry is considered a high technological industry. It is a fertile field for university staff to contribute to their societies. Such role have always been played in both the east and the west. This approach have stimulated establishing an industrial company to produce scientific instruments locally in Egypt. Such company has produced many instruments and equipment under registered patents besides some foreign licenses. The trainer presented in this paper is one of the products of this company. The trainer is locally designed and produced in Egypt. One have to say that in scientific instruments industry most devices are tailor made. So manufacturing cycle starts before production and normally leads to a development phase. The company like all international scientific instruments is established by some engineers and scientists mainly having strong links with the university. Such core have attracted some university professors who design and develop scientific and educational equipment for the company. Those university staff have found it efficient to practice their knowledge in a productive way besides their work at the university. Such approach have led to truly producing some scientific instruments with an acceptable international standard for sale not only in Egypt but also abroad. This doesn't say that manufacturing high-tech products in our societies is an easy thing; but it says it is possible to produce such items. To be fair one have to say that such industry needs a lot of support from the state and from the university staff themselves. University professors are a part and from the university staff themselves. University professors are a part of the society with its weakness and strength but with different degrees. Such statement is not a favorable one as the university should lead by work not by words. University should put the example in supporting local products having acceptable standard and not supporting products of low quality. University should set also the example for the society to do duties before asking for rights.

3. The Trainer

The idea behind the system was to design a rugged instrument to stand rough usage with minimum running cost, suitable for training, teaching and development work [5].

A general purpose trainer is designed and precisely manufactured using CNC machinery to attain high precision in performing both training tasks and development work. It has three main modules two of which are for general purpose signals and indicators, while the third module is for applications. Many self contained experiments are performed on this module. Mostly one can perform one set (a group) of experiments in a specific topic, on each module [6]. For development work a bread boarding module consisting of 4x640 pin breadboards give enough space for most moderate circuits. In some cases where more facilities are needed an expander module with three versatile modules could be added easily to the system Extra expanders with only general purpose signals are optional to the system.

Fig. 17.1: The trainer showing its three modules

Fig. 17.1 shows the system with a solid state experiment module placed in the middle slot of the trainer. It is also clear from the figure that all writing on the trainer front panel are in Arabic to go with the experiments manuals written in Arabic to push Arabization a step forward [7, 8].

3.1. System hardware [9, 10]

3.1.1. The two standard modules of the system give the following outputs:

3.1.1.1. Three signals (sine, square and sawtooth waves) in the frequency range 20 Hz - 20 KHz. Frequency and amplitude of output wave are adjustable allowing different experiments in the digital and analog fields to be performed on the system.

3.1.1.2. A clock of 1 KHz. This extra output allows digital and analog experiments to be performed simultaneously on the unit.

3.1.1.3. Four regulated stabilized DC output voltages of +5, -5, +12 & -12 volts. Each output can supply 1 amp. Adding and subtracting output voltages to obtain higher or other voltages are easily obtained. The four output allows us use different digital and analog integrated circuits of different families and moreover mix them on the same unit. For example CMOS and TTL logic families could be used simultaneously on the system. Experiments utilizing desecrate components could be used equally on the system.

3.1.1.4. Variable regulated stabilized DC voltages of 1 Amp. this output could be added or subtracted from the other four voltages to get other output voltages.

3.1.1.5. Low tension AC voltage of 50 Hz and 1 Amp. This helps us to execute different AC circuits on the unit.

3.1.1.6. A positive and a negative push button. A true signal pulse is a standard output signal in the device to help perform many logic experiments on the unit.

3.1.1.7. Eight logic signal switches. These give 8 true logic 1 or logic 0 signals to be used in logic circuits. In a smaller version of the system we have only four switches.

3.1.2. The Standard unit has the following inputs:

3.1.2.1. Eight Led indicators for logic circuits. These allow indicating eight logic signals simultaneously. In a smaller version of the system we have only four LED's.

3.1.2.2. A seven segment display to be used in many logic experiments. Extra meters are attached to different experiments modules. A CRT is normally needed in some electronics experiments.

3.1.3. A bread-boarding are of 640 pins is standard on the trainer main chassis.

3.1.4. The experiments modules: Through the use of the dedicated modules of the trainer we can perform specific experiments. These are mostly contained in a single physical module to be fitted in the middle slot of the system, to allow ease of using the system. The experiments modules allow performing many experiments in: Physics, Electricity, Electronics and Logic. They could be used as a stand alone experiments setups; but their utmost use is through their use within the trainer. Each module is dedicated to a specific subject. They are designed to allow diversified and progressive study of the technical materials under study. They could be used in a variety of ways according to the educational planning of different educational curricula. the list of experiments presently running on the system covers a good portion in physics, electricity, electronics and logic [11].

Many modules are being added constantly to the trainer due to its open ended features.

Fig. 17.1 shows also an experiment module for optoelectronics[12]. The experiment module as every experiment module is to be placed in the middle slot of the trainer. The figure shows how mechanical requirements could integrate electronic requirements is such experiments modules. The figure also shows Arabic instructions written on the experiments modules.

3.2. System software

Experiments manuals reflect our system approach of teaching electronics, electricity, logic and physics through experimentation. It shouldn't be looked at as a complimentary service to the training system but as an integral part of it. Our system relay upon a well defined logical sequence in grasping the technical materials.

This has been made possible through a good collaboration between some university professors and the industry [12, 13]. Working instructions on the device goes well with the Arabic experiments manuals.

*3.2.1. **Flip flop module:*** As an example of the logical sequence of the technical material covered by the experiments modules; we list the steps performed in the Flip Flop construction and types experiments module which are:

3.2.1.1. The basic S-R flip-flop circuits.

3.2.1.2. Clocked S-R flip-flop.

3.2.1.3. D-Type flip-flop.

3.2.1.4. Edge-Triggered D flip-flop.

3.2.1.5. J-K flip-flop.

3.2.1.6. J-K Master-Slave flip-flop.

3.2.1.7. J-K Edge- Triggered flip-flop.

3.2.1.8. T-Type flip-flop.

The experiment constructs each step from a previously constructed type. This approach not only simplifies the technical materials but also teaches the students the engineering sense of constructing the circuits [15].

3.3. System design features

The system is mechanically and electronically a rugged one. Such raggedness is attained due to a well put philosophy making it possible to design mechanical parts parallel to designing the electronic circuitry of the system. Such mechanical design has taken into consideration the availability of components in the market. The use of CNC machinery with a versatile software made it possible to tailor the system in case components are short in the local market and we have to replace such components with others of different mechanical dimensions. The system could well suite the limited budgets of educational and training institutions while not sacrificing neither quality nor the simplicity of performing the experiments. Moreover many experiments are performed in a variety of ways to suite different courses in universities and training institutions. The trainer is having the following characteristics:

*3.3.1. **Expandability:*** The system allows many experiments covering different courses (physics, electricity, electronics and logic) to be performed on the system. Thus allowing the use of the system for different courses simultaneously as the application module is the only part to be changed to perform different experiments. Many new experiments are always added to the system. Such feature means that a tight link should be formed between the factory and the designers not only during production phase but also after sales.

*3.3.2. **Cost per experiment:*** Having almost a general purpose trainer would certainly lower the cost of performing an experiment per trainee; as the system main cost would be distributed over many experiments.

*3.3.3. **Size and cost of the equipment:*** Using a pin connectors allow us to lower the size and decrease the cost of the system; inspite of the many features the unit is having and its rugged metal construction. This makes the system well suited for many budgets.

*3.3.4. **Cost of maintaining the equipment:*** Having a protection on all DC power outputs extends the life time of the equipment. Behavior of students from different cultural backgrounds vary much and care have to be made when designing the system to minimize system malfunctions. The use of a no banana strapped colored wires vanishes the need for extra bananas to keep the system uprunning as the cost of wires are within the limited budgets of any laboratory.

*3.3.5. **Versatility:*** Experiments are been performed in many study levels allowing the system to even spread more. In an introductory level experiments components are placed underneath the front panel of the experiments modules with its symbols drawn in front of the student. A step higher is to display actual components on the front panel. Another further step is to ask students to plug-in components on a pre-drawn schematic diagram. A breadboard with different overlays for different circuits could be used at this stage either on the main device breadboard or on the bread boarding module.

A more advanced level of performing experiments; just below using normal components on the breadboard; is the semi-versatile boards with components in and without having any schematic diagram drawn on the front panel. This last approach could well suit certain students tests.

The system is patented and have been field tested and proved to be well suitable in many situations. It is presently been sold to many universities, undergraduate and postgraduate vocational institutions and training centers in Egypt and abroad.

3.3.6. Laboratory work space: With a compact; yet versatile; trainer of 41 cm × 25 cm base and a tilted working front face making the unit height from 6 cm to 11 cm, we have a friendly but efficient instrument. With such system dimensions we can save about 30 per cent of needed working space over normal available trainers and would save about 50 per cent of needed working space if we use normal conventional equipment; as normal experiments setups would require about three equipment at least. This has a straight forward relationship on laboratories areas and hence on their costs and on the number of experiments allowed per class provided that same equipment facilities level have to be given to each student.

4. Conclusion

A combined electricity, electronics, logic and physics trainer is described. The system is modular in design and upgradable to accommodate an ever increasing number of experiments. It consists of some fixed genera purpose modules and some dedicated modules to perform specific experiments.

Working instructions on the device is in Arabic to go with the Arabic experiments manuals. The system was built using advanced CNC machinery, showing that mechanical design factors must go parallel to electronic design factors and to usage convenience.

The system could well suite the limited budgets of educational and training institutions while not sacrificing neither quality nor the simplicity of performing the experiments. Moreover many experiments are performed in a variety of ways to suite different courses in universities and training institutions.

The trainer has been designed and manufactured in Egypt. It presently supports many experiments in electricity, electronics, logic and physics. The experiments software is done in a well structured logical sequence to assure best usage of the trainer. Examples of experiments modules are presented.

The trainer is a result of an efficient long-term university-industry working relationship.

References

1. Mohamed A. El Hamalaway, "A Novel Electricity, Electronics, Logic and Physics Trainer", 20th International Conference on Statistics, Computer Science and its Practical Applications, Cairo, Egypt, April 3-8th, 1995; pp. 177-189.
2. Mohamed A. El Hamalaway, "Towards a Working Relation to Establish the Needed Interaction between University and Industry", The First International Conference on University-Industry Interaction; Cairo, Egypt, March 22-24, 1994, pp. 85-91. (In Arabic).
3. Mohamed A. El Hamalaway, "Towards a Real Protection of the Real National Industry Conference on Settling Technology for Industrial and Social Development", Alexandria, Egypt, January 24-26th, 1995, pp. 288-296 (In Arabic).
4. Osama Abu El Hagag, Mohamed H. El Zayat, Mohamed A. El Hamalaway and Nabil N. El Hefnawy, "Towards Establishing a Numerical Evaluation Procedure when Purchasing a Computer", Sixth Conference on Computer Theory and Applications, Alexandria, Egypt, Sept. 3-5th, 1996, pp. 353-359 (In Arabic).
5. Mohamed A. El Hamalaway, "Requirement of an Ideal Teaching System For Microcomputers", International Federation of Automatic Control (IFAC) Conference; Cairo, Egypt, November 26-29th, 1977; pp. 201-2-3.
6. Mohamed A. El Hamalaway and Ahmed A. El Hamalaway, "An Innovative Physics Trainer", Second International Conference on Engineering Mathematics and Physics (ICEMP-94); Cairo, Egypt, December 27-19th, 1994; pp. 291-300.
7. Mohamed A. El Hamalaway, "Reimplanting Arabic into Science Map", Symposium on Requirements for Teaching University courses in Arabic, Cairo, Egypt, April 13, 1994. (In Arabic)
8. Mohamed A. El Hamalaway, "Arabizing the Nation", First Workshop on Arabizing Engineering Education, Cairo, Egypt, April 5-6th, 1995 (In Arabic).
9. Mohamed A. El Hamalaway, "A Versatile Trainer", Patent No. 10967, 1994, Egypt.
10. Mohamed A. El Hamalaway, "An Electricity, Electronic and Logic Trainer", Patent No. 10968; 1994, Egypt.
11. Trainers Catalogue, Misr Fatramo Co., P. O. Box 5648 West Heliopolis, Cairo 11771, Egypt.
12. Mohamed A. El Hamalaway, "Experiments Modules for Electricity, Electronics", Logic and Physics Trainer, patent bending, 1996, Egypt.

13. Mohamed A. El Hamalaway, "Manufacturing Scientific Instruments in Egypt: A Case Study", Small Scale Scientific Instruments: Manufacturing and Investment Development Seminar, Cairo, Egypt, March 24th, 1990. (In Arabic)
14. Abd El Shakour El Samahy and Mohamed A. El Hamalaway, "High Technology Industries: A Real Example Seminar on Cooperation between the University and the Industry", National Seminar on Cooperation between Faculties of Engineering and the Industry & Production Establishments, Cairo, Egypt, October 8-9th, 1990, pp. 119-121. (In Arabic).
15. Mohamed A. El Hamalaway, *Logic Laboratory Notebook*, Al Azhar University, Egypt, 1991.
16. Paul B. Zbar et al., *Basic electronics, A Text-Lab Manual*, Sixth Edition, McGraw-Hill Co., U.S.A., 1990.
17. N. Nelkon and J. M. Ogborn, *Advanced Level Practical Physics*, Fourth Edition, ELBS Co., England, 1987.